THE CAREERS HAND BOOK

THE GRAPHIC GUIDE TO FINDING THE PERFECT JOB FOR YOU

Penguin
Random
House

DK India

Project Editor Rupa Rao
Senior Art Editor Anis Sayyed
Project Art Editor Mahipal Singh
Editorial team Priyanka Kharbanda, Deeksha Saikia,
Neha Pande, Antara Moitra, Anita Kakar
Art Editor Pooja Pipil
Assistant Art Editors Tanvi Sahu, Deepankar Chauhan
DTP Designer Shanker Prasad
Senior DTP Designer Harish Aggarwal
Jackets Designer Suhita Dharamjit
Managing Jackets Editor Saloni Talwar
Pre-production Manager Balwant Singh
Managing Editor Kingshuk Ghoshal
Managing Art Editor Govind Mittal

DK London

Project Editor Ashwin Khurana
Art Editor Jemma Westing
Editorial team Suhel Ahmed, Chris Hawkes, Andrea Mills
Jacket Editor Maud Whatley
Jacket Designer Mark Cavanagh
Jacket Design Development Manager Sophia MTT
Producer, pre-production Lucy Sims
Senior Producer Mandy Inness
Managing Editor Gareth Jones
Managing Art Editor Philip Letsu
Publisher Andrew Macintyre
Publishing Director Jonathan Metcalf
Associate Publishing Director Liz Wheeler
Design Director Phil Ormerod

Cobalt ID

Editor Richard Gilbert
Editorial Director Marek Walisiewicz
Art Director Paul Reid

First published in Great Britain in 2015
by Dorling Kindersley Limited
80 Strand, London WC2R ORL

Copyright © 2015 Dorling Kindersley Limited

A Penguin Random House Company

10 9 8 7 6 5 4 3 2 1
001–197162–02/15

A CIP catalogue record for this book
is available from the British Library.

ISBN: 978-0-2410-0692-4

Printed and bound in China by
Hung Hing Printing Group Ltd

Discover more at

www.dk.com

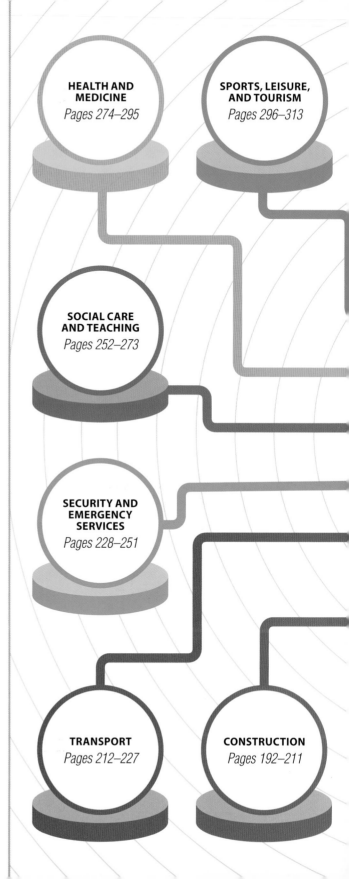

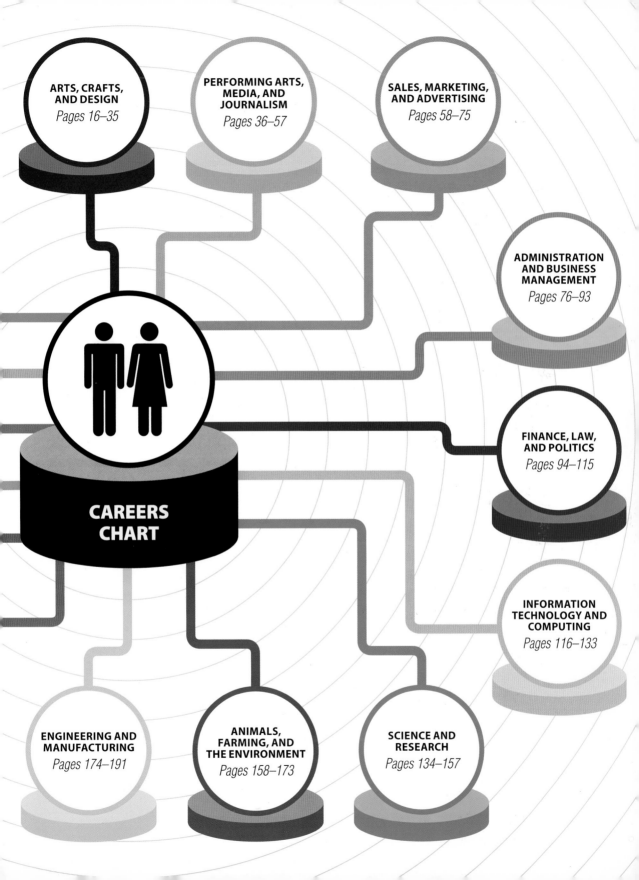

ARTS, CRAFTS, AND DESIGN
Pages 16–35

PERFORMING ARTS, MEDIA, AND JOURNALISM
Pages 36–57

SALES, MARKETING, AND ADVERTISING
Pages 58–75

ADMINISTRATION AND BUSINESS MANAGEMENT
Pages 76–93

CAREERS CHART

FINANCE, LAW, AND POLITICS
Pages 94–115

INFORMATION TECHNOLOGY AND COMPUTING
Pages 116–133

ENGINEERING AND MANUFACTURING
Pages 174–191

ANIMALS, FARMING, AND THE ENVIRONMENT
Pages 158–173

SCIENCE AND RESEARCH
Pages 134–157

SALES, MARKETING, AND ADVERTISING
58

60 Sales executive
62 Store manager
64 Buyer
66 Estate agent
68 Marketing executive
70 Market researcher
72 Advertising account manager
74 Public relations officer

ADMINISTRATION AND BUSINESS MANAGEMENT
76

78 Customer service manager
80 Human resource manager
82 Project manager
84 Management consultant
86 Personal assistant
88 Events manager
90 Charity fundraiser
92 Translator

INFORMATION TECHNOLOGY AND COMPUTING
116

118 Software engineer
120 Systems analyst
122 Database manager
124 Network engineer
126 IT support executive
128 Web designer
130 Games developer
132 Cyber-security analyst

FINANCE, LAW, AND POLITICS
94

96 Bank manager
98 Trader
100 Investment analyst
102 Accountant
104 Actuary
106 Financial adviser
108 Economist
110 Solicitor
112 Barrister
114 Politician

174 ENGINEERING AND MANUFACTURING

176 Civil engineer
178 Drilling engineer
180 Chemical engineer
182 Mechanical engineer
184 Motor vehicle technician
186 Electrical engineer
188 Telecoms engineer
190 Aerospace engineer

192 CONSTRUCTION

194 Architect
196 Structural engineer
198 Quantity surveyor
200 Town planner
202 Builder
204 Construction manager
206 Carpenter
208 Electrician
210 Plumber

296 SPORTS, LEISURE, AND TOURISM

298 Sports professional
300 Personal trainer
302 Beauty therapist
304 Hotel manager
306 Travel agent
308 Airline cabin crew
310 Chef
312 Museum curator

274 HEALTH AND MEDICINE

276 Doctor
278 Nurse
280 Midwife
282 Dentist
284 Pharmacist
286 Radiographer
288 Physiotherapist
290 Speech and language therapist
292 Occupational therapist
294 Optometrist

THINKING ABOUT YOUR CAREER

Thinking about your future career is exciting, but it can also be quite daunting. You need to select subjects to study at school, make choices with regard to further and higher education, and think about the interests you want – and would like – to pursue. It is best to think of choosing a career as a process rather than a single decision. Think of it as a journey, during which you will experience a variety of influencing factors.

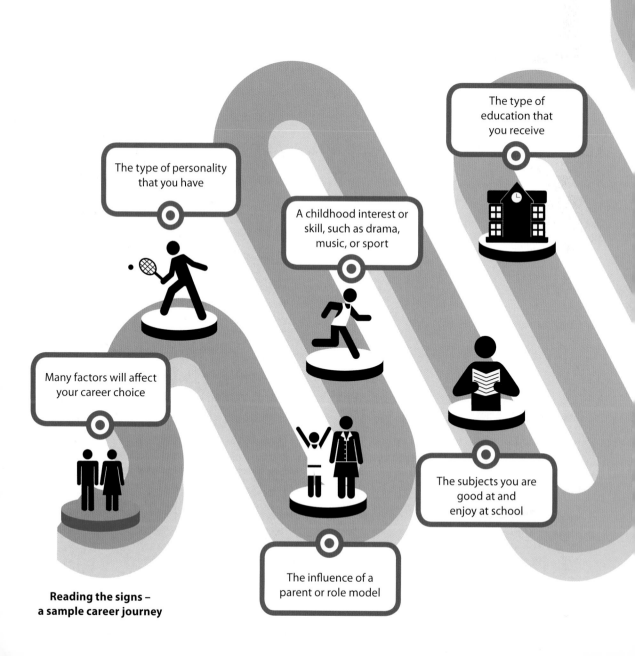

The type of education that you receive

The type of personality that you have

A childhood interest or skill, such as drama, music, or sport

Many factors will affect your career choice

The subjects you are good at and enjoy at school

The influence of a parent or role model

Reading the signs – a sample career journey

University study or an apprenticeship

The work-life balance you would like in your life

Finding the job that is right for you.

Exam results at university

Where you live now and where you would like to live

A desire for professional status

Exam results at school

A desire for wealth and comfort

A desire to challenge yourself

Work experience

UNDERSTANDING YOURSELF

We are all individuals with our own personality, interests, skills, and values. To find a good career match, you first need to think about yourself, not only about what interests you, but your skills, personal qualities, motivators, and character. This reflection will help you plan future training and work experience, strengthen your CV, and make well-informed career decisions.

WHAT SUBJECTS DO YOU LIKE?

Which subjects do you enjoy at school? Which are you best at? How can you improve your performance in the subjects you like the most?

Understanding yourself

WHAT OTHER INTERESTS DO YOU HAVE?

Do you play sports? Employers look for a range of interests beyond school work. Taking part, and succeeding in, activities such as sport demonstrates that you can work well with others – an important part of many jobs.

Many people have hobbies that develop into careers, and not always in obvious ways. If you enjoy drama, for example, you might go on to forge a career as an actor, but you will also have skills that could be used in giving presentations or working as a teacher.

Think about your hobbies and interests and how they could be put to use in the workplace.

WHAT MOTIVATES YOU?

What is most important in your life? Do you want fame, status, and high earnings, or would you gain more satisfaction from helping others in the community? Do you seek excitement and challenge in your life, or are stability, freedom, and comfort more valuable?

WHAT SKILLS DO YOU HAVE?

Whether you are still at school, or have already gained work experience, think about the skills you have developed. You may be highly creative, be a great communicator, or have advanced IT skills; you may be good at problem-solving, or excel at working with your hands.

WHAT ARE YOUR PERSONAL QUALITIES?

While you might be able to learn new skills to pursue a career, it is far more difficult to change your personality. Think about what kind of person you are – and ask others to describe how they see you. Choosing a job that fits with your personality will make you happier in your career and far more likely to be an effective employee.

WHAT ARE YOUR CIRCUMSTANCES?

Do you want to work in a particular place – close to family and friends, for example – or are you prepared to relocate?

Do you have any health conditions that may affect your applications?

What are the costs of education and training in your chosen area – can you realistically afford them?

To focus your thoughts, make a checklist that you can refer to throughout your career journey.

 FAVOURITE SUBJECTS

 INTERESTS

 MOTIVATORS

 PERSONALITY

 SKILLS

 OTHERS

TAKING ACTION

Once you have a greater understanding of who you are, what you are good at, and what type of job you would like to do, you can start to explore the world of education, training, and work. Start by looking at the job profiles in this book – they will give you a flavour of the types of careers available, and help you to broaden your current ideas and learn about new opportunities.

SEEK ADVICE
Read up about your career or industry of interest. Talk to friends, family, teachers, or careers advisers about your options.

SET SOME GOALS
Ask yourself what you want to achieve in your life and what you need to do in the short term to get to where you want to be.

TAKE ACTION
Once you have decided on the career you would like to pursue, you can do several things to make yourself stand out to potential employers.

GET EXPERIENCE
Try and get a place on a work experience programme. This will give you an excellent opportunity to talk to employees.

START NETWORKING
Try contacting employers to see if they run open days. Use social networks to connect with companies.

JOB

TRAINING AND LEARNING
Do your research to find out what qualifications you will need to enter a particular career.

BECOME A VOLUNTEER
Offer your time to a company, charity, or other organization. By doing so you will make valuable contacts and learn new skills.

RESEARCH EMPLOYERS
Find out all there is to know about a range of employers in your chosen sector.

BUILD AN ONLINE BRAND
Use the Internet to set up, and actively manage, profiles on networking sites such as LinkedIn and Facebook.

GETTING THE JOB

Presenting your skills, talents, and experience to potential employers – in writing or in person – is a key part of getting any job. Research and preparation are the key to success when applying for jobs and when attending interviews.

CHOOSE YOUR WORDS

Think carefully about the words you use to describe your skills and achievements. Try to mirror the language used in the job description or on the company's website.

RESEARCH

Use the Internet to do some online research into your potential employer. What do they do? What makes them distinctive? What is happening in their sector of the market?

APPLYING FOR A JOB

Whether responding to an advertised job or approaching an employer, take time to think about your job application.

READ THE JOB DESCRIPTION

Make sure you read the job description very carefully. Employers usually specify skills and qualifications that are essential to the job, so make sure your application indicates that you meet the specific job requirements.

FINE-TUNE YOUR CV

Don't send out the same, standard CV to all potential employers. Think about what each employer is looking for and try to include evidence of success in these areas.

PREPARE AND RELAX

Make sure you prepare thoroughly for the interview. Remember that it is natural to feel nervous beforehand, so try to find ways to relax: you could play music or do some breathing exercises.

DRESS FOR SUCCESS

You should always be well-groomed and smart for an interview. This does not always mean wearing a suit: try to match the style of dress within the organization.

INVITATION TO INTERVIEW

GETTING THROUGH THE INTERVIEW
If an employer is impressed by your application, you may be invited to attend an interview.

GET THE JOB

HAVE ANSWERS TO STANDARD QUESTIONS

Prepare answers for some of the most common interview questions, such as: "Tell me about yourself"; "Why are you interested in this role?"; "Why are you right person for this job?"

KNOW YOURSELF

Make sure you review your CV or application form before you attend the interview. Be clear about the skills and qualifications you have to offer the employer, and think of examples of your achievements.

ARTS, CRAFTS, AND DESIGN

If you have artistic talent and an eye for what looks stylish, you could consider a career in arts, crafts, and design. In this sector you may be involved in creating new products, making illustrations for magazines, styling home interiors, or dreaming up the latest fashion trends.

PRODUCT DESIGNER

JOB DESCRIPTION

Almost every object or device used in everyday life – from a chair to a computer – has been shaped by a product designer. In addition to creating new items, a product designer may also improve existing ones or make them more cost-effective. The design process is collaborative – product designers develop ideas with clients, work on prototypes with engineers, and assist marketing staff to promote the product to buyers.

SALARY

Product designer ★★☆☆☆
Design engineer ★★★★☆

INDUSTRY PROFILE

Highly competitive • Huge demand for innovative product designers • Jobs available with manufacturers or specialist product design agencies

▼ RELATED CAREERS

▶ **INTERIOR DESIGNER** *see pp. 34–35*

▶ **ARCHITECTURAL TECHNICIAN** Supports an architect on the practical aspects of a construction project. An architectural technician prepares drawings and blueprints, sources suitable materials, and oversees legal and planning issues.

▶ **DESIGN ENGINEER** Conceptualizes and develops new products as well as their manufacturing processes. Testing prototypes to ensure products function correctly and are reliable is also part of this job.

> There are more than 40,000 product designers working in the USA alone.

AT A GLANCE

YOUR INTERESTS Art and design • Engineering • Craft technology • Graphic design • Physics • Mathematics • History • Information Technology (IT)

ENTRY QUALIFICATIONS An undergraduate degree in product design, industrial design, or engineering is essential to enter this profession.

LIFESTYLE Product designers work regular office hours, but need to be flexible to meet deadlines. Most of the design work is done on computers.

LOCATION Most product designers are based in offices or studios, but may need to travel to meet clients or conduct research with the product's users.

THE REALITIES This is a competitive field in which designers need to keep up with new technologies and design trends. Networking is key to career progression.

CAREER PATHS

A qualified product designer needs to build a portfolio of successful work to get established. There are many fields in which you can specialize, but you may need a postgraduate qualification for some of the more technical fields, such as biomedical engineering.

ASSISTANT Before undertaking a degree, you can gain work experience as a design assistant with an engineering company or design consultancy.

GRADUATE You require a degree-level qualification and may then need to join a professional design association to gain practical training.

PRODUCT DESIGNER The work requires you to consult with clients, research the needs of users, and then sketch ideas and develop them into plans using specialist software. With experience, you can specialize in a number of different areas.

SKILLS GUIDE

A high level of creativity in devising fresh ideas and new product features that will appeal to buyers.

The ability to plan and organize all stages of a project to ensure delivery on time and to budget.

Excellent numerical skills for calculating the dimensions and proportions of a product.

The ability to explain complex ideas to clients clearly, both verbally and in writing.

Good IT skills for working on specialist Computer-aided Design (CAD) programs.

Close attention to detail when working to technical specifications or client briefs.

VEHICLE DESIGNER Works in the transport industry, creating new concepts for car bodies, lighter seats for aircraft, or clearer instrument panels for trains.

HEALTH CARE ENGINEER Applies engineering and design principles in the field of health care to create medical products, such as prosthetics and robotic surgical instruments.

CONSUMER PRODUCT DESIGNER Specializes in developing better consumer products, such as glassware, vacuum cleaners, computers, and hand-held electronics.

ERGONOMIST Focuses on the functionality of the products people use at home and in office spaces. Designs new products, such as desks, kitchen equipment, or industrial tools, and tries to make them safe, comfortable, and easy to operate.

TEXTILE DESIGNER

JOB DESCRIPTION

A textile designer designs woven, knitted, and printed textiles that are used to make clothes, fabrics, and furnishings. With an understanding of materials, dyes, patterns, and manufacturing processes, they produce designs for a range of decorative, durable, or protective fabrics. The work involves producing sketches and samples, and liaising with marketing and buying staff to make products that will sell.

SALARY

Newly qualified textile designer ★★★★★
Experienced textile designer ★★★★★

INDUSTRY PROFILE

Increasingly competitive sector, with more applicants than vacancies • Growing demand for textile designers in specialist markets, such as protective clothing and seating for car interiors

AT A GLANCE

YOUR INTERESTS Art • Craft • Fashion • Sewing • Knitting • Design technology • Mathematics • Chemistry • Information Technology (IT)

ENTRY QUALIFICATIONS A degree in textile or fashion design is desirable, but it is possible to learn on the job while working in the industry.

LIFESTYLE Regular office hours are the norm, but designers may have to work overtime to meet deadlines. Freelance designers can work from home.

LOCATION Primarily based in an office or a studio, but designers may need to visit factories during production, or attend client briefings and trade shows.

THE REALITIES The work is creatively rewarding. Most textile businesses are based in large cities, so relocation may be necessary to find a good position.

▼ RELATED CAREERS

▶ **JEWELLERY DESIGNER** *see pp. 28–29*

▶ **CLOTHING AND TEXTILE TECHNOLOGIST** Manages the design, manufacture, and quality control of fabrics, yarns, and textiles. An expert in this field may work on fabrics for clothing, furnishings, medical supplies, or textiles for the car industry.

▶ **FURNITURE DESIGNER** Designs furniture pieces and fittings, such as cupboards. Some furniture designers work for manufacturers, creating designs for mass production; others produce items of furniture for individual clients.

In 2012, 4 million people were employed in the manufacturing of clothing and footwear in the USA.

CAREER PATHS

Without a relevant degree, it may be possible to enter the textile industry as a pattern cutter, creating fabric templates from drawings, or as a machinist, making garment samples. On-the-job training could lead to higher qualifications.

MACHINIST OR PATTERN CUTTER You can study for a vocational qualification while working as a machinist or pattern cutter, which will give you valuable experience of the textile industry.

GRADUATE Taking a degree in textile design, fashion, or a related subject can help you develop the skills, creative confidence, and industry contacts to progress as a designer.

TEXTILE DESIGNER Once qualified, you may work with fashion houses, architects, interior designers, or fabric manufacturers and retailers. You can specialize in areas such as interiors – upholstery, furnishings, and carpets – or technical fabrics, such as those used in fireproof clothing.

TEXTILE CONSERVATOR Works with museums, heritage organizations, and in the antiques trade to restore valuable textiles, such as tapestries, clothing, and wall and floor coverings. This job requires a thorough knowledge of design history, textile structure, and traditional manufacturing methods.

WALLPAPER DESIGNER Creates patterns and textures for wallpapers and other wall coverings. Most opportunities in this specialist field are freelance, or in working for textile or wall-covering manufacturers.

FASHION DESIGNER Designs accessories, shoes, or clothes – for mass-production or limited editions for niche markets – that mimic current trends in fabric, colour, and shape, or create a new style.

INTERIOR DESIGNER Uses a knowledge of pattern, colour, texture, and design techniques to produce interior schemes – which may include textile elements – for interior design studios and architectural firms.

GRAPHIC DESIGNER

JOB DESCRIPTION

Using images, colours, and text, graphic designers create compositions on screen to convey information and messages for print or electronic media. Designers must assess their clients' requirements to produce advertisements, promotional material, or logos that appeal to their target audience. Most of the work is computer-based, but may also involve working with suppliers, such as illustrators and photographers.

SALARY

Trainee graphic designer ★★★★★
Experienced graphic designer ★★★★★

INDUSTRY PROFILE

Industry continually evolving due to technological developments • Wide range of employers • Self-employment common • Worldwide demand

AT A GLANCE

YOUR INTERESTS Art and design • Information Technology (IT) • Photography • Illustration • Project management

ENTRY QUALIFICATIONS Most designers have a degree, but some train on the job. Qualifications in art or IT are useful.

LIFESTYLE Designers tend to work normal office hours. However, overtime may be required to meet pressing deadlines and tight schedules.

LOCATION Although designers will usually work in a studio or office, they may need to travel to meet clients for a briefing or to present their work.

THE REALITIES Nearly one-third of all graphic designers are freelance. More expect to have to work in a number of different companies.

SKILLS GUIDE

Strong written and verbal communication skills to articulate designs and ideas clearly.

Expertise in using the latest design software, and the ability to adapt to new technology.

Excellent design flair, artistic abilities, and creative ideas to produce innovative designs.

The ability to listen to clients and fully understand their specific requirements and ideas.

Good organizational skills to handle multiple projects at the same time.

An eye for detail to ensure designs are accurate, conveying the correct messages required by the client.

▼ RELATED CAREERS

▶ **ILLUSTRATOR** *see pp. 26–27*

▶ **INTERIOR DESIGNER** *see pp. 34–35*

▶ **ADVERTISING ACCOUNT MANAGER**
see pp. 72–73

▶ **WEB DESIGNER** *see pp. 128–129*

▶ **ADVERTISING ART DIRECTOR** Creates visual ideas to convey each particular message for advertising campaigns. Works closely with a copywriter, who writes persuasive text, or copy, for a specific target audience.

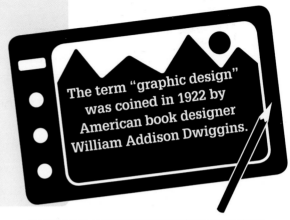

The term "graphic design" was coined in 1922 by American book designer William Addison Dwiggins.

CAREER PATHS

Most graphic designers have a degree in graphics or art, and find work in companies involved in marketing, communications, advertising, or publishing. They usually specialize in one area, such as designing children's books, magazines, websites, or user interfaces for applications.

ASSISTANT As a school-leaver, you may be able to find work as a design assistant, then train on the job and progress into more creative roles.

GRAPHIC DESIGNER As a graphic designer, you will continue learning throughout your career, keeping in touch with new directions in commercial design and changes in technology. You may choose to work freelance or develop your career in an individual company.

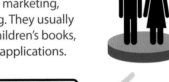

GRADUATE You can enter the career with a degree-level qualification in graphic design or a related arts subject.

ART DIRECTOR
Steers the design of a brand, campaign, or publication, usually heading a team of designers or other creative staff.

WEB DESIGNER
Specializes in website design, from creating logos to providing visual content for their clients' brands.

EXHIBITION DESIGNER
Designs displays for exhibitions, conferences, or museums. A strong interest in 3-D design definitely helps in this role.

MARKETING CONSULTANT
Uses design expertise to provide advice on marketing strategy and branding.

PHOTOGRAPHER

JOB DESCRIPTION

Photographers combine artistic flair with technical knowledge of cameras and digital imaging to produce photographs. They work across a range of industries, from newspapers and magazines, to fashion and advertising. Some are self-employed, selling their images to picture libraries and media agencies. Others are hired for special events, such as school portraits and weddings.

SALARY

Assistant photographer ★★★★★
Experienced photographer ★★★★★

INDUSTRY PROFILE

Many different opportunities to specialize • Growing industry • Freelance work common • Very competitive area

AT A GLANCE

YOUR INTERESTS Photography • Art and design • Travel and culture • Information Technology (IT) • News and current affairs

ENTRY QUALIFICATIONS A degree in photography is desirable, but it is possible to train on the job as a photographer's assistant.

LIFESTYLE The work schedule may be arranged at short notice. Photoshoots can include evening and weekend work, plus travel to long-haul destinations.

LOCATION Some photographers may work outdoors or overseas to capture specific landscapes. Most work in studios and will spend time on computers.

THE REALITIES Competition is intense and fees vary enormously. Professional networking and building a reputation help build a successful career.

▼ RELATED CAREERS

▶ **GRAPHIC DESIGNER** *see pp. 22–23*

▶ **JOURNALIST** *see pp. 54–55*

▶ **WEB DESIGNER** *see pp. 128–129*

▶ **ANIMATOR** Brings characters and images to life on-screen by using animation software to create visual effects and movements. Animators work in the TV, film, or computer games industries.

▶ **ART EDITOR** Oversees the visual style and content of a printed book, magazine, or website. Responsibilities include ensuring the work meets the client's brief, and is delivered on time and to budget. With a strong background in design, art editors lead and manage creative teams.

▶ **TV CAMERA OPERATOR** Prepares and sets up equipment ready for use. Under the instruction of a director of photography, a camera operator records images to film or digital media. Multi-taskers who can think and react quickly, camera operators may have to film scenes outside on location, as well as carrying out work in a studio.

CAREER PATHS

Most photographers are self-employed and focus on one or more areas of work. Creating a portfolio (presentation book) of images and skills – as well as developing contacts – helps in securing regular work.

ASSISTANT After finishing school, you may be able to gain experience working as an assistant to an established photographer.

GRADUATE A degree in photography or related arts or design subject is useful, in addition to gaining experience as an assistant.

PHOTOGRAPHER As your career progresses, business acumen and self-promotion are as important to your success as technical and creative skills. You will need to keep up to date with new technology and emerging markets for images.

MEDICAL PHOTOGRAPHER Makes photographic records of medical procedures, diseases, injuries, or operations for teaching purposes.

GENERAL PRACTICE PHOTOGRAPHER Works with the general public at theatrical performances, weddings, end-of-year dance events, and for family portraits.

FASHION PHOTOGRAPHER Takes shots of designers' clothing and accessories to promote fashion brands, especially in magazines. Usually works in a studio or on location.

PRESS PHOTOGRAPHER Produces photographs of events and the people associated with them, usually for newspapers and magazines. May need to work under pressure to meet deadlines.

CORPORATE PHOTOGRAPHER Works in the corporate world to produce images that record or promote an organization's activities or showcase its products and brands to customers.

ILLUSTRATOR

JOB DESCRIPTION

Illustrators are commercial artists who produce paintings and drawings to accompany text in books, magazines, brochures, and advertisements. They usually specialize in one particular area, such as producing drawings for children's books, cartoons for newspapers, or technical illustrations for manuals. While some illustrators still use a pen or brush, many work on computers with specialist graphics software.

SALARY

Illustrator ★★☆☆☆

INDUSTRY PROFILE

Majority of illustrators work as freelancers • Volume and type of work subject to changing trends in media industries • Bulk of jobs available in print and online media

CAREER PATHS

There is no formal career path into this creative industry. Illustrators need to assemble a collection of their best work into a portfolio and present this to prospective clients. In this role, your success depends not only on your artistic and technical skills, but also on your ability to promote and market yourself.

ASSISTANT You can gain useful experience and make potential contacts by working as a design assistant or technical artworker within a media or publishing company. This may be enough to give you a start in the industry.

GRADUATE An undergraduate degree or equivalent qualification in illustration, fine art, or graphic design offers proof of your skills. However, potential clients will judge your ability on the quality of your portfolio and its suitability for their needs.

CARTOONIST Uses their acute sense of humour and observational skills to draw cartoons or devise graphic stories. A cartoonist's work may be used in newspapers, books, or magazines, or by advertisers to promote products.

ILLUSTRATOR Developing one of several artistic styles, you can find work through personal contacts or register with agents who promote your work and take a commission on any jobs they find for you. With experience, you may choose to take one of a number of different career paths.

SKILLS GUIDE

 A strong proficiency in computer applications and graphic design software.

 Effective communication skills for dealing with clients, agencies, and potential employers.

 A high level of creativity to produce eye-catching work and generate new ideas.

 Good commercial awareness for negotiating fees with clients and working in a competitive market.

 The flexibility to take on different types of work when opportunities in a specialism become scarce.

 The ability to follow a client's brief and accurately produce specialist technical illustrations.

 BOOK OR MAGAZINE ILLUSTRATOR Draws images that accompany articles in magazines, or which illustrate and enliven text in books.

 **MEDICAL OR TECHNICAL ILLUSTRATOR** Produces images of medical conditions and procedures that help people understand complex information in textbooks, instruction manuals, or sales brochures.

▼ RELATED CAREERS

▶ **GRAPHIC DESIGNER** *see pp. 22–23*

▶ **GAMES DEVELOPER** *see pp. 130–131*

▶ **ANIMATOR** Draws multiple images by hand, or uses software, to animate a character or object on screen. An animator may produce work for cartoon films, commercials, computer games, websites, and other media.

▶ **ART DIRECTOR** Leads and directs a team responsible for the design of visual concepts and images in creative industries, such as advertising, publishing, film and TV, or web design.

▶ **STORYBOARD ARTIST** Draws sequences of illustrations that show the key points in a story, which are then used as a basis for filming.

AT A GLANCE

 YOUR INTERESTS Art • Drawing and painting • Graphic design • Information Technology (IT) • English • Science • Mathematics

 ENTRY QUALIFICATIONS Illustrators need a good basic education and a strong portfolio of creative work, or a degree in art, illustration, or graphics.

 LIFESTYLE Freelance illustrators can set their own working hours; those employed by companies work regular office hours.

 LOCATION Although illustrators can work at home or in a studio, they may need to visit a client's office to discuss briefs and promote their work.

 THE REALITIES Paid commissions may be sporadic for freelance illustrators, so many have a second job to maintain a regular income.

JEWELLERY DESIGNER

JOB DESCRIPTION

Jewellery designers need a keen eye for detail, a flair for fashion, and a love of creating intricate objects to succeed in their profession. They design jewellery and accessories, and make the items in their workshop using materials such as gold, silver, precious stones, and wood. Designers without access to a workshop use the services of specialist companies to manufacture their designs.

SALARY

Newly qualified designer ★★☆☆☆
Established manufacturer ★★★★☆

INDUSTRY PROFILE

Competitive industry • Most jewellery manufacturers concentrated in "jewellery quarters" of large cities • Traditional jewellery stores have declined in number

AT A GLANCE

YOUR INTERESTS Craft design and technology • Art • Information Technology (IT) • Science • English • Mathematics

ENTRY QUALIFICATIONS A degree in a relevant discipline is an advantage, but many jewellery designers are self-taught or take vocational courses.

LIFESTYLE Jewellery designers generally work regular hours, but they may travel to meet suppliers, retailers, clients, and manufacturers, and to attend trade fairs.

LOCATION Jewellery designers usually work in a studio or workshop. They may also work at a manufacturer's office, sharing a space with other designers.

THE REALITIES Building a reputation is vital for success, so jewellery designers need to work hard to promote their work in galleries and stores.

CAREER PATHS

Aspiring jewellery designers do not require formal qualifications – skills and experience are much more important. However, a relevant degree will increase your chances of finding a job with a large jewellery company, or give you the confidence to start your own design business, selling your work online or through galleries and stores.

TRAINEE As a school-leaver, you can start a traineeship with a large jewellery company, learning practical skills on the job.

GRADUATE When you apply for a job, a prospective employer will value certain degree courses, such as jewellery design, gemology (the science of natural and artificial gems), art and design, 3-D design, fashion design, or textile design.

▼ RELATED CAREERS

▶ **PRODUCT DESIGNER** *see pp. 18–19*

▶ **FASHION DESIGNER** *see pp. 30–31*

▶ **CERAMICS DESIGNER** Shapes and fires clay to produce objects such as kitchenware, tableware, and tiles. Some ceramic designers work with manufacturers, while others design and make one-off items.

▶ **WATCHMAKER** Makes and repairs watches and other timepieces. Many watchmakers are self-employed, while others work in jewellery shops and department stores. The traditional skills of the watchmaker are in renewed demand because of an upsurge of interest in classic and antique timepieces.

SKILLS GUIDE

 A high level of creativity and innovation to prepare designs to commissioned briefs.

 Good communication skills for interacting with designers, manufacturers, and clients.

 Proficient computer skills, such as the ability to operate Computer-aided Design (CAD) software.

 The ability to use fine tools to create and repair intricate pieces of jewellery.

 Commercial awareness for marketing designs and products to clients and manufacturers.

 Good attention to detail for carrying out complex design work accurately.

JEWELLERY MANUFACTURER
Uses specialized equipment in order to make jewellery. A manufacturer will usually make jewellery in a factory or large workshop.

SILVERSMITH Specializes in, and principally works with, silver to make jewellery, silverware, vases, and other artistic items. May use other metals, such as gold, copper, steel, and brass.

JEWELLERY DESIGNER
You may specialize in a specific type of work, such as bracelets or wedding rings. Once established, you may move into manufacturing, or run your own business.

GEMOLOGIST Gives valuations of precious jewellery for insurance purposes. This role requires formal training in the identification, grading, and pricing of gems.

Demand for gems and jewellery goes up in good times, and down when an economy is flat, so a designer's income can fluctuate.

FASHION DESIGNER

JOB DESCRIPTION

Fashion designers create clothing, shoes, and other accessories. They use their creative expertise and knowledge of textiles, sewing, and manufacturing processes to set trends in colour, fabric, and style. Designers with a high profile often specialize in creating expensive one-off items, whereas the majority of designers work on clothing for the mass market, focusing on certain lines, such as sportswear, men's suits, or knitwear.

SALARY

Junior designer ★★★★★
Head of design ★★★★★

INDUSTRY PROFILE

Market dominated by small- to medium-sized fashion houses located in large cities • Jobs in high-fashion (*haute couture*), ready-to-wear (*prêt-a-porter*), and high-street retail

CAREER PATHS

This is a highly competitive industry. A degree is not essential to earn your first break, but you do need to show evidence of your interest, such as a portfolio of fashion sketches, and have lots of determination. With experience, you can reach more senior creative positions in a fashion house or clothing manufacturer, or even start your own business.

ASSISTANT If you are a naturally gifted designer, work experience in a retail store or hands-on dressmaking skills will make you more attractive to employers. With talent and a good portfolio, you may gain an entry-level job in fashion design.

GRADUATE Studying for a degree in fashion or textile design develops your skills and teaches you the technical aspects of clothing design, which will improve your chances of finding a job in the industry.

SPECIALIST DESIGNER Focuses on designing clothes for a specific area of the industry, such as menswear, footwear, or swimwear.

FASHION DESIGNER In the beginning, you work to a tight brief to fill a specific gap in the market. Creative freedom comes with seniority, or when you start your own company or label.

SKILLS GUIDE

 The ability to generate lots of ideas and translate them into viable sketches and designs.

 Strong numeracy in setting dimensions and scale in patterns and calculate production costs.

 Effective communication skills for interacting with design team and conveying ideas clearly.

 Strong market awareness and business skills, especially for self-employed designers.

 Strong computer skills for working on Computer-aided Design (CAD) software and other applications.

 **TECHNICAL DESIGNER** Bridges the gap between fashion house designers and the manufacturer, focusing on producing patterns that make the most economical use of fabric, and are cost-effective and easy to manufacture.

 **FASHION STYLIST** Advises individuals on fashion to make them as attractive as possible. Stylists are usually employed within the modelling, photography, and film industries.

 **FASHION BUYER** Works for retail stores, purchasing stock to sell to the store's customers. Because buyers usually purchase merchandise several months in advance, they must be able to anticipate trends in fashion to meet future demand.

AT A GLANCE

 YOUR INTERESTS Art • Fashion • Craft and design • Sewing • Information Technology (IT) • Mathematics

 ENTRY QUALIFICATIONS A degree-level qualification in fashion, art, or design is helpful. However, a strong portfolio of work is essential.

 LIFESTYLE Fashion designers work regular hours, but usually stay late and work weekends in the lead up to fashion shows and other launches.

 LOCATION The role is based in a studio or workshop. Fashion designers may have to travel abroad to attend fashion shows and fairs.

 THE REALITIES A fashion designer's work is often subject to harsh criticism. Deadlines are tight, especially when they are preparing a new collection.

▼ RELATED CAREERS

▶ **COSTUME DESIGNER** Designs clothes and accessories that actors wear in plays or films. These outfits need to be appropriate for the characters in a production and suit the period or fictional world in which the play or film is set.

▶ **DRESSMAKER/TAILOR** Creates made-to-measure items of clothing for customers, and usually runs small independent businesses, specializing in a particular type of clothing, such as customized suits or bridal wear.

▶ **FASHION MODEL** Models clothes in order to promote fashion lines to customers and the media. Models appear in fashion shows or in photographs for catalogues, magazines, newspapers, and advertising campaigns.

MAKE-UP ARTIST

JOB DESCRIPTION

Make-up artists work in the film, TV, theatre, music, and fashion industries. They apply make-up and style hair for models or performers, whether they are trying to create a dynamic look for a model, a natural look for a TV presenter, or a dramatic image for a rock musician. In TV or theatre, they might also work with production and costume designers to create a desired style or to capture a certain historical period.

SALARY

Make-up artist ★★★★★
Make-up designer ★★★★★

INDUSTRY PROFILE

Many opportunities for freelance work • Employers generally based in large cities • High-profile make-up artists can charge high fees

▼ RELATED CAREERS

▶ **FASHION DESIGNER** *see pp. 30–31*

▶ **BEAUTY THERAPIST** *see pp. 302–303*

▶ **COSTUME DESIGNER** Designs clothes and accessories that actors wear in their performances. Costume designers combine their own creative instincts with extensive research into the clothes and styles associated with a particular era or location. They must ensure that costumes are authentic, as well as comfortable for the performers to wear.

▶ **HAIRDRESSER** Cuts, colours, or shapes a client's hair to create the style they want. Training can either be on the job or at college.

▶ **WIGMAKER** Creates wigs for a film, TV, or theatrical production. Wigmakers may work with a costume designer or director to decide on a specific look. They also design and create wigs and hairpieces for patients with medical conditions.

AT A GLANCE

 YOUR INTERESTS Make-up and hair • Fashion • Art • Photography and videography • Design • Drama • History • Film and theatre studies

 ENTRY QUALIFICATIONS A diploma in make-up or hairdressing followed by work experience at a beauty salon is the most common entry route.

 LIFESTYLE This is a demanding job with no regular schedule. Working hours are long and can stretch into the night if working on a film or video shoot.

 LOCATION A make-up artist works mainly in theatres, film and TV studios, or in the offices of commercial video companies. Overseas travel is common.

 THE REALITIES Competition for work is tough and success depends on experience and the ability to build a network of contacts in the industry.

CAREER PATHS

An aspiring make-up artist can gain valuable experience by working for amateur theatre groups, or in student fashion shows or film productions. Training at college is useful and may help you get a job assisting an established make-up artist, where you can build up your knowledge and industry contacts.

SCHOOL-LEAVER You can study for a diploma in make-up design, hairdressing, or fashion design at college, but will need specialist training to work in any aspect of the media.

ASSISTANT You may be able to assist an experienced make-up artist, by maintaining a make-up station, and freshening make-up between shots.

MAKE-UP ARTIST In most cases, your work is based around contracts that run for the duration of a film or other production. You can choose to specialize in a number of areas.

SKILLS GUIDE

 Creative flair and the distinctive style to stand out in this highly competitive industry.

 The ability to create intricate styles of make-up and hair for prosthetics and wigs.

 Excellent interpersonal skills to work calmly with actors and models, often under pressure.

 The ability to work well within a production team, and meet the production designer's brief.

Physical and mental stamina to cope with the long hours and heavy demands of the job.

Attention to detail, particularly when trying to ensure continuity during filming.

MAKE-UP AND HAIR DESIGNER Oversees the look of hair and make-up in a film or theatre production. The best film make-up designers are in great demand and may win awards for their work.

WEDDING MAKE-UP STYLIST Provides customized make-up and hairstyles for weddings, end-of-year dances, and other events. Often runs their own business.

PROSTHETICS ARTIST Helps create special effects, such as fake wounds or fantasy characters, using sculpting and crafting techniques. Most of this work is for film or TV.

COSMETICS DEVELOPER Works with a cosmetics company to develop new products. Cosmetic developers may run promotional sessions in stores, trying out new products on potential customers, or they can showcase products through photoshoots.

INTERIOR DESIGNER

JOB DESCRIPTION

Interior designers shape the look and feel of living and working spaces in homes, offices, shops, hotels, and other buildings. They may work on their own or alongside other professionals, such as architects and builders, to create interiors that are both functional and attractive. Their work may range from advising on structural alterations to helping select and coordinate furnishings, colour schemes, and lighting.

SALARY

Junior interior designer ★★☆☆☆
Consultancy partner ★★★★★

INDUSTRY PROFILE

Demand for interior designers rising steadily • Main employers include design consultancies and architectural practices • Self-employment common among interior designers

AT A GLANCE

YOUR INTERESTS Interior design • Architecture • Design technology • Drawing • Arts and crafts • Materials • Science • Mathematics

ENTRY QUALIFICATIONS A relevant qualification is essential to practise. Accreditation by a professional body may also be required.

LIFESTYLE The work is often demanding and may require long or irregular hours to complete a job to a set deadline.

LOCATION Interior designers work in their clients' homes, in an office, or at industrial sites. They may also have to attend exhibitions and trade fairs.

THE REALITIES Clients can be unreasonable if their vision differs from that of the interior designer. Competition for work is fierce.

CAREER PATHS

A degree-level art or design qualification is often required to become an interior designer, although many colleges also offer courses in interior design. Before you practise, you may also need to become a member of a professional design body. With experience, you can specialize in areas such as lighting and furniture.

ASSISTANT You may start by working alongside an established designer, sourcing materials or producing mood boards – used to illustrate the style a designer is trying to achieve. To progress, you will need to study for a degree or diploma on the job.

GRADUATE A degree or other higher-level qualification in design, architecture, or art history is essential for you to work in some companies.

▼ RELATED CAREERS

▶ **ARCHITECT** *see pp. 194–195*

▶ **COLOUR THERAPIST** Uses colour to help people with physical, neurological, or emotional problems.

▶ **EXHIBITION DESIGNER** Designs exhibitions held in museums, galleries, and heritage centres, or focuses on commercial exhibitions, such as trade shows and conferences.

▶ **PAINTER AND DECORATOR** Applies paint and coverings, such as wallpaper, to enhance the look of surfaces in buildings or to protect them from the elements.

▶ **SET DESIGNER** Creates sets and scenery for use in theatre productions of plays and musicals, and for films and TV programmes.

SKILLS GUIDE

 Creativity and imagination in designing new concepts in line with contemporary trends.

 Good communication skills to explain ideas, and negotiate with clients and suppliers.

 Excellent organizational skills to ensure each project is completed on time and within budget.

 Commercial awareness for negotiating contracts with clients and attracting new business.

 Adaptability to work on different briefs simultaneously and to follow new trends.

 Excellent numerical skills for working out costs and the amount of materials needed for a job.

 **HEAD OF PRACTICE** Heads a design team or establishes their own practice to work on interior-design projects.

 ARCHITECTURAL DESIGNER Specializes in working with architects at the planning stage of a new building. Designs interior fittings, and may help with creating floor plans.

LIGHTING DESIGNER Produces functional and appealing designs for lighting. Creates lighting concepts for a project, such as a new building, and then plans how to implement the scheme liaising with engineers, electricians, and architects.

INTERIOR DESIGNER
In this role, you may work on residential or corporate projects or focus on buildings with a specialized function, such as hospitals, restaurants, or hotels.

 FURNITURE DESIGNER Creates new designs for furniture, balancing creativity with comfort. Some furniture designers make one-off items, while others may work for large manufacturers of office or home furniture.

PERFORMING ARTS, MEDIA, AND JOURNALISM

Performing on stage, playing an instrument, writing articles, or communicating through visual media – such as TV, film, and the Internet – can all be pursued as careers. However, each field is fiercely competitive and you will need tenacity, dedication, and perseverance to succeed.

MUSICIAN
Page 38

Combining musical talent with enthusiasm, determination, and a flair for performance, musicians entertain a listening audience with their melodies and compositions.

DANCER
Page 40

With an inherent feel for music, and movement, together with years of practice, dancers bring stories, themes, and emotions to life through rhythmic steps and routines.

ACTOR
Page 42

Whether working in TV, film, and theatre, or commercials and training videos, actors use their dramatic skills to portray and develop the characters they play.

TV/FILM DIRECTOR
Page 44

Using commercial instinct and technical expertise, the director is the creative force inspiring actors and crew to fulfil the overall vision of a TV show or film.

TV/FILM PRODUCER
Page 46

Successful TV and film productions are big business. The producer ensures they make it to the screen by studying scripts, securing funding, and hiring cast and crew.

CAMERA OPERATOR
Page 48

Filming dramatic performances, musical pieces, news items, and nature events, camera operators use technical skill and creativity to capture the scene in front of the lens.

SOUND ENGINEER
Page 50

Rigging up equipment and checking sound levels at concerts and shows, sound engineers create pitch-perfect acoustics for the listening audience.

WRITER
Page 52

With a mastery of story and language, writers use their creativity and research skills to produce fiction and non-fiction pieces for publication across a range of media.

JOURNALIST
Page 54

Digging up the facts behind newsworthy events, journalists are seasoned professionals who investigate every angle to get to the heart of a story.

EDITOR
Page 56

Working with the written word across books and other media, editors have overall responsibility for the quality and accuracy of the text content in a publication.

MUSICIAN

JOB DESCRIPTION

For most musicians, music is not so much a career as a lifelong passion. To succeed, you need natural ability, dedication, and a lot of practice. Musicians may need formal training, especially in classical music or composition, but many are self-taught. Their earnings come from performing, recording, or writing music, either alone or as part of a group or an ensemble.

SALARY

Orchestral player ★★☆☆☆
Successful artist ★★★★★

INDUSTRY PROFILE

Competitive industry • Mostly part-time and freelance work, although full-time roles in military bands and large orchestras available • The Internet has changed the industry's business model

AT A GLANCE

YOUR INTERESTS Music • Entertainment • Songwriting and composition • Performance arts and culture

ENTRY QUALIFICATIONS A degree is not essential, but one must be able to either sing or play an instrument, and perform to a very high standard.

LIFESTYLE Rehearsals and recordings in a studio, or live performances during gigs and tours, can involve long hours. Schedules are highly irregular.

LOCATION Musicians may work in a recording studio, theatre, school, or even a church. If touring, international travel may be required.

THE REALITIES This is a hugely competitive field. Performances can be tiring and stressful, whether live or in a studio.

CAREER PATHS

A musician's future depends partly on the genre of music chosen. If you play in an orchestra, your chances of becoming a soloist are low; if you play in a popular group, you could achieve huge, but often short-lived, commercial success.

AMATEUR Taking music classes and exams, and playing in a local band or orchestra will help you develop your skills, give you exposure to an audience, and may help you start a professional career in music.

GRADUATE If you study music at university or college, you will gain an understanding of theory, history, and technique. A degree is not a guarantee of success as a performer, but may give you access to other parts of the music business.

▼ RELATED CAREERS

▶ **ARTS ADMINISTRATOR** Supervises activities and events that promote the arts in theatres, museums, galleries, and music festivals.

▶ **MUSICAL INSTRUMENT MAKER/REPAIRER** Uses specialist skills to create new instruments or repair ones that have been damaged.

▶ **MUSIC TEACHER** Gives music lessons to people of all ages and abilities. Music teachers can teach students in a college, school, or private centre, or tutor individuals at home.

▶ **MUSIC THERAPIST** Uses music creatively to help people address social, emotional, or physical problems. Music therapists take sessions in a variety of settings with people of all ages and social backgrounds.

SKILLS GUIDE

 A high level of musical ability and the confidence to perform before an audience.

 Dedication and motivation to practise and rehearse for several hours every day.

 The ability to work closely with other musicians in orchestras, and sound recordists in studios.

 Excellent social skills and the ability to self-promote in order to find paid work.

 Attention to detail and perfect timing, especially when performing with other musicians.

POPULAR MUSICIAN
Plays pop, jazz, or another contemporary musical genre. Only a few achieve great success, but many more make a living playing in informal settings, such as small venues, bars, restaurants, and at events such as weddings.

CLASSICAL MUSICIAN Performs live or in recordings as part of an orchestra, a smaller ensemble, or as a soloist. Skill in playing more than one instrument can improve the musician's prospects.

CONDUCTOR Interprets musical scores, and uses a baton or hand gestures to give musical or artistic directions to performers. Some classical musicians undergo further training to become conductors in orchestras and ensembles.

MUSICIAN As a musician, you can work in various roles, as a performer on stage, in the theatre, or as a session musician, working as a non-permanent member of a group in a recording studio or at a live performance. Many trained musicians become instrument teachers or work with record companies.

COMPOSER Creates original music for artists and orchestras, as well as for TV and film soundtracks, computer games, and advertising jingles.

DANCER

JOB DESCRIPTION

Dancers use their bodies to perform routines to music, tell stories, and express ideas for the entertainment of audiences. They can work on stage as members of a dance company or theatre group, or perform in films, TV shows, and music videos. Dancers spend years training to hone their skills, and build up their fitness and flexibility. They usually specialize in one genre, such as ballet, jazz, or street dance.

SALARY

Junior in dance company ★★★★★
Experienced dancer ★★★★★

INDUSTRY PROFILE

Opportunities exist in dance, ballet, opera, and theatre companies • Highly competitive industry • Many dancers are self-employed

CAREER PATHS

Most dancers begin their training in childhood, attending ballet classes or dance school. If you choose this career, you can continue training at vocational dance colleges or at universities that offer undergraduate and postgraduate programmes in dance. The physical demands and brevity of this career mean that most dancers have an additional line of work, possibly in dance teaching or therapy.

DANCE NOTATOR
Records dance moves in a score (a plan of a dance), using figures and graphic symbols. This allows ballets and other dance pieces to be recreated at a later date or by other companies.

ASSISTANT In this role, you help out with classes at a dance school. You may lead students through exercises, help with choreography, or play accompanying music. Many dance students reduce their school fees by working as part-time assistants.

GRADUATE An undergraduate degree in dance or in the performing arts can give your career a boost. You can also train in your chosen genre of dance at a private dance school and pass examinations set by various accredited bodies.

DANCER Performance is an important but relatively small part of a dancer's life. You spend the bulk of your time practising to maintain your skills and fitness, rehearsing or preparing for auditions for new roles. After gaining experience, you can become a dance notator, dance teacher, or choreographer.

SKILLS GUIDE

 Excellent interpersonal skills for communicating with dancers and choreographers about routines.

 The ability to work in a team with a troupe of dancers, choreographers, and others.

 The ability to master new types of dance and to meet the demands of an ongoing performance.

 A high level of physical fitness and stamina to brave the rigorous cycles of training and performance.

 Creativity and innovation to add flair and individuality to footwork, while following a choreographed routine.

 Motivation and the self-discipline to train and rehearse regularly, and maintain high levels of fitness.

 DANCE TEACHER Trains students of all ages in different types of dance. Dance teachers work in dance and stage schools, colleges, and universities, and may also teach related subjects, such as drama or performing arts.

 CHOREOGRAPHER Works in theatre, film, and television to create routines for dancers and other performers. Planning movements to fit the music and staging, choreographers need to work closely with musical directors and costume designers.

▼ RELATED CAREERS

▶ **MUSICIAN** *see pp. 38–39*

▶ **ACTOR** *see pp. 42–43*

▶ **ARTS ADMINISTRATOR** Plans and oversees programmes of arts activities and events in theatres, museums, galleries, and music festivals. This may be a new career for dancers who have retired from performance.

▶ **CHILDREN'S ENTERTAINER** Provides shows and entertainment for children at parties, on cruise ships, or in family-centred hotels. Jobs can be sporadic or seasonal, and most entertainers have another line of work to supplement their income.

AT A GLANCE

 YOUR INTERESTS Dance • Music • Drama • Art • Mime • Musical theatre • Self-expression • Fitness and sport

 ENTRY QUALIFICATIONS Training at a stage school, dance academy, or ballet school is essential. A degree in dance and choreography may help.

 LIFESTYLE Working hours can be long and dancers may have to rehearse and tour a lot. Keeping fit is crucial because the job is physically demanding.

 LOCATION Dancers can work in film and TV studios, as well as in opera, theatres, nightclubs, hotels, and festivals. They may have to travel.

 THE REALITIES Income may be irregular. Self-confidence to pursue goals is important when facing rejections at auditions.

ACTOR

JOB DESCRIPTION

Actors portray a character through a combination of speech, movement, and body language. They work mainly in theatre, film, TV, and radio, but can also appear in corporate videos, advertisements, and record voice-overs. Usually, they interpret the words of a playwright or screenwriter, mostly working from a script under the instruction of a director, but sometimes they may improvise on a theme.

SALARY

Actor in regional theatre ★★★★★
Film or TV actor ★★★★★

INDUSTRY PROFILE

Intense competition for roles • Diverse opportunities, ranging from theatre to theme parks, and from TV to teaching • An expanding industry

AT A GLANCE

YOUR INTERESTS Drama • Film • Arts and literature • Languages • History • Poetry • Music • Dance • Mime • Sport and fitness

ENTRY QUALIFICATIONS Although a degree in drama, or training at a stage school or drama college, is not essential, it will help break into the industry.

LIFESTYLE Actors work irregular hours. In film and TV, days can be long and involve a lot of waiting. Actors may work far from home on location or on tour.

LOCATION Actors work in theatres, TV, film, commercial studios, and even in open-air locations, such as parks, gardens, and forests, around the world.

THE REALITIES Actors need to audition for every role, and rejection can be tough. There is little job security and most actors spend a lot of time looking for work.

▼ RELATED CAREERS

▶ **MUSICIAN** *see pp. 38–39*

▶ **DANCER** *see pp. 40–41*

▶ **DRAMA THERAPIST** Uses drama and theatrical techniques, such as vocal expression, role play, and improvisation, to help people through traumatic experiences or emotional, physical, or behavioural problems. Works closely with teachers, social workers, and psychologists, as well as hospital and prison staff.

▶ **SCREENWRITER** Creates ideas and writes scripts for films or television shows. Screenwriters may also adapt existing works, such as novels or plays, for the screen.

In William Shakespeare's time, in the late 16th and early 17th centuries, there were no female actors. Men played all the female roles.

CAREER PATHS

An actor's career can be unpredictable. Training and talent may help you land good and well-paid roles, but you also need luck and perseverance to be spotted and to be selected at auditions. Finding a respected agent to represent you may help you get noticed.

AMATEUR ACTOR Joining an amateur drama group, or appearing in student films or stage productions, can help you get noticed as a young, aspiring actor.

GRADUATE You can study for an academic degree in drama or theatre studies at university or choose a course focused on acting at a drama school.

ACTOR You may need to join a professional body or an actor's union to be considered for some acting roles. You will need to learn new skills throughout your career, such as stage fighting and perfecting dialects, to win roles.

VOICE ACTOR Works on radio dramas, or provides voice-overs for commercials, animations, training materials, or audiobooks. Voice actors are hired for the quality of their voices.

FILM ACTOR Performs in front of cameras on movie sets, often repeating scenes several times in different "takes". Many actors start their careers in low-budget independent movies.

TV ACTOR Performs a role for a TV show, such as a soap opera or period drama. Some TV actors may also find work in corporate videos, or TV and online advertisements.

STAGE ACTOR Performs in front of audiences in a range of venues, from large theatres or smaller studios, to open-air theatres, or even on the street.

STUNT PERFORMER Stands in for other actors on set, when the film or TV script calls for a scene that is physically dangerous or which requires specialized skills.

TV/FILM DIRECTOR

JOB DESCRIPTION

Directors oversee the production of a film or TV show, and make the creative decisions that guide the rest of the crew. They link together experts in various disciplines, including actors, costume and set designers, and camera operators, and are ultimately responsible for developing a vision for the TV show or film by defining its overall shape, structure, and style.

SALARY

Independent director ★★☆☆☆
Experienced director ★★★★★

INDUSTRY PROFILE

A fast-evolving industry • Corporate production is booming • Rise in independent film-making due to affordable film equipment and more investors

CAREER PATHS

There is no formal route to becoming a director, but experience, reputation, and creative energy are all important. Aspiring directors often work on low-budget independent productions early in their careers, and often come from diverse backgrounds, such as acting or screenwriting.

GRADUATE You can study for a degree in film or cinematography, in which you will be taught technical skills in composition, lighting, and direction, and develop your creative instincts.

CAMERA OPERATOR If you start your career as a camera operator, you can progress to the senior position of director of photography. From there, you can go on to direct films and TV shows.

RUNNER As a runner (or gopher), on a TV or film set, you run errands for the production team. Hard work may gain you promotion to production-based or creative roles, which may eventually lead to an assistant director position.

Steven Spielberg and James Cameron, two of the most successful film directors of all time, did not go to film school.

ASSISTANT DIRECTOR As the director's second-in-command, you are responsible for many practical tasks, such as managing schedules and allowing the director to concentrate on the creative process.

SKILLS GUIDE

 Strong leadership skills to take charge of a cast, technical crew, and production teams.

 Excellent communication skills to ensure the cast and crew understand what to do.

 Creative flair in interpreting a script, framing shots, and giving clear direction to actors.

 Endurance and stamina to maintain the fast pace of filming under potentially difficult conditions.

 The ability to complete the project, working within the budgets set by the producer.

AT A GLANCE

 YOUR INTERESTS Film • Drama • Art • Music • English • Mathematics • Languages • Information Technology (IT)

 ENTRY QUALIFICATIONS A degree-level qualification in film production or cinematography is helpful, but not essential.

 LIFESTYLE Directors keep regular hours when planning and rehearsing. However, they often work long and irregular hours during shoots.

 LOCATION Film directors work in production studios, film-editing suites, on film sets, or outdoor locations, some of which are far from home.

 THE REALITIES This is a highly competitive field. Working on set can be both physically and emotionally demanding.

PRODUCER Steers a TV show or film from its earliest stages – securing funds, rights, and scripts – through production, all the way to release, promotion, and distribution. Not all producers have experience as a director.

TV/FILM DIRECTOR You will oversee the entire production of a film or TV show. With experience and success, you may take on progressively larger and more ambitious projects. You may choose to move into production – the business end of the industry.

▼ RELATED CAREERS

▶ **FILM OR VIDEO EDITOR** Works closely with the director after the filming has finished to select shot sequences, and arranges them in an order and style that creates a convincing and coherent story.

▶ **SCREENWRITER** Creates ideas and writes scripts for films or television shows. Screenwriters may also adapt existing works, such as novels or plays, for the screen.

▶ **THEATRE DIRECTOR** Interprets a dramatic script or musical score and directs actors and technicians. A theatre director is involved at all stages of the creative process, from casting actors and managing rehearsals, through to the final performance.

TV/FILM PRODUCER

JOB DESCRIPTION

The producer is the lynchpin of any TV or film production. The role involves assessing scripts, buying the rights to adapt books for the screen, and securing finance before filming. The producer hires a director and crew, organizes the shooting schedule, and is responsible for ensuring that the project is completed on time and to budget, using a blend of business acumen, creativity, and technical expertise.

SALARY

Assistant producer ★★☆☆☆
Experienced producer ★★★★★

INDUSTRY PROFILE

Most jobs based in large cities • Fiercely competitive industry • Permanent, salaried jobs becoming rare • Growing opportunities in cable and satellite TV

▼ RELATED CAREERS

▶ **TV/FILM DIRECTOR** see pp. 44–45

▶ **CAMERA OPERATOR** see pp. 48–49

▶ **SOUND ENGINEER** see pp. 50–51

▶ **PROGRAMME RESEARCHER** Contributes ideas for programmes, sourcing contacts and contributors. Programme researchers also collect, verify, and prepare information for film, TV, and radio productions.

▶ **RUNNER** Acts as a general assistant on a film or TV production, carrying out basic tasks, such as carrying equipment and making deliveries. For hard-working and motivated individuals, this entry-level job can lead to further opportunities in the industry.

The most successful producers are often paid a percentage of a film's box-office takings.

AT A GLANCE

YOUR INTERESTS Film • TV • Drama • Theatre • Photography • Videography • Crafts and design technology • English • History • Arts • Economics

ENTRY QUALIFICATIONS There are no defined entry qualifications. A degree in film production or similar is useful, and a showreel of work is essential.

LIFESTYLE Producers work long and irregular hours to ensure that projects finish on time. Working during weekends and holidays is common.

LOCATION Based in an office, producers need to travel to studios and casting sessions, and to oversee location shoots, some of which may be abroad.

THE REALITIES Finding work is tough in this competitive industry. Balancing the creative, practical, and financial aspects of a project can be stressful.

CAREER PATHS

There is no set path to becoming a film or TV producer, and no defined route for progression. However, many producers start as production assistants, then specialize in a particular area after gaining experience in the industry.

ASSISTANT You can gain experience in production work in the role of an assistant. You will perform administrative tasks, such as delivering props and scripts.

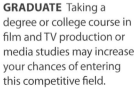

GRADUATE Taking a degree or college course in film and TV production or media studies may increase your chances of entering this competitive field.

SKILLS GUIDE

 Strong organizational skills for managing creative and technical processes on time and to budget.

 Excellent communication and interpersonal skills for teamwork during the production process.

 Creative flair to help interpret how a script can be presented through visual images and sound.

 Endurance and stamina for dealing with a range of responsibilities, often within tight timescales.

 Commercial awareness to manage resources effectively and raise the necessary finance for projects.

TV/FILM PRODUCER Working as an associate producer – who performs many of the tasks of a producer, under their direct supervision – can be a stepping stone to becoming a producer yourself. You can then specialize in a particular type of production.

EXECUTIVE PRODUCER Oversees the work of a producer on behalf of a studio or a project's backers. Usually focuses on the financial and creative aspects of production, as opposed to technical issues.

COMMERCIAL PRODUCER Produces TV commercials for advertisers, working on every aspect of the project, from writing to shooting and editing.

CORPORATE VIDEO PRODUCER Manages the production of videos for a range of purposes, such as business training and conferences, or award ceremonies and industry conventions.

VIDEO GAME PRODUCER Handles different aspects of video game development to ensure that it is being produced on schedule and to budget. This role requires an undergraduate degree in game design, computer science, or digital media.

CAMERA OPERATOR

JOB DESCRIPTION

The role of a camera operator involves recording moving images for films, TV shows, music videos, or commercials using digital video and film cameras. Camera operators use both technical and creative skills to follow a script, visualize and frame shots under instructions from a director, and work closely with performers as well as other members of the crew during the shoot.

SALARY

Camera assistant ★★★★★
Experienced operator ★★★★★

INDUSTRY PROFILE

Freelance work common • Full-time employment opportunities with large broadcasting companies • A number of jobs available in corporate and training video production

AT A GLANCE

YOUR INTERESTS Photography and videography • Cinema, film, and video • Art • Electronics • Design technology • Media • Travel

ENTRY QUALIFICATIONS A degree is useful, but practical knowledge of videography and work experience in the industry can be enough to get a job.

LIFESTYLE Long hours and tight deadlines are common. Operators may also have to travel to distant or extreme locations, such as deserts or war zones.

LOCATION Camera operators may work primarily in a studio or on location. They may need to spend extended periods away from home.

THE REALITIES Competition for jobs is intense, and many camera operators are self-employed, moving from one contract to another.

CAREER PATHS

Many camera operators get their foothold in the industry by working as runners, or as trainees with a production company. Your progress will depend on your talent and commitment, as well as on the way in which you develop a network of contacts in the industry.

ASSISTANT With some technical knowledge of film-making, you may become a camera assistant. Your job is to assemble the cameras, and keep shots in focus. With experience you can become a camera operator.

GRADUATE You can study for a degree-level qualification in photography, film and TV production, cinematography, or media studies, but technical ability and experience count for more than academic study.

▼ RELATED CAREERS

▶ **SOUND ENGINEER** *see pp. 50–51*

▶ **GRIP** Works with camera operators in the film and video industries. Grips are responsible for mounting camera equipment onto fixed or moving supports, such as cranes, and setting up lighting rigs safely. They also order and prepare the required equipment, and transport it to a film location.

▶ **LIGHTING ENGINEER** Sets up and operates all of the lighting equipment for video, film, TV, and theatre productions. Lighting engineers visit locations to assess requirements for lighting and special effects.

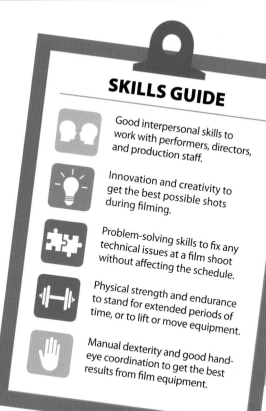

SKILLS GUIDE

Good interpersonal skills to work with performers, directors, and production staff.

Innovation and creativity to get the best possible shots during filming.

Problem-solving skills to fix any technical issues at a film shoot without affecting the schedule.

Physical strength and endurance to stand for extended periods of time, or to lift or move equipment.

Manual dexterity and good hand-eye coordination to get the best results from film equipment.

More than 20,000 camera operators work in the USA alone.

DIRECTOR OF PHOTOGRAPHY Works with the director of the film or TV show to establish its visual style. The job involves determining how a scene should be lit, which lenses and equipment should be used, and instructing camera and lighting crews.

IMAGE TECHNOLOGIST Develops new equipment and techniques that push the boundaries of what is possible to record on film or digital media. Imaging companies may recruit camera operators with expertise in the technical side of film-making to fill this role.

CAMERA OPERATOR You usually specialize in one area of work. This could be covering news stories for TV, making corporate videos, or recording sports events or concerts. With experience, it is possible to advance into more creative roles.

SOUND ENGINEER

JOB DESCRIPTION

Sound engineers work with musicians and film or TV producers to make high-quality recordings of music, speech, and other sounds. They oversee recording sessions, usually in a studio but sometimes on location. They set up microphones and other equipment, record different instruments or voices separately, and then mix these different recordings (known as tracks) together electronically to craft the desired overall sound.

SALARY

Junior sound engineer ★★★★★
Experienced sound engineer ★★★★★

INDUSTRY PROFILE

Opportunities in a range of industries, including broadcasting, music, TV, and computing and advertising • A growing sector continually evolving with development of new technology

CAREER PATHS

Formal training in sound engineering or music technology is an advantage in this competitive industry, but some studios and broadcasting companies take on talented trainees from school or college. You will need to learn continually to keep up to date with digital recording technologies if you are to be considered for more senior and creative roles.

TRAINEE You may be able to find an employer to take you on as a trainee. This route is very competitive and you will need good grades in mathematics, physics, and computer science. Any experience you may have from working on school productions or amateur gigs will be useful.

MIXING ENGINEER
Mixes or remixes music or sound. Mixing engineers edit the sound and manipulate the volume and pitch of individual tracks to achieve a finished mix (an electronic blend of music tracks or sounds) with the desired qualities.

GRADUATE A degree in sound or acoustic engineering gives you an excellent foundation in the technical and creative aspects of this career.

SOUND ENGINEER As a sound engineer, you record and mix sounds to realize the creative vision of the artist or film or TV producer. With experience, you can go on to manage a studio, or move into specialized roles in TV, film, or music production.

SKILLS GUIDE

 Good team-working skills to deal with artists and producers, often under intense time pressure.

 A good knowledge of operating a mixing console and other equipment to set sound levels.

 Scrupulous attention to detail for monitoring audio signals and keeping a log of all recordings.

 Physical strength for setting up equipment in a studio or on location at concerts and events.

 Excellent computer skills to operate state-of-the-art digital systems for recording music.

 Flexibility to work the long hours needed to accommodate performers and events.

 **SOUND DESIGNER** Takes responsibility for the entire sound of a production, which may be a film, video, or computer game. Sound engineers create and edit music and sound effects, using a range of digital equipment.

 MUSIC PRODUCER Brings together artists, songwriters, and technical know-how to create an original recorded work. Many music producers work for record companies or are hired by artists who are looking for a distinctive sound.

▼ RELATED CAREERS

 BROADCAST ENGINEER Sets up and operates the sophisticated electronic systems used in TV, radio, and other digital media broadcasts. Broadcast engineers work as part of a team with producers and presenters in recording studios, control rooms, or on location in all weather conditions. They also oversee the updating and repair of equipment, installing hardware, software, and other digital systems.

LIGHTING ENGINEER Prepares, sets up, and operates the lighting equipment for TV, film, or video productions, and live events, such as concerts and theatre productions. An excellent understanding of the effects achieved with different types of lighting is essential for any lighting engineer.

AT A GLANCE

 YOUR INTERESTS Music • Sound technology • Electronics • Physics • Mathematics • Information Technology (IT)

 ENTRY QUALIFICATIONS A relevant degree is desirable, but good technical skills and experience can get one started in this career.

LIFESTYLE Hours can be long and irregular. Sound engineers may be expected to work at night when studio time is less expensive.

 LOCATION Sound engineers may work in a studio or on location at concerts, on a film set, or at another live event. They may have to travel extensively.

 THE REALITIES The work can be demanding, but working as part of a creative team with talented artists can be highly rewarding.

WRITER

JOB DESCRIPTION

Writers work to inform, educate, or entertain their readers. They are skilled at using the written word to convey meaning or to tell stories, and work in a huge range of industries in diverse roles. Some writers achieve fame by writing novels or working as journalists or film scriptwriters, but many more make their living by writing articles for magazines and websites, press releases, or copy for advertisements.

SALARY
Varies enormously depending on the type of writing and experience

INDUSTRY PROFILE
Increasing demand for writers in online media • Fierce competition for work in every sector • Work predominantly freelance-based

AT A GLANCE

YOUR INTERESTS Writing • Languages • Literature and reading • Performing arts • Drama • Technical and scientific subjects

ENTRY QUALIFICATIONS No specific qualifications are required. Some writers have higher degrees in creative writing, but others have little formal education.

LIFESTYLE Many writers are self-employed and set their own working hours. They usually need to meet deadlines set by publishers.

LOCATION Writers may work on a computer in an office, a library, or at home. They sometimes need to travel to meet clients or conduct interviews.

THE REALITIES A writer's earnings can be as unpredictable as their workload. Writing is an isolating experience and all writers need great perseverance.

CAREER PATHS

The majority of writers work on a freelance basis, specializing in one of many areas, from children's books to technical manuals. As with many other creative jobs, there is no formal career structure, and some people can become writers without undergoing any training. Reputation and experience count for more than any qualifications.

BLOGGER Writing an online blog or contributing to a college magazine gives you a chance to develop your writing skills. Showing your work to online or print publishers may win you a paid commission.

GRADUATE A degree in English or creative writing is useful, but not essential. You may be better off taking a degree in another subject that enables you to become a writer on a specialized subject.

▼ RELATED CAREERS

▶ **JOURNALIST** *see pp. 54–55*

▶ **EDITOR** *see pp. 56–57*

▶ **PROOFREADER** Checks documents for accuracy, grammar, spelling, and consistency before their publication.

▶ **WEB CONTENT EDITOR** Writes text, and researches and collects images for publication on websites. Web content editors ensure that the content is accurate and that it is arranged correctly, as well as checking that links to other pages function properly.

A successful writer needs determination: J.K. Rowling's first novel, *Harry Potter and the Philosopher's Stone*, was rejected by 12 publishers.

SKILLS GUIDE

 Excellent writing and communication skills for creating lively and readable text.

 A high degree of creativity in inventing stories, characters, themes, and dialogue.

 Perseverance in the face of criticism from clients or the rejection of work from publishers.

 Good knowledge of Information Technology (IT), as almost all text is submitted electronically.

 Strong organizational skills to manage a schedule when working on your own.

An eye for detail to ensure that text is accurate and free from grammatical and spelling errors.

REVIEWER Analyses a variety of artistic works, including books, films, and theatrical performances, and then critiques them, in newspapers, magazines and journals, or online.

 POET Expresses an emotion or tells a story through verse. Some poets write with the aim of being published; others choose purely to perform to audiences.

 NOVELIST Writes fictional stories to entertain readers. There are many genres of novels, from science fiction to romance.

 SCREENWRITER Produces scripts for films and TV productions, sometimes adapting existing novels. Can also find work writing speeches for business leaders and politicians.

WRITER In this career, you may get lucky enough to be commissioned to write by a publisher. Otherwise you can write speculatively, hoping to sell your completed work. As an experienced writer, you can move into several other fields of work.

JOURNALIST

JOB DESCRIPTION

Journalism consists of two main related areas: researching and gathering information, and writing or presenting content. As a journalist, you will often need to be "on the go" to report events as they happen or to interview people on location. You will usually work on a specific subject area assigned to you.

SALARY

Newly qualified journalist ★★★★★
Experienced journalist ★★★★★

INDUSTRY PROFILE

Opportunities in traditional print journalism in decline • Many journalists write for online publications • Highly competitive • Deadline-driven industry

CAREER PATHS

Many journalists begin by writing for student publications. Once qualified, they can find work in diverse media – including newspapers, magazines, TV, and online – and choose to specialize in one field, such as sport or politics. They can progress to an editorial role, which involves managing a section of a publication or broadcast.

BROADCAST JOURNALIST Works for radio or TV stations broadcasting via air, cable, or the Internet. Broadcast journalists research, write, and often present stories for broadcast.

TRAINEE You may be able to find a trainee position if you lack a degree. A portfolio of work for school publications, blogs, or local magazines will help prove your abilities and commitment to employers.

GRADUATE You can apply for a trainee post with a media company after completing your degree. Many employers seek out applicants with postgraduate qualifications in journalism.

JOURNALIST After gaining the necessary qualifications and work experience for a local newspaper or radio station, you can choose to pursue one of a variety of specialisms in the field of journalism.

SKILLS GUIDE

 Excellent verbal and written skills to express ideas clearly to varied readerships or audiences.

 The ability to work with people in many teams, including editors, designers, and producers.

 Perseverance and a "can-do" attitude to create and present a story for the target audience.

 The flexibility to take on stories that arise without warning and to follow them as events unfold.

 Good organizational skills to meet tight deadlines, especially when juggling stories.

AT A GLANCE

 YOUR INTERESTS Writing • Research • Meeting and interacting with people • Media • Social media • Information Technology (IT)

 ENTRY QUALIFICATIONS A degree followed by postgraduate training in journalism is desirable; traineeships are also available.

 LIFESTYLE Work is project-based, with often long and irregular hours, which can extend to weekends and holidays. Some jobs require frequent travelling.

 LOCATION The work may be office-based, but travel is essential to conduct research and interviews depending on the chosen field.

 THE REALITIES Tight deadlines and long hours are common. Working conditions can be poor or dangerous, for example in war or disaster zones.

NEWSPAPER JOURNALIST
Provides information to the public about events, people, and ideas. The role involves detailed research, writing, and fact-checking.

MAGAZINE JOURNALIST
Researches and writes news articles and features for a variety of periodicals, including popular titles, business journals, and trade publications.

ONLINE JOURNALIST Produces content for online publication on one or many different topics. This requires good journalistic and IT skills, plus the ability to work in a variety of media – including video and sound.

▼ RELATED CAREERS

► **WRITER** see pp. 52–53

► **EDITOR** see pp. 56–57

► **ADVERTISING COPYWRITER** Produces the concise and persuasive written words, or copy, for advertisements. This can range from slogans and text for printed advertisements and leaflets to radio jingles and scripts for television commercials.

As global newspaper sales continue to fall, more people are choosing the Internet and radio for their daily news.

EDITOR

JOB DESCRIPTION

Editors of books and journals are responsible for the editorial content of their publications. In this role, your duties may range from evaluating manuscripts and commissioning writers to produce text, to checking text for accuracy, spelling, and grammar. Editors may work directly with subject experts, graphic designers, and picture researchers, and liaise with sales, marketing, or production staff to promote and print the publication.

SALARY

Editorial assistant ★★★★★
Editor ★★★★★

INDUSTRY PROFILE

Strong competition for entry-level jobs • Low pay levels for junior roles • Book and journal publishers increasingly turning to online publication • Jobs in book publishing not always advertised

CAREER PATHS

Most editors enter publishing as editorial assistants, helping with research, fact-checking, and basic editorial tasks. With experience they can gain promotion to manage the publication of a book or journal, and then a "list" – a themed category – of books. Some editors diversify into other roles in publishing, such as marketing or management.

GRADUATE To become an editor, you need a degree in English or a subject related to the type of publishing you intend to specialize in. An internship with a publishing company will give you useful experience, and you can also take industry-accredited courses in editing and proofreading.

▼ RELATED CAREERS

▶ **WRITER** see pp. 52–53

▶ **JOURNALIST** see pp. 54–55

▶ **ADVERTISING ACCOUNT MANAGER** see pp. 72–73

▶ **FILM/VIDEO EDITOR** Assembles pictures and sound for film or television. A film or video editor needs a good sense of timing, attention to detail, and the ability to meet deadlines. Due to the competitive and fast-paced nature of the industry, technical skills and experience are valued just as highly as formal qualifications.

EDITOR After gaining experience at editorial assistant level, you can choose to specialize in a particular type of book or journal publishing.

AT A GLANCE

 YOUR INTERESTS Reading · English · Literature · Languages · Graphic design · Information Technology (IT) · Creative writing

 LOCATION Editors are largely office- or home-based. Occasional travel to trade shows – sometimes overseas – or meetings may be required.

 ENTRY QUALIFICATIONS A degree is essential; English is preferred by some employers, but degrees in other subjects are useful for specialist publishing.

 THE REALITIES Editors must put in long hours of meticulous editorial work. Schedules can be demanding, especially if working on multiple projects.

 LIFESTYLE Editors in full-time jobs keep regular office hours, but evening and weekend work is often required, especially if freelancing.

SKILLS GUIDE

 Excellent verbal and written skills to express themes, ideas, and concepts clearly to the reader.

 Strong team-working skills for liaising with authors, designers, and other publishing departments.

 A creative flair, critiquing skills, and commercial awareness to improve and refine a publication.

 Flexibility and adaptability, as publishing schedules may be revised at short notice.

 Good organizational skills to handle heavy workloads on several ongoing projects.

 FICTION EDITOR Works with the author of a novel or short story to prepare the manuscript for publication. Assesses the author's work, suggests changes to make the text more engaging, corrects errors, and may advise on marketing and production.

 NON-FICTION EDITOR Develops, commissions, and checks content for non-fiction books, such as biographies, histories, and cookery, travel, or fitness books. Non-fiction editors may liaise with subject specialists to consult on the text.

 **REFERENCE EDITOR** Plans, commissions, and ensures the accuracy of text for a range of reference works, such as dictionaries, encyclopedias, directories, and academic or scientific works.

 ACADEMIC JOURNAL EDITOR Prepares scholarly or scientific articles for publication and distribution to academics and researchers. Ensures that articles are read and validated by expert consultants.

 ONLINE EDITOR Sources, edits, and collates text and imagery for publishing on websites. Online editors are trained in specialist web-design and editing software.

SALES, MARKETING, AND ADVERTISING

Commercial flair, an interest in selling, and a knowledge of customers are vital in this fast-paced industry. Job roles are diverse and range from creating adverts to writing press releases and predicting the public's spending habits.

SALES EXECUTIVE
Page 60

The aim of sales is to grow a firm's profits by increasing revenue from its products or services. Sales executives do this by approaching clients to win new business.

STORE MANAGER
Page 62

Using their leadership skills to motivate staff to achieve sales targets, store managers oversee the shops and supermarkets in which we purchase the goods we need.

BUYER
Page 64

With an eye on the latest trends and consumer demands, buyers make decisions about what will sell, which products to stock, and how to price them.

ESTATE AGENT
Page 66

Estate agents link home buyers and sellers, negotiating property sales on behalf of their clients. They are most in demand when the property market is booming.

MARKETING EXECUTIVE
Page 68

Clear and creative communication is the key to successful marketing. This is how marketing executives promote products, services, and ideas to customers.

MARKET RESEARCHER
Page 70

Combining numerical skills with knowledge of consumer behaviour, market researchers survey consumers' preferences to improve existing products and services.

ADVERTISING ACCOUNT MANAGER
Page 72

Interpreting the goals of their clients, advertising account managers work alongside a creative team to develop campaigns for print, television, and online media.

PUBLIC RELATIONS OFFICER
Page 74

The public perception of a product, service, or company is vital to its sales and popularity. Public relations officers promote a positive public image for their company.

SALES EXECUTIVE

JOB DESCRIPTION

Sales executives make contact with potential customers – either individuals or businesses – to sell their company's goods or services. They develop a thorough understanding of their company's products so that they can address a customer's queries with confidence to complete a sale. Sales executives must have a good understanding of both customer psychology and sales strategies to be successful.

SALARY

Retail sales worker ★★★★★
Business sales executive ★★★★★

INDUSTRY PROFILE

Job opportunities in all commercial sectors • Demand for sales executives varies with market conditions • Financial rewards often linked to sales targets

AT A GLANCE

YOUR INTERESTS Sales • Marketing • Customer service • Finance • English • Business studies • Mathematics • Advertising • Languages

ENTRY QUALIFICATIONS A degree is not essential for most sales jobs, but may be required when selling technical or financial products.

LIFESTYLE Sales executives may need to work long hours to meet sales targets or to deal with customers in other countries and time zones.

LOCATION Depending on the sector, sales executives may be based in stores or offices; they may travel widely to visit clients at their premises.

THE REALITIES Competition between colleagues and rivals can be intense. The role demands a thick skin to deal with rejection from customers.

▼ RELATED CAREERS

▶ **BRAND MANAGER** Promotes a company or a product by managing its profile and reputation among its customers and the wider public. Uses a variety of techniques, such as advertising and public relations, to enhance the brand's image.

▶ **INTERNET MARKETING MANAGER** Develops strategies to attract customers to an online store, and ensures that the design and usability of a retail website helps to increase sales.

▶ **RETAIL MANAGER** Manages the day-to-day operations of supermarkets and shops.

More than 12 per cent of all jobs in the USA are full-time sales positions.

CAREER PATHS

Sales executives need to be ambitious and determined because career progress depends entirely on hitting sales targets. Successful salespeople are typically promoted to handle larger and more valuable clients, and may go on to join a company's management team. Sales skills are highly transferable, and it is not unusual for sales executives to move between different industries.

SKILLS GUIDE

 Excellent communication skills for presenting product information to potential customers.

 Good interpersonal skills to handle queries and complaints in a professional manner.

 Strong organizational skills and self-motivation in planning and making sales calls and visits.

 A sound knowledge of business practices, and an awareness of customer expectations.

Good numerical skills for calculating percentages, discounts, and profits on sales.

JUNIOR EXECUTIVE You may begin your career in an administrative role, supporting senior salespeople. Your employer is likely to teach you about the company's products and sales techniques before you start to deal with customers.

SALES EXECUTIVE As a sales executive, you will represent an organization's products or services, and build and manage relationships with customers. With experience, you can move into several other fields of work.

SPECIALIST SALES EXECUTIVE Works in the financial sector, selling products such as mortgages and investments, or in other fields, selling products such as pharmaceuticals or Information Technology (IT) systems.

KEY ACCOUNT MANAGER Takes on responsibility for dealing with their employer's most valuable clients or product areas.

MARKETING EXECUTIVE Researches customer needs and behaviour and plans a company's strategy to promote its products.

SALES MANAGER Coordinates a company's sales operations in a region or country, setting targets and advising staff on ways to improve their performance.

STORE MANAGER

JOB DESCRIPTION

Store managers run the day-to-day business activities of a retail store. In this role, you lead and inspire a team of sales assistants, manage staff recruitment, organize pricing, displays, and promotions and special events, and deal with customer queries. You analyse sales data to forecast future stock requirements, and are also responsible for the health and safety of customers and staff in the store.

SALARY

Sales assistant ★★★★★
Head office manager ★★★★★

INDUSTRY PROFILE

Vast range of potential employers • Recent decline in business for some high-street stores • Many retailers also sell online, with store managers overseeing click-and-collect facilities

▼ RELATED CAREERS

▶ **SALES EXECUTIVE** *see pp. 60–61*

▶ **BUYER** *see pp. 64–65*

▶ **INTERNET MARKETING MANAGER** Develops Internet-based strategies to raise public awareness of an organization's activities.

▶ **MERCHANDISE MANAGER** Decides which goods to stock, sets prices, predicts future demand, and monitors supply levels.

▶ **SALES ASSISTANT** Works on the sales floor, replenishing stock, pricing, and ticketing, using checkout facilities, and serving customers.

In 2012, Switzerland had the highest retail sales per member of population in the world, at US$ 6,545.

AT A GLANCE

YOUR INTERESTS Business studies • Marketing • Dealing with people • Economics • Mathematics • Psychology • Information Technology (IT)

ENTRY QUALIFICATIONS A good general education is sufficient, but a degree in business or retail management will hasten promotion.

LIFESTYLE Shift and weekend work is normal at most stores. Overtime is to be expected in busy periods, such as stocktakes or during seasonal sales.

LOCATION Work is split between an office in the store and the sales floor. Some travel for training and to meetings with management is required.

THE REALITIES Store management is competitive and fast-paced. Long hours on the sales floor and pressure to meet sales targets can be tiring and stressful.

CAREER PATHS

There are two main routes to becoming a store manager: by joining a company as a sales assistant and gaining promotion through merit, or joining a retailer's training scheme, which may be open to school-leavers or graduates. The prospects for progression are good, with vacancies available with retailers of all sizes and specialisms.

SKILLS GUIDE

The ability to communicate well with customers and staff while maintaining a calm disposition.

Excellent team-working skills for motivating staff to achieve a store's sales targets.

Creativity and innovation in sales techniques and product display to increase store revenues.

Strong leadership skills to inspire staff to reach their potential and deliver excellent service.

Business-management skills, commercial awareness, and the ability to spot future trends.

SCHOOL-LEAVER You can join a retailer as a sales assistant and work your way up, or enrol in the company's management training programme.

GRADUATE A degree in any discipline will enable you to join a graduate training scheme, but employers favour subjects such as business studies, retail management, and marketing.

STORE MANAGER After gaining experience, you can seek promotion to work in a larger branch, or in one of the business areas of retailing, such as buying, human resources, or marketing.

OPERATIONS MANAGER Works with store managers and regional managers to help a business to increase its profits through methods such as marketing, more efficient stock control, or improved customer service.

RETAIL IT MANAGER Responsible for a store's technology systems, such as point-of-sale, stock ordering, and cash accounting, IT managers install updates and resolve computer problems as and when they occur.

HUMAN RESOURCE (HR) MANAGER Deals with staffing issues for a large store or for a number of stores, organizing recruitment, training, payroll, and staff rotas.

REGIONAL MANAGER Takes responsibility for the retail activities and profitability of a number of stores in a certain area, and liaises with senior management.

BUYER

JOB DESCRIPTION

Every retail business needs stock – the items it sells to its customers in store, online, or by mail order. A buyer's job is to source, select, and purchase these goods. Buyers must anticipate customer demands and predict market trends. By combining excellent people skills and deep industry knowledge, they negotiate prices with suppliers and agree delivery schedules to get the best deals for their company.

SALARY

Junior buyer ★★☆☆☆
Senior buyer ★★★★☆

INDUSTRY PROFILE

Demand for buyers set to grow • Plenty of job opportunities in all industry sectors • Growth in certain sectors depends on market trends

AT A GLANCE

YOUR INTERESTS Business studies • Economics • English • Mathematics • Law • Information Technology (IT) • Languages • Travel

ENTRY QUALIFICATIONS Relevant work experience may be enough, but some companies may expect a degree.

LIFESTYLE Buyers keep regular office hours. Workload may vary considerably if working in an area such as fashion, in which buying activity is seasonal.

LOCATION Most work is office-based, but buyers need to travel regularly to meet suppliers and attend industry events and trade fairs.

THE REALITIES This is a demanding job as buyers make decisions that impact a company financially. Success often leads to management-level roles.

CAREER PATHS

Buying is a key activity in the retail industry. With experience, buyers move on to manage ever-larger contracts with suppliers, or take responsibility for numerous product lines. This opens the door to higher management roles in planning, logistics (the transportation of goods), and marketing.

TRAINEE As a school-leaver, you can join a retail chain's management programme. You may then work as an assistant buyer, checking stock levels and placing orders while training on the job.

GRADUATE Your best route to becoming a buyer is to study for a degree in business and then take a postgraduate qualification in purchasing offers.

▼ RELATED CAREERS

▶ **SALES EXECUTIVE** *see pp. 60–61*

▶ **STORE MANAGER** *see pp. 62–63*

▶ **CONTRACT MANAGER** Manages the process of selecting suppliers by providing them with (detailed) information about the goods required and asking them to offer their best price. Contract managers arrange a formal contract between the buyer and seller, and manage the ongoing relationships with suppliers.

▶ **PURCHASING MANAGER** Buys the equipment, goods, and services needed by government departments or large industries.

SKILLS GUIDE

Good communication skills to explain buying choices and negotiate prices with suppliers.

A sharp analytical approach for comparing offers from various suppliers and selecting the best.

Confidence with numbers to calculate the best deals offered by suppliers and estimate profit margins.

An awareness of commercial needs and trends to ensure customer requirements are met.

Good attention to detail to ensure the right goods are purchased at the right time.

Depending on the item, or season, buyers will often buy merchandise six months before it is sold in stores.

MERCHANDISING MANAGER Controls all of the selling activities in a store or group of stores. This job includes tasks such as analysing the market, planning product lines and sales promotions, buying, and pricing goods.

COST ESTIMATOR Analyses data to predict the costs of future business activities and so determines if selling certain items will make a profit for a retail chain. The factors taken into consideration include the costs of labour, materials, storage, and transport.

BUYER As a buyer, you can specialize in diverse areas – from fashion to food. To progress, you usually need to gain accreditation by a professional body.

LOGISTICS MANAGER Oversees the transport of products from suppliers, through distribution centres, and onto the shelves of stores.

ESTATE AGENT

JOB DESCRIPTION

Estate agents organize the sale, purchase, and letting (renting) of properties. They meet sellers or landlords, value and market the house or flat, and present it to potential buyers or tenants. Sales agents handle all of the negotiations between the buyer and seller, and liaise with surveyors and lawyers to ensure the sale runs smoothly. Letting agents finalize the contractual details between landlords and tenants.

SALARY

Trainee estate agent ★★★★★
Experienced manager ★★★★★

INDUSTRY PROFILE

Many job opportunities, especially in big cities • Industry sensitive to economic change and housing demand • Estate agents often move between companies

CAREER PATHS

Estate agents handle the sales of residential and commercial properties, or focus on the rental property market. Once they have gained experience and seniority, they may progress to handling larger property deals, conduct property auctions, or choose to manage their own agencies.

LETTING AGENT You will oversee all aspects of letting a property, from valuing it to finding tenants. With experience, you will go on to become an assistant branch manager.

TRAINEE You can start your career as a trainee negotiator after leaving school or college. Employers may offer a short induction course, and encourage you to study for further qualifications.

The world's largest estate agent, Century 21, has more than 7,100 offices in 74 countries.

SALES AGENT You will oversee all aspects of the sale of a property, from valuing it and finding potential buyers, to supervising the completion of the sale. With experience, you will go on to become an assistant branch manager.

SKILLS GUIDE

 Excellent verbal communication skills to promote properties to potential clients.

 Flexibility to deal with a variety of challenging negotiations between a wide range of clients.

 The ability to understand the requirements of potential clients and adapt responses accordingly.

 Organizational skills to deal with many sales or rentals going through at the same time.

 Awareness of current commercial trends, and escalating or declining prices in the property market.

ASSISTANT BRANCH MANAGER Assists the branch manager with the overall running of an estate agency. Has a proven track record in sales, valuation, and property listing.

BRANCH MANAGER Handles the branch's staff and administration, and is responsible for increasing the profitability of the branch.

AGENCY DIRECTOR Owns or runs an estate agency, overseeing all aspects of the business, from employing staff to attracting new clients in both the sales and rental property markets.

▼ RELATED CAREERS

▶ **QUANTITY SURVEYOR** *see pp. 198–199*

▶ **DOMESTIC ENERGY ASSESSOR** Calculates how much energy a property uses and comes up with ways to make it more energy-efficient. Makes recommendations to home owners to save them money on their energy bills.

▶ **LICENCED CONVEYANCER** Handles all the legal matters involved in the sale and purchase of properties. Licenced conveyancers must pass related exams before they can start practising.

▶ **PROPERTY DEVELOPER** Buys, improves, then sells properties to make money. May invest in a wide range of properties, from new developments to homes requiring renovation, before selling them for a profit.

AT A GLANCE

 YOUR INTERESTS Marketing • Sales • Property • Customer service • Estate management • Business studies • English

 ENTRY QUALIFICATIONS After leaving school or college, one can begin as a trainee with a company, which may provide induction courses.

 LIFESTYLE Outside of regular office hours, estate agents may need to attend property viewings in the evenings and weekends.

 LOCATION Estate agents usually deal with properties within a defined location. The flexibility to travel quickly to properties in that area is essential.

 THE REALITIES There is an intense pressure to meet sales targets. Basic salaries are often low and supplemented by bonuses on commissions.

MARKETING EXECUTIVE

JOB DESCRIPTION

Marketing is the art – and science – of creating demand for a product or service. Executives in this area work to communicate positive messages about products and brands to potential customers through print, TV, and online advertising. They may also use social media, or make direct contact via email, post, or telephone.

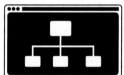

SALARY

Marketing manager ★★☆☆☆
Marketing director ★★★☆☆

INDUSTRY PROFILE

Competitive and fast-paced industry • Opportunities in company marketing departments and stand-alone agencies • Digital and social media becoming increasingly important

AT A GLANCE

YOUR INTERESTS Business studies • Economics • Mathematics • English • Science • Information Technology (IT) • Psychology • Sociology

ENTRY QUALIFICATIONS A business-related degree is a great advantage, although training on the job as a marketing assistant is an option.

LIFESTYLE Most marketing executives keep regular office hours, but may need to work evenings and weekends when launching a new campaign.

LOCATION Based in an office, marketing executives need to travel to present work to clients at their premises or to attend conferences.

THE REALITIES Job specifications – and salaries – vary widely. Pressure to deliver results can be high, and junior roles may offer limited creativity.

CAREER PATHS

Some marketing executives work for one individual company that makes and sells products and services; others are employed by specialist marketing agencies who develop and deliver campaigns for numerous clients. It is possible to move between the two sectors to gain promotion and responsibility for larger and higher-profile campaigns.

ASSISTANT In this entry-level job, you assist a marketing team by preparing presentations and dealing with clients. With experience, you can progress to the role of marketing executive.

GRADUATE In order to enter marketing at an executive level, you will need to study for a degree in a related subject, such as marketing, communications, business management, or advertising.

▼ RELATED CAREERS

▶ **MARKET RESEARCHER** *see pp. 70–71*

▶ **ADVERTISING ACCOUNT MANAGER**
see pp. 72–73

▶ **PUBLIC RELATIONS OFFICER** *see pp. 74–75*

▶ **ADVERTISING MEDIA BUYER** Negotiates
on behalf of clients to buy advertising space in
print and on billboards, as well as airtime on TV,
radio, and digital media, with the aim of reaching
the target audience for as little cost as possible.

▶ **SALES DIRECTOR** Oversees a company's sales
and its position in the marketplace, directing
sales strategy and managing sales staff.

SKILLS GUIDE

 Good evaluative skills to help
analyse market trends and
competitors' products and services.

 Excellent numerical skills for
preparing and managing
budgets and accounts.

 Strong communication skills
for presenting reports to senior
managers and directors.

 The ability to manage, inspire,
and support a team, and take
the lead in client meetings.

 Creative thinking to come up
with new marketing concepts
and strategies.

 Good business awareness and the
ability to identify target markets
and analyse market-research data.

DIRECT MARKETING MANAGER
Promotes a company's products
and services by engaging directly
with customers through channels
such as mail shots, competitions,
displays in shops, and money-off
or loyalty schemes.

ONLINE MARKETING MANAGER
Promotes products and services through
websites, social media, and email
campaigns. Works to build awareness
of a company or product, and to attract
Internet traffic to its website.

EVENT MARKETING MANAGER
Markets products or services by
sponsoring or placing promotions,
such as branded displays or handing
out free samples, at public events.

MARKETING EXECUTIVE Most marketing
executives gain experience on the job, but many
employers will encourage you to study for
professional qualifications. You can specialize in a
particular type of marketing, or after three or more
years in the job, aim for promotion to senior roles.

FREELANCE CONSULTANT Provides
advice to companies on how best to
present their products to customers.
Usually possesses an in-depth knowledge
of consumer activity and buying trends
within a specific industry.

MARKET RESEARCHER

JOB DESCRIPTION

Market researchers gather information to help organizations understand the needs and preferences of customers, and to assist with developing new products. They carry out surveys by telephone, post, online, or in person, and analyse the results to produce reports of people's opinions about a product, brand, or a political or social issue.

SALARY

Market researcher ★★☆☆☆
Market research director ★★★★★

INDUSTRY PROFILE

Marketing agencies are largest employers • Industry in decline in the Middle East and Europe, but growing in most other parts of the world

CAREER PATHS

A degree is usually required to enter the market research sector, which includes marketing agencies, businesses, government departments, or charities. Early in their career, market researchers collect and analyse information, but with experience, may choose to conduct research for clients, give presentations, or manage teams on projects.

DATA ANALYST Specializes in using statistical and mathematical methods to analyse market research data. Data analysts interpret the results and present their findings to clients.

SCHOOL-LEAVER You can find work as a market research assistant if you have good literacy and numeracy skills; experience in customer service is also beneficial. You can combine working as an assistant with taking a part-time degree in a related subject.

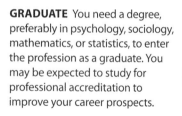

GRADUATE You need a degree, preferably in psychology, sociology, mathematics, or statistics, to enter the profession as a graduate. You may be expected to study for professional accreditation to improve your career prospects.

MARKET RESEARCHER You can stay in touch with advances in research methods by taking courses run by professional bodies. You can specialize in areas such as ethnographic research – observing people at home or work to understand their needs better – or move into management roles.

SKILLS GUIDE

Strong interpersonal skills to put people at ease while conducting market research interviews.

Good writing skills for scripting questionnaires and preparing reports and presentations.

Perseverance and self-motivation for completing research tasks in order to meet projected targets.

Flexibility to work irregular hours, and to adapt to different research methods and interview styles.

Excellent attention to detail when completing market research surveys and collating the results.

Good numerical and analytical skills to interpret data using statistical methods.

RESEARCH MANAGER Oversees the planning, execution, and analysis of market research projects, from setting goals with the client to choosing a survey method and preparing reports.

ACCOUNT DIRECTOR Manages client accounts for a marketing agency, ensuring that market research is carried out in the best way and among the right customer group to suit the client's goals.

Market research was developed in the 1930s by US advertising pioneer Daniel Starch.

AT A GLANCE

YOUR INTERESTS Psychology • Sociology • Anthropology • Statistics • Mathematics • Information Technology (IT) • Business studies • Economics

ENTRY QUALIFICATIONS A degree-level qualification is usually required. Prior marketing experience or working in a customer-facing job is useful.

LIFESTYLE Most researchers keep regular office hours, but conducting face-to-face surveys may require working on evenings and weekends.

LOCATION Most of the work is office-based. Researchers may need to travel to conduct surveys or to run consumer focus groups.

THE REALITIES Workload can be high as researchers often manage several studies at once. An appealing job for those who enjoy dealing with people.

▼ RELATED CAREERS

▶ **MARKETING EXECUTIVE** *see pp. 68–69*

▶ **INVESTMENT ANALYST** *see pp. 100–101*

▶ **CONSUMER SCIENTIST** Researches the tastes, needs, and preferences of existing and potential customers, and advises commercial clients on improvements to products and services.

▶ **INFORMATION SCIENTIST** Acquires, manages, and utilizes electronically stored information – such as online databases – for commercial, public-sector, or charitable uses.

▶ **STATISTICIAN** Collects, analyses, and interprets complex quantitative data, then presents it in a comprehensible form using graphs and charts.

ADVERTISING ACCOUNT MANAGER

JOB DESCRIPTION

In the advertising industry, the account manager is the most important link between an agency's creative team and its clients. In this role, you work with your creative team to create an effective advertising campaign that fulfils the client's goals. You track each campaign stage to ensure that the client is happy, and that the team sticks to deadlines and budgets.

SALARY

Junior account manager ★★★★★
Account director ★★★★★

INDUSTRY PROFILE

Highly competitive, fast-paced industry • Roles available in public and private sectors • Opportunities across the world

CAREER PATHS

An advertising account manager works on the business side of the advertising industry, and it is rare for individuals to move from this area into creative roles, and vice versa. Experienced account managers may, however, move into marketing roles within larger companies.

ACCOUNT DIRECTOR Looks after a team of advertising account managers, and usually works on larger, more complex projects with high-profile clients.

ASSISTANT Some advertising agencies take on school-leavers to work in an administrative role, for example, in their media buying departments. From here, you may be able to apply for internal promotion.

GRADUATE A degree in any discipline will allow you to apply for the graduate training schemes run by many agencies. These schemes will train you to become an advertising account executive.

ADVERTISING ACCOUNT MANAGER This role is linked to your reputation, which you can build by working on high-profile projects and networking within the industry. Managers tend to work for clients in one specific industry, such as in food or financial services. After gaining experience, you can go on to become an account director or work on a freelance basis.

SKILLS GUIDE

 Excellent written and verbal communication skills to tailor campaigns to meet client needs.

 The ability to lead, inspire, and motivate a creative team to produce successful campaigns.

 Good organizational skills to manage many complex and varied advertising projects at once.

 The drive and motivation to succeed, and the ability to develop this attitude among team members.

 An extensive knowledge of market trends, current media, and the client's business and competitors.

GROUP ACCOUNT DIRECTOR
Supervises the advertising accounts and staff of a whole group of advertising companies, and possibly even advertising branches across the world.

FREELANCE ADVERTISING ACCOUNT MANAGER
Chooses to work freelance as either an advertising consultant or start up a new advertising company.

> The skills base of an advertising account manager is changing to adapt to advances in the latest digital technology.

▼ RELATED CAREERS

▶ **JOURNALIST** *see pp. 54–55*

▶ **MARKETING EXECUTIVE** *see pp. 68–69*

▶ **PUBLIC RELATIONS OFFICER** *see pp. 74–75*

▶ **ADVERTISING ART DIRECTOR** Creates visual ideas to convey a clear message for advertising campaigns. Works with a copywriter, who writes text, or copy, for the target audience.

▶ **MEDIA BUYER** Organizes and purchases advertisement space in magazines, newspapers, TV, and online resources on behalf of clients to promote their products and services.

▶ **SALES PROMOTION EXECUTIVE** Organizes promotional marketing campaigns to encourage consumers to purchase products and services.

AT A GLANCE

 YOUR INTERESTS Media • Social media • Current affairs • English • Communications • Business management • Art • Design

 ENTRY QUALIFICATIONS Although there are no set entry requirements, a degree will help join a graduate training scheme with an employer.

 LIFESTYLE Official working hours are usually regular, but most account managers may need to put in overtime if they need to complete a project.

 LOCATION The work is office-based, but travel may be needed to meet clients and collect market research data, or go abroad for international campaigns.

 THE REALITIES This is a high-profile job with a lot of responsibility. It can be stressful at times, but greater experience produces financial rewards.

PUBLIC RELATIONS OFFICER

JOB DESCRIPTION

Organizations hire Public Relations (PR) officers to manage and boost their reputations. As a PR officer, you produce campaigns to promote awareness of a company and its products or services. You can achieve this using conventional media, such as newspapers, or online social media, or by creating promotional film, literature, and other materials.

SALARY

Publicity assistant ★★★★★
Account director ★★★★★

INDUSTRY PROFILE

Highly competitive job market • Majority of work in large firms • Most work located in big cities • Global opportunities • Freelance possible

CAREER PATHS

PR officers can work within organizations, communicating with both staff and the wider public, or for agencies hired by corporate clients. Progress in either arena depends much on their abilities and commitment.

ASSISTANT Straight after school you can take an administrative role in the PR department of a large organization, or within a PR agency.

GRADUATE You can study PR at college, but most employers welcome candidates with degrees in disciplines such as English, journalism, business studies, or marketing.

▼ RELATED CAREERS

▶ **MARKETING EXECUTIVE** *see pp. 68–69*

▶ **ADVERTISING ACCOUNT MANAGER** *see pp. 72–73*

▶ **EVENTS MANAGER** *see pp. 88–89*

▶ **CHARITY FUNDRAISER** *see pp. 90–91*

▶ **ADVERTISING COPYWRITER** Produces text, or copy, for marketing and advertising materials. Also liaises with clients, designers, and the rest of the creative team to agree on campaign style and content.

PUBLIC RELATIONS OFFICER To progress as a PR officer, you may be expected to study for professional qualifications in order to progress to more senior roles.

AT A GLANCE

 YOUR INTERESTS Media • Marketing and communication • Social media • Business studies • Advertising • Current trends

 ENTRY QUALIFICATIONS There are no set entry requirements, but many employers expect a degree in a relevant subject, such as communications.

 LIFESTYLE Working hours are regular, although it may be necessary to attend social events and launches in the evenings.

 LOCATION PR officers usually work in an office, but may have to travel to meet clients or for promotional events, requiring short periods away from home.

THE REALITIES Flexibility is essential to attend various events scheduled at different times. Work and social life can often merge into one.

> PR specialists in government are known as press secretaries.

SKILLS GUIDE

 Excellent written and verbal skills to craft original and memorable campaigns.

 An ability to grasp a client's needs quickly and handle multiple PR campaigns at once.

 A clear understanding of the interests, aims, and requirements of the client and target audience.

 Exceptional planning and organizational skills for running different projects.

 Knowledge of global events and current business trends to help create effective PR strategies.

 ACCOUNT MANAGER Manages a small team and, within a PR agency, provides the primary point of contact for a particular client.

 **ACCOUNT DIRECTOR** Liaises with senior managers to develop and deliver effective campaigns, and is often responsible for managing a large team of PR officers.

 COMMUNICATIONS MANAGER Leads a team within a company to deliver consistent news and business messages to all staff.

 DIGITAL COMMUNICATIONS MANAGER Deals with managing and promoting organizations through various channels, such as digital, online, and social media.

 HEAD OF COMMUNICATIONS Executes complex, innovative, and high-profile projects. This senior internal role requires excellent leadership skills.

ADMINISTRATION AND BUSINESS MANAGEMENT

Decision-making and organizational abilities are key aspects of administration and business management. There are many sectors of employment within this field, and you will need a range of skills – from problem-solving to expertise in leadership to teamworking – to excel.

CUSTOMER SERVICE MANAGER
Page 78

The public face of a business or organization, customer service managers work to ensure that clients are happy with the products and services they provide.

HUMAN RESOURCE MANAGER
Page 80

People are the most valuable asset of any organization. Human resource managers recruit and train staff, and deal with personnel issues, such as equal-opportunity policies.

PROJECT MANAGER
Page 82

Working in virtually every industry and sector, project managers ensure that projects are well-organized, run smoothly, and within budget.

MANAGEMENT CONSULTANT
Page 84

Contracted by firms to identify problems and recommend solutions, management consultants are business experts with the skills to cut to the heart of key issues.

PERSONAL ASSISTANT
Page 86

Busy executives rely on their personal assistants to organize their diaries, deal with correspondence, and supervise administrative staff.

EVENTS MANAGER
Page 88

Commercial, charitable, and public events require careful planning, whatever their scale. Running them are events managers, who ensure that every aspect runs smoothly.

CHARITY FUNDRAISER
Page 90

Fundraising is fundamental to the operation of every charity, and fundraisers must develop exciting and innovative approaches to bringing in donations.

TRANSLATOR
Page 92

Drawing on their linguistic skills and an understanding of other cultures and traditions, translators convert written or audio material from one language to another.

CUSTOMER SERVICE MANAGER

JOB DESCRIPTION

The experience of buying products or using services is enhanced by impressive customer support. A customer service manager works for an organization to ensure that its clients are satisfied. Leading a dedicated team, managers handle customer queries, offer product advice, and resolve complaints. More senior managers develop a company's policies and procedures.

SALARY

Customer service assistant ★★★★★
Experienced manager ★★★★★

INDUSTRY PROFILE

Many opportunities available across a wide range of organizations • More jobs resulting from the growth in online retailing • Customer service skills in high demand • Target-driven work

CAREER PATHS

Most people begin their careers as customer service assistants, learning on the job by dealing directly with clients. With experience they can progress into supervisory and then managerial roles. Customer service managers are employed in businesses such as retail, telecommunications, and financial services, and public sector areas, such as health care and social security.

SENIOR CUSTOMER SERVICE MANAGER Develops policies, procedures, and staff training programmes to improve customer service standards across the business.

ASSISTANT As a school-leaver, you can begin your career as an assistant. Employers will train you on products and services, and on customer service procedures and protocols.

GRADUATE If you have an undergraduate degree in a subject such as business or management, you can start as a trainee customer services manager with a large corporation.

CUSTOMER SERVICE MANAGER Experience is crucial if you want to move up the ladder in your organization. In bigger companies, you can progress into one of several specializations or move up into a more senior role.

SKILLS GUIDE

 Communication and motivational skills to deal with both customers and colleagues.

 Good team-working skills to work closely with customer service agents to keep them happy and driven.

 The ability to lead and inspire staff to get the best out of them, and also reflect well on the company.

 Genuine understanding and empathy to resolve a range of customer queries and problems.

 Excellent organizational skills and the ability to manage staff and high volumes of caller queries.

 Great problem-solving skills to provide effective responses to various customer complaints.

AT A GLANCE

 YOUR INTERESTS Business studies • Administration • Retail • Customer care • Information Technology (IT) • Psychology

 ENTRY QUALIFICATIONS An undergraduate degree in business or management can boost chances of landing a job as a trainee.

 LIFESTYLE Customer service managers work regular hours. Shift work is sometimes necessary to cover evenings and weekends.

 LOCATION The work is mainly office-based. Out-of-town call centres are becoming common as they are cheaper to run than city offices.

 THE REALITIES The industry is driven by meeting quality targets. Though irate clients can be frustrating, it is satisfying to resolve their problems.

 CUSTOMER SERVICE ASSESSOR Trains and develops staff who are new to the customer service role. Assessors use training techniques to ensure that candidates reach the required standards of work.

 **BUSINESS MANAGER** Influences strategic business decisions based on customer satisfaction in order to push up sales. Works as part of the senior management team.

▼ RELATED CAREERS

▶ **HUMAN RESOURCE MANAGER** *see pp. 80–81*

▶ **HOTEL MANAGER** *see pp. 304–305*

▶ **CALL CENTRE MANAGER** Oversees the day-to-day running of a call centre, where call centre operators answer customer enquiries via telephone or email. Managers organize the staff, explain their duties, and set their targets.

▶ **OFFICE MANAGER** Organizes and supervises administrative and IT tasks to ensure the smooth running of an office.

▶ **RETAIL MANAGER** Runs shops and department stores, while also managing staff. Has strong commercial skills and uses displays and pricing methods to maximize revenue.

HUMAN RESOURCE MANAGER

JOB DESCRIPTION

Human Resource (HR) professionals deal with people in the workforce. They work for organizations and are responsible for hiring new staff, and for ensuring that employees uphold company standards and procedures. They also represent staff, negotiating their benefits and offering them new training and development opportunities.

SALARY

HR assistant ★★★★★
HR manager ★★★★★

INDUSTRY PROFILE

Competitive but growing industry •
Jobs in companies' own HR divisions and also in external HR agencies •
Industry very sensitive and responsive to movements in the economy

AT A GLANCE

YOUR INTERESTS Project management • Employment law • Marketing and communication • Psychology • English

ENTRY QUALIFICATIONS A degree in business, management, law, or a similar subject is desirable. Some companies hire trainees at junior levels.

LIFESTYLE Working hours are regular. As the "face" of an organization, HR managers have to look professional and well-presented at all times.

LOCATION An HR manager will probably be based at the head office of a business. Travel is likely as a company may have branches in different locations.

THE REALITIES Dealing with people is not easy. It is important to be strong and resilient, while showing sensitivity when handling their professional issues.

▼ RELATED CAREERS

▶ **MANAGEMENT CONSULTANT** *see pp. 84–85*

▶ **EMPLOYEE RELATIONS MANAGER** Facilitates effective working relationships between management and employees. May cover all communications between the two, including employment contracts, changes to workforce planning, and trade unions.

▶ **LEARNING AND DEVELOPMENT PROFESSIONAL** Delivers training sessions to all employees to improve business practices and outcomes.

▶ **OCCUPATIONAL HEALTH PROFESSIONAL** Provides health support to employees while at work. Plays an important role in promoting health and advising on safety issues. Treating staff who become unwell at work, occupational health professionals also maintain detailed health records for all employees.

▶ **RECRUITMENT PROFESSIONAL** Finds and helps select suitable candidates for employment. Recruitment professionals conduct necessary background checks for potential candidates.

CAREER PATHS

Some colleges offer programmes in HR management, but a business-related degree is usually enough to apply for entry-level jobs. In larger companies, it may be possible to specialize in one area of HR, such as recruitment and selection, or learning and development.

SKILLS GUIDE

 Good communication skills to interact and negotiate effectively with colleagues.

 Leadership skills and the vision to implement difficult policies and measure the impact of decisions.

 Sensitivity towards diverse viewpoints and empathy for employees' issues at work.

 Decisive problem-solving to help make individual employees productive and happy at work.

Precision and an eye for detail in HR activities, such as recruitment drives and payroll administration.

HR OFFICER Joining a company as an HR officer, you start in a general role, gaining an overview of relevant activities. The work can be routine and repetitive.

EMPLOYEE RELATIONS OFFICER If you have a background in law, this is a suitable role that involves negotiating legal aspects with employees.

HR MANAGER While HR management is a common position in most companies, with experience you may be able to progress into more senior roles or various specialisms.

TALENT MANAGER Sources, recruits, and retains key personnel for a business. Works with senior management to ensure that the needs of a business are being met by its current and future workforce.

LEARNING AND DEVELOPMENT MANAGER Identifies the training needs of employees, including inductions for newcomers, and ongoing technical training for staff and management.

HR DIRECTOR Plays the lead role in shaping and driving an organization's HR policies, from recruitment to training.

INDEPENDENT HR CONSULTANT Provides HR expertise to client companies. This role is suitable for senior HR managers who want the freedom to choose their clients.

PROJECT MANAGER

JOB DESCRIPTION

Project managers work in a range of industries to ensure that projects are completed on time and to budget. In this role, you will need to draw upon organizational and interpersonal skills to agree the project's goals with your client, draft a plan, identify risks, and assemble a team of consultants and specialists to carry out the work. You then monitor the progress of the project until its goals have been achieved.

SALARY

Project manager ★★★☆☆
Senior project manager ★★★★★

INDUSTRY PROFILE

Good pay levels • Opportunities in public and private sectors • Key role in a wide range of industries • Size and number of available projects depends on state of economy

▼ RELATED CAREERS

▶ **MANAGEMENT CONSULTANT** *see pp. 84–85*

▶ **EVENTS MANAGER** *see pp. 88–89*

▶ **SYSTEMS ANALYST** *see pp. 120–121*

▶ **CONSTRUCTION MANAGER** *see pp. 204–205*

By 2012, the number of project managers awarded Project Management Professional status had reached 470,000 around the world.

AT A GLANCE

YOUR INTERESTS Business studies • Economics • Management • Accounting • Information Technology (IT) • Mathematics • English • Psychology

ENTRY QUALIFICATIONS A degree in project- or business-management, or in a subject directly relevant to the industry, is essential.

LIFESTYLE Project managers generally work longer hours than project staff in order to ensure that the project hits targets and deadlines.

LOCATION Managers often alternate between an office and a project site, which may be outdoors. Local and international travel are common.

THE REALITIES The job may involve changing location, colleagues, and clients for each new project. Inactivity while awaiting a new project can be frustrating.

CAREER PATHS

Most project managers hold a degree related to the sector in which they work, or a qualification in business administration. They usually specialize in managing projects in one sector, such as IT or construction.

ASSISTANT This role enables you to learn on the job by taking a distance-learning degree and lending support to project managers.

GRADUATE A degree followed by a postgraduate qualification in project management offers you the best way into this career.

SKILLS GUIDE

 Strong written and verbal skills for briefing teams and making progress reports.

 The ability to coordinate, lead, and monitor a diverse team with different skills and specialisms.

 Excellent numerical and statistical skills for planning budgets and managing accounts.

 Strong IT skills for using project-management planning and monitoring software.

 Excellent problem-solving skills to find effective and timely solutions to problems.

PROJECT MANAGER
After gaining experience of supervising and managing projects, you can choose to specialize in one of a number of sectors. You can also seek sponsorship from your employer to study for professional qualifications in project management.

CONSTRUCTION PROJECT MANAGER
Oversees the successful delivery of construction projects, such as new housing, roadways, airports, or retail parks.

CONSERVATION PROJECT MANAGER
Plans, oversees, and delivers projects such as breeding programmes or habitat protection for wildlife trusts, conservation bodies, or environmental agencies.

ARTS PROJECT MANAGER Supervises and delivers arts-related ventures such as community arts projects, installations and exhibitions, and arts-education projects.

IT PROJECT MANAGER Coordinates IT projects such as installing or upgrading computer systems, networks, hardware, and software for new or existing businesses and organizations.

ENGINEERING PROJECT MANAGER Manages engineering projects such as the building of railways, bridges, power stations, telecommunications systems, and energy networks.

MANAGEMENT CONSULTANT

JOB DESCRIPTION

Management consultants provide businesses with specialist research and advice to help them grow and increase their profits. The largest consultancies advise on all business areas, from Information Technology (IT) and finance to human resources, while smaller companies may specialize in one specific area of business.

SALARY

Graduate consultant ★★☆☆☆
Experienced consultant ★★★★☆

INDUSTRY PROFILE

The largest consultancies employ thousands of staff and have offices all over the word • Some clients retain consultants for long-term projects

AT A GLANCE

YOUR INTERESTS Management science • Business studies • Economics • Accounting • Marketing • Mathematics • Statistics • Political science

ENTRY QUALIFICATIONS A degree is essential. Most employers will expect a postgraduate degree or experience that is relevant to their area of activity.

LIFESTYLE Long working hours and frequent travel are common. Management consultants may have to spend long periods away from home.

LOCATION Management consultants are usually office-based in a large city, but may have to visit clients at different locations, some of them abroad.

THE REALITIES The financial rewards are high, but management consultants have to work hard, and may have to spend long periods away from home.

CAREER PATHS

Management consultancy firms offer internships and training programmes to high-achieving graduates. Following a period of training, management consultants usually specialize in one area, such as helping companies re-brand, or analysing a client's competitors or sales strategies.

BUSINESS PROFESSIONAL

Your chances of becoming a management consultant are higher if you have solid experience or formal training in a profession such as law, finance, accountancy, or IT.

GRADUATE

You can join a management consultancy as an intern after completing a degree. Competition for places is intense, but for ambitious graduates they offer the best route into the profession.

▼ RELATED CAREERS

▶ **HUMAN RESOURCE MANAGER** *see pp. 80–81*

▶ **ACCOUNTANT** *see pp. 102–103*

▶ **ECONOMIST** *see pp. 108–109*

▶ **POLITICIAN** *see pp. 114–115*

▶ **COMPANY EXECUTIVE** Responsible for directing a company, setting its policies and targets, and ensuring that the company's managers work towards these goals. Most company executives specialize in one area of business activity, such as finance or human resources, and are part of a board of executives with different skills and responsibilities.

SKILLS GUIDE

 Good communication skills to work with senior managers and executives.

 Leadership and authority to implement change in a business or organization.

 The ability to understand and interpret complex numerical data and financial reports.

 Strong mathematical skills for collecting and processing data, and making financial projections.

 A thorough understanding of business processes, taxes, and the impact of business decisions.

 An eye for detail for analysing data and other business-related information accurately.

FINANCIAL CONSULTANT

Reviews a company's financial systems and evaluates its business plans in order to help it identify ways of raising money to grow. Financial consultants usually come from an accountancy background.

STRATEGY CONSULTANT

Analyses a business and provides advice on issues, such as how to improve the value of the company's shares, or how to diversify the company's activities. Works closely with senior management.

OPERATIONS CONSULTANT

Focuses on helping a company improve its productivity by analysing the workflow between employees, and looking at a company's structures and policies.

MANAGEMENT CONSULTANT In this role, you examine a client company's working methods and strategies, applying your own expert knowledge to help solve a variety of business problems. With experience you can move into a number of different roles.

PERSONAL ASSISTANT

JOB DESCRIPTION

Personal Assistants (PAs) support business executives and senior managers in their day-to-day work. They set up meetings for their employer, manage their correspondence, organize their travel requirements, and file documents. Experienced PAs may even represent their employers at meetings.

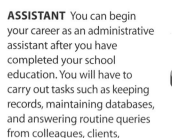

SALARY

Junior PA ★★★★★
PA to company chairman ★★★★★

INDUSTRY PROFILE

High demand for candidates with computing and language skills • PAs required in every sector of business

CAREER PATHS

The role of a PA can vary enormously depending on the employer. The most senior PAs command good salaries and have a detailed understanding of their employer's business. Ultimately, they may even move into management roles themselves.

RECEPTIONIST Highly experienced receptionists can move into more administrative work, such as a PA role within a company.

ASSISTANT You can begin your career as an administrative assistant after you have completed your school education. You will have to carry out tasks such as keeping records, maintaining databases, and answering routine queries from colleagues, clients, or suppliers.

GRADUATE If you have a degree and good administrative skills, you may find a job as a PA for a senior executive. Proficiency in languages or knowledge of the employer's business sector is an advantage in most roles.

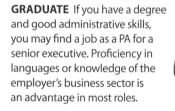

PERSONAL ASSISTANT With experience, you will develop knowledge of the business in which you work. You can move into more senior roles, such as human resources or office management.

SKILLS GUIDE

 Good communication skills for negotiating with others, writing reports, and dealing with enquiries.

 Team-working skills to deal with people at all levels in an office or organization.

 The ability to remain calm under pressure, prioritize work, and multitask when necessary.

 A thorough knowledge of standard office software and Internet research methods.

 A good understanding of business, book-keeping, and management techniques.

 MEDICAL PA Works with senior doctors to manage their patient lists, arrange appointments, and ensure patients receive the appropriate treatment. The job requires a thorough knowledge of medical terminology.

 VIRTUAL PA Operates from home and provides administrative support to one or more business clients via the telephone and the Internet.

 EXECUTIVE PA Combines the role of a general PA with organizing an employer's personal and social calendar. Usually works for wealthy, high-level executives.

AT A GLANCE

 YOUR INTERESTS Computing • Administration • English • Foreign languages • Business studies • Law • Mathematics

 ENTRY QUALIFICATIONS PAs can usually find work with good school qualifications, but they may need a degree to work for some companies.

 LIFESTYLE Regular office hours are the norm, but tight deadlines or other demands may require overtime. A smart appearance is essential.

 LOCATION PAs are usually office-based, but they may need to accompany managers to meetings. This may involve international travel.

 THE REALITIES Some managers can be very demanding. Working very closely with one individual can be difficult.

▼ RELATED CAREERS

▶ **BOOK-KEEPER** Maintains thorough records of a company's financial transactions, such as purchases, invoices, wages, and taxes paid.

▶ **OFFICE MANAGER** Oversees the efficient day-to-day operation of an office. This includes supervising administrative staff, arranging supplies of business equipment and stationery, and maintaining a healthy office environment.

▶ **PARALEGAL ASSISTANT** Supports lawyers in carrying out administrative or routine legal tasks to enable them to prepare for client meetings or court appearances.

EVENTS MANAGER

JOB DESCRIPTION

Great people skills, a "can do" attitude, and the ability to multitask make a successful events manager. In this job, you are responsible for organizing and running all types of events, including festivals, weddings, conferences, and parties. The role involves understanding a client's needs before coming up with event ideas, sourcing venues, hiring and managing a work force, negotiating costs, and promoting the occasion.

SALARY

Events administrator ★★☆☆☆
Events manager ★★★★☆

INDUSTRY PROFILE

Multiple entry points into the field • Business expected to grow significantly • Global opportunities • Almost equal proportion of males and females in the industry

AT A GLANCE

YOUR INTERESTS Planning events • Hospitality • Marketing • Working with people • Business administration • Management • Law

ENTRY QUALIFICATIONS A degree is fast becoming a requirement, but work experience and a good standard of school education may be acceptable.

LIFESTYLE Attending events in the evenings and on weekends may be needed. This is a social business and event managers will be surrounded by people.

LOCATION Much of the event planning is office-based, but travel – sometimes over long distances or abroad – can also be a feature of this career.

THE REALITIES In this fast-paced job, it is not acceptable to be late. Events managers who are highly organized and thrive on deadlines are likely to succeed.

CAREER PATHS

An events manager may work on a variety of social, business, or commercial events, or specialize in one kind of event. Progress in this career depends on contacts, energy, and networking abilities as much as on formal education.

ASSISTANT If you have a positive attitude, you may be able to find employment as an assistant or a trainee in an events company after leaving school. You can progress to the level of events manager as you build up experience.

GRADUATE A degree in hospitality management combined with relevant work experience is a typical example of a route into this career.

▼ RELATED CAREERS

▶ **MARKETING EXECUTIVE** *see pp. 68–69*

▶ **PUBLIC RELATIONS OFFICER** *see pp. 74–75*

▶ **HOTEL MANAGER** *see pp. 304–305*

▶ **FOOD SERVICES MANAGER** Supervises the daily operation of restaurants and other outlets serving prepared meals. The role involves managing the kitchen and waiting staff to make sure customers are happy with the food and service.

▶ **LEISURE SERVICES MANAGER** Manages recreational venues, such as spas and gymnasiums. The role's main responsibilities may include managing staff, organizing budgets and activities, taking care of the health and safety of visitors, and overseeing the day-to-day running of a venue.

SKILLS GUIDE

 Good communication and negotiation skills to liaise effectively with clients.

 The ability to coordinate and manage teams when working on multiple projects.

 Excellent business skills to manage the potentially large budgets involved with big events.

 Strong organizational skills to carry an events project from concept to completion.

Keen multitasking skills in order to juggle a client's many needs.

WEDDING PLANNER Organizes and manages weddings for clients, booking venues, caterers, decorators, and entertainers.

 **CONFERENCE DIRECTOR** Arranges conferences by booking speakers and venues that will attract paying delegates.

EXHIBITION PLANNER Works with businesses and organizations exhibiting to the public or at trade fairs and conferences. The planner helps design and produce exhibition stands, then delivers and installs them on site.

EVENTS MANAGER Junior events managers are responsible for tasks such as registration of visitors and sales of exhibition space. As you gain more experience in the role, you may deal with larger clients and negotiate contracts with suppliers. There are numerous future career options.

 CONCERT PROMOTER Sets up concerts or other public events by booking artists and venues, publicizing the event, and selling tickets to the public.

CHARITY FUNDRAISER

JOB DESCRIPTION

Charities depend on the financial support of individuals, organizations, and governments. Fundraisers use various methods to increase these donations. They organize events or collections, carry out postal campaigns to donors, promote the charities through the media, or seek to get sponsorship from companies.

SALARY

Charity fundraiser ★★☆☆☆
Fundraising manager ★★★★☆

INDUSTRY PROFILE

Demand for fundraisers set to grow as government funding falls • Job opportunities exist around the world • Salaries vary depending on the size and location of the charity

CAREER PATHS

A charity will expect a fundraiser to be highly committed to the cause it promotes. Some of the larger organizations provide training in fundraising and marketing skills. With experience, you may be able to move into the management of the charity, helping to set its goals and determining its fundraising strategies.

VOLUNTEER MANAGER
Recruits, trains, and manages volunteers to carry out different tasks within a charity or other voluntary organizations.

VOLUNTEER If you are interested in becoming a charity fundraiser, you should seek out experience as a volunteer in your charity of interest. Some offer unpaid internships, which can be a good way for you to build contacts.

GRADUATE You stand a better chance of getting hired as a charity fundraiser if you have a degree in business or marketing, or one that is related to the activities of your chosen charity, such as a degree in development studies for an aid organization.

CHARITY FUNDRAISER You may specialize in one area of revenue, such as arranging corporate sponsorship, street collections, or legacies if working for a larger charity. Fundraisers in smaller charities combine all these roles.

SKILLS GUIDE

 Good communication skills across all forms of media, from social media to television.

 The ability to work in a team on a variety of tasks, such as making phone calls to writing mail shots.

 Great interpersonal skills and the ability to manage negative responses appropriately.

 Organizational skills to coordinate the work of untrained, but enthusiastic, volunteers.

 Motivation and commitment to drive a fundraising project with limited funds and resources.

 Financial knowledge and commercial awareness to work with business donors.

AT A GLANCE

 YOUR INTERESTS Fundraising • Planning • Psychology • Sociology • Politics • Journalism • Business studies • English • Economics

 ENTRY QUALIFICATIONS A relevant degree is useful, but hard work and commitment to the charity's causes may be sufficient to find a job.

 LIFESTYLE Jobs can be part- or full-time. Weekend and evening work is common in roles that involve organizing events with the public.

 LOCATION Much of the work is office-based, but fundraisers may need to visit potential donors, attend events, or organize street collections.

 THE REALITIES Competition for jobs is intense when starting out, but experienced fundraisers can command high salaries.

 LEGACY MANAGER Persuades and encourages a charity's supporters to leave part of their wealth to the charity in their wills. Legacies are a very important source of income for most charities.

 **LOBBYIST** Represents charities in meetings with politicians or government officials. Using their skills of persuasion, lobbyists encourage people to increase funding to the organization to help it achieve its aims.

▼ RELATED CAREERS

▶ **MARKETING EXECUTIVE** *see pp. 68–69*

▶ **AID WORKER** Travels to countries affected by disaster, war, or poverty and helps the local people. Aid workers provide practical aid in medicine, education, or engineering, or coordinate the transport and distribution of essential supplies, such as food or medicine.

On average, people give 3–5 per cent of their income to charitable causes.

TRANSLATOR

JOB DESCRIPTION

A translator converts words from one language to another while making sure that the original meaning is retained. Translators are fluent in more than one language and have highly developed written and verbal skills. They also often have a good understanding of the cultures of the countries associated with the languages they are translating.

SALARY

Newly qualified translator ★★★★★
Experienced translator ★★★★★

INDUSTRY PROFILE

Freelance work is common • Most full-time jobs in governments • Increasing demand for translation to and from Chinese, Russian, Arabic, and minority European languages

SKILLS GUIDE

 Excellent written and verbal communication skills to translate clearly for clients.

 Fluency in multiple languages in order to translate efficiently, easily, and accurately.

 A good understanding of different cultural values and how people communicate in different regions.

 The perseverance to handle complex, technical, and lengthy projects, and still meet deadlines.

 Attention to detail and the ability to understand and convey the correct meaning of words.

AT A GLANCE

YOUR INTERESTS Languages • Literature • Science • Writing and speaking • Law • Business studies • Politics • Travel and culture

ENTRY QUALIFICATIONS Most employers require a degree in languages and a postgraduate qualification in translation. Work experience is valuable.

LIFESTYLE Much of the work is done on computers and driven by deadlines, which means long hours may be needed in order to finish a project.

LOCATION Most company employees are office-based; freelancers usually work from home. Both may need to visit clients to discuss the work required.

THE REALITIES Jobs may not be regular as freelance work is more common in this industry. Pay rates vary according to the language.

▼ RELATED CAREERS

▶ **BILINGUAL SECRETARY** Uses a knowledge of one or more foreign languages to translate business communications and research materials, and liaise with overseas clients face-to-face or by telephone. Administration skills are also essential in this job.

▶ **HOLIDAY REPRESENTATIVE** Looks after groups of tourists on holiday in international resorts. Proficiency in the local language and the languages of clients is highly desirable.

▶ **TECHNICAL AUTHOR** Writes user manuals, technical guides, and online blogs for a wide range of industries and products. Technical authors are highly skilled at presenting technical information in a user-friendly form.

Working on country-specific versions of computer games is a new opportunity for translators.

CAREER PATHS

Translation is a degree-level profession, but postgraduate degrees in translation can greatly enhance employment opportunities. Fluency in two or more languages is a key requirement and knowledge of a specialist sector, such as business, finance, or technology, is an advantage.

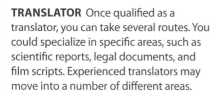

TRANSLATOR Once qualified as a translator, you can take several routes. You could specialize in specific areas, such as scientific reports, legal documents, and film scripts. Experienced translators may move into a number of different areas.

GRADUATE To find work in this field you need a degree in modern languages and preferably a postgraduate qualification in translation. However, diplomas are available to those who already speak more than one language fluently and do not hold a university degree.

GOVERNMENT TRANSLATOR
Works for government departments, such as border control, security, and intelligence services. Governments can offer a clear and structured career path in this field.

INTERPRETER Converts the spoken word from one language to another between people who do not speak the same language. A clear, strong voice is essential.

TRANSLATION AGENCY MANAGER Sets up an independent business, and employs freelance workers to provide translation services to clients in government and the private sector.

FREELANCE TRANSLATOR
Registers with agencies or finds translation jobs using their own contacts. This option is usually for more experienced translators who are confident to work on a freelance basis.

FINANCE, LAW, AND POLITICS

Careers in this area require keen intellect, the ability to process and retain large amounts of information, numerical aptitude, and an understanding of legal and business issues. People skills are also vital, as these careers involve working with other professionals and the public.

BANK MANAGER
Page 96

Working in a retail banking setting, bank managers oversee the delivery of a range of financial services for personal and business customers.

TRADER
Page 98

Through buying and selling investments such as shares and currencies, traders use their knowledge of financial markets to make profits for their clients.

INVESTMENT ANALYST
Page 100

By researching financial data and economic and political trends, investment analysts advise banks, investors, and fund managers on the best ways to generate income.

ACCOUNTANT
Page 102

Financial accounting is fundamental to businesses of every kind. Accountants are the skilled analysts who gather and examine complex financial data.

ACTUARY
Page 104

With an advanced knowledge of statistics and economics, actuaries are skilled mathematicians who give risk advice to organizations to help them plan and make decisions.

FINANCIAL ADVISER
Page 106

The growth of the financial services industry has led to a vast array of saving and investment products. Financial advisers help their clients make the right financial choices.

ECONOMIST
Page 108

An understanding of economic theory is vital for business strategy and government policy. Economists are the experts who give economic advice to decision-makers.

SOLICITOR
Page 110

From employment rights and divorce proceedings to criminal and corporate law, solicitors advise and act on behalf of their clients across a range of legal matters.

BARRISTER
Page 112

Barristers are expert legal practitioners who use their specialized legal knowledge to provide advice on the law and represent clients in a tribunal or in court.

POLITICIAN
Page 114

Representing the interests of their political party and voters, politicians campaign to win support for their policies in order to achieve social and political change.

BANK MANAGER

JOB DESCRIPTION

Managers in retail banks provide banking and financial services to individuals and businesses. They supervise the day-to-day work of the branch's staff and ensure that procedures are followed. Bank managers are also responsible for attracting new clients, generating sales of financial products, such as mortgages and credit cards, assessing applications for loans, and reporting to the bank's head office.

SALARY

Management trainee ★★☆☆☆
Senior bank manager ★★★★★

INDUSTRY PROFILE

Opportunities available worldwide • Competitive sector, but pay levels good and bonuses common • Branch closures among certain banks due to recent economic events

▼ RELATED CAREERS

▶ **INVESTMENT ANALYST** *see pp. 100–101*

▶ **ACCOUNTANT** *see pp. 102–103*

▶ **FINANCIAL ADVISER** *see pp. 106–107*

▶ **INVESTMENT BANKER** Provides advice to companies about strategic issues, such as taking over businesses or merging existing ones. Raises money from investors to fund the growth and expansion of companies.

Globally, mortgage lending is the largest sector in retail banking, and was valued at US$24 trillion in 2010.

AT A GLANCE

YOUR INTERESTS Financial services • Accounting • Business studies • Economics • Mathematics • Statistics • English • Information Technology (IT)

ENTRY QUALIFICATIONS Bankers need a good standard of general education. School-leavers and graduates can join work-based training programmes.

LIFESTYLE Working hours are regular, although some branches remain open in the evenings and on Saturday mornings.

LOCATION Bank managers work at a specific branch or at a bank call centre. Some travel is needed to meet business clients and liaise with the head office.

THE REALITIES Trainee managers often have to work long hours to gain promotion and may be under pressure to meet strict sales targets.

CAREER PATHS

There are three main routes into retail bank management. Entrants can join a graduate training scheme if they have a degree, work in a customer services role and work their way up, or take an apprenticeship in bank management.

SCHOOL- OR COLLEGE-LEAVER You can join a bank's structured work-based training scheme and gain relevant qualifications on the job to progress to more senior roles.

GRADUATE Most of the large retail banks offer management training programmes to attract graduates. You can apply with a degree in almost any discipline.

SKILLS GUIDE

Commercial awareness and a strong interest in economic affairs and financial markets.

Excellent communication skills for handling customers and managing staff.

Strong leadership skills and the ability to motivate staff to meet targets.

Good organizational skills to manage a high workload and lead a large team.

The ability to use computerized systems and banking-specific software efficiently.

BANK MANAGER To become a manager, you must work in a range of banking areas – from personal loans to business accounts – and complete an apprenticeship or in-house management training course. Most managers go on to senior or specialist roles.

PRODUCT DEVELOPMENT MANAGER Conducts research and analyses data about the needs of bank customers in order to develop and target new products, such as loans, credit cards, and mortgages.

REGIONAL MANAGER Takes responsibility for a number of bank branches, devising and implementing a regional business plan, and ensuring that branch staff follow company policies.

BANK CALL CENTRE MANAGER Leads and motivates staff at telephone and online banking centres, and makes decisions about staff targets, lending, and day-to-day operations.

RISK MANAGER Identifies potential threats to the bank's profitability, such as fraud or risky lending practices, and recommends solutions.

TRADER

JOB DESCRIPTION

Traders are employed by financial institutions – such as investment banks – to trade investments by buying and selling them on the world's financial markets. These trades are made on behalf of individuals, companies, or institutional investors, such as pension funds and banks. Traders work in a fast-paced environment, using their judgement and experience to create a profit for their clients.

SALARY

New entrant ★★★☆☆
Senior trader ★★★★★

INDUSTRY PROFILE

Highly competitive industry • Financial rewards, particularly bonuses, are potentially substantial • Jobs available across the world

AT A GLANCE

 YOUR INTERESTS Economics • Finance • Mathematics • Financial markets • Accountancy • Business studies • Information Technology (IT)

 ENTRY QUALIFICATIONS A degree or higher is essential – employers favour subjects related to business, finance, or mathematics.

 LIFESTYLE Traders work long hours every day to track movements in markets around the world. Much of the work is screen-based.

 LOCATION Traders work in an office. Most job opportunities exist in the world's major financial centres, such as London, New York, and Tokyo.

 THE REALITIES The job can be very demanding and stressful. Traders must excel in a fiercely competitive and pressurized work environment.

CAREER PATHS

Prospective traders must pass a rigorous recruitment process that may include aptitude and personality tests. Most entrants then spend two years working in a junior trading role and studying for professional qualifications. With experience, they may manage a team of traders in a particular type of financial market, or specialize in a specific trading area.

GRADUATE Due to strong competition for jobs, you need high grades in an undergraduate degree in a technical, financial, or business-related subject when applying for jobs as a trader.

POSTGRADUATE You can increase your chances of becoming a trader by gaining a postgraduate degree in a subject such as economics, finance, mathematics, or business.

SKILLS GUIDE

 Excellent communication skills and high levels of confidence to negotiate trading options.

 Strong numerical skills to manipulate financial data when compiling and analysing reports.

 Strong IT skills for using computerized financial systems to conduct efficient financial trades.

 In-depth knowledge and awareness of issues that might affect financial markets.

 Attention to detail and the ability to react swiftly and decisively to market changes.

▼ RELATED CAREERS

▶ **INVESTMENT ANALYST** *see pp. 100–101*

▶ **ECONOMIST** *see pp. 108–109*

▶ **INVESTMENT BANK ACTUARY** Conducts research to assess the potential risks of investment decisions, such as buying or selling particular shares. Investment bank actuaries are among the most influential and best-paid professionals in the world of finance.

▶ **STOCKBROKER** Buys and sells stocks, shares, and other investments on behalf of businesses and individual clients, rather than for large financial institutions, taking a percentage of clients' fees.

PROPRIETARY TRADER
Working as an employee of a bank or other financial institution, a proprietary trader increases profits for an employer by using the company's money – rather than that of a client – to buy and sell on the financial markets.

TRADER You will need to gain professional qualifications before you can perform all the functions of a trader. With experience, you can progress into a specialist role.

SALES TRADER Works to create new business for banks by identifying and talking to potential clients, and liaising between the client and the traders who will handle the investments.

COMMODITY BROKER Buys and sells contracts for physical commodities – such as oil, gas, metals, and foods – on behalf of companies.

STRUCTURER Develops, models, and sets the pricing structure for sophisticated financial products, such as derivatives, the price of which may vary according to the value of a linked asset, such as a share.

QUANTITATIVE ANALYST (QUANT) Develops and runs complex mathematical formulae, or algorithms, that determine the prices of shares or other financial products and assess risks. Also identifies profitable trading opportunities.

INVESTMENT ANALYST

JOB DESCRIPTION

Working in the world's financial markets, analysts research the economic, business, and market conditions that affect the value of investments, such as stocks and shares. They then advise their clients, which may be companies or individuals or funds, on which investments to buy or sell to make the highest profit.

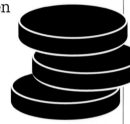

SALARY

Graduate trainee ★★★★★
Senior analyst ★★★★★

INDUSTRY PROFILE

Intense competition for entry into profession • Rise in jobs with expanding range of financial products • Emerging global markets creating opportunities to work abroad

CAREER PATHS

Analysts work for buyers or sellers of investments, such as pension funds, hedge funds, banks, insurance companies, stockbrokers, and traders. There are many opportunities for experienced analysts who could, for example, specialize in a specific type of investment or region, or choose to manage an investment firm.

ACCREDITED ANALYST Advises high-profile clients. An industry-recognized accreditation is necessary to qualify for the position, which may take several years of study.

GRADUATE TRAINEE You will need a degree from a good university; employers may prefer subjects that include mathematical analysis. Your employers usually sponsor your training while you work under a senior analyst. To move into senior positions, you may need a postgraduate degree in business administration (known as a Masters of Business Administration, or MBA) or in finance.

INVESTMENT ANALYST In this role, you research the past and project the future performance of a company to forecast its value on a stock exchange. You may produce reports that guide clients on their investment decisions. Experienced investment analysts can specialize in a number of different areas.

SKILLS GUIDE

 Acute commercial awareness and maturity to make judgements about complex markets.

 Excellent communication skills to develop working relationships with people at all levels.

Good organizational and research skills to gather relevant, time-sensitive information.

Strong mathematical skills and the ability to interpret statistical data.

 The ability to work under pressure and to deadlines, within and outside business hours.

AT A GLANCE

 YOUR INTERESTS Financial management or accountancy • Business studies • Economics • Mathematics • Statistics

 ENTRY QUALIFICATIONS A degree is essential. A postgraduate degree in mathematics or business is usually necessary to progress to senior positions.

 LIFESTYLE The job can bring big financial rewards but it is very pressurized. Employers expect analysts to work very long hours.

 LOCATION Investment analysts mostly work from the offices of large financial institutions, but travel to visit investors and companies.

THE REALITIES The work is closely scrutinized – mistakes can be very costly. Progress to senior positions demands lengthy periods of study.

 STOCKBROKER Acts as an agent for businesses or personal clients, and buys and sells shares and other financial products in markets around the world.

 WEALTH MANAGER Guides wealthy individuals on how to invest their money to maximize returns, and also advises them on tax payments.

 FUND MANAGER Looks after specialist investment funds that focus on buying and selling shares in a particular type of company, such as firms working in mining or pharmaceuticals.

▼ RELATED CAREERS

► **BANK MANAGER** *see pp. 96–97*

► **TRADER** *see pp. 98–99*

► **ACTUARY** *see pp. 104–105*

► **FINANCIAL MANAGER** Works within a business to guide its financial affairs. Financial managers monitor activities, produce financial statements, and develop plans based on business objectives.

 Annual bonuses in this job can range between 40 and 150 per cent of your salary.

ACCOUNTANT

JOB DESCRIPTION

Accountants play a vital role in the operation of virtually every business and organization, ensuring that financial systems run smoothly and that tax laws and other regulations are followed. They calculate annual accounts and produce financial reports, and may specialize in other areas, such as fraud detection. Senior accountants may play a strategic role, advising the leaders of a business or organization.

SALARY

Trainee ★★★★★
Senior partner ★★★★★

INDUSTRY PROFILE

Consistent demand for industry professionals • Highest salaries in banking and finance accountancy • Fierce competition for training positions in large firms

AT A GLANCE

YOUR INTERESTS Finance • Accounting • Economics • Mathematics • Statistics • Information Technology (IT) • Business studies

ENTRY QUALIFICATIONS Applicants can join accountancy firms as assistants and learn on the job, or as trainees after completing a degree in any discipline.

LIFESTYLE Regular office hours are the norm, although some overtime may be required to complete reports or financial audits to tight schedules.

LOCATION The work is largely office-based. Travel to meet clients and conduct audits – an official examination of accounts – is a vital part of the job.

THE REALITIES Although the financial rewards can be high, evening and weekend work is often required to meet deadlines during busy periods.

CAREER PATHS

There are two main types of accountancy: public practice, in which accounting services are provided to clients; and management accountancy, in which accountants work in-house for a public- or private-sector organization or business. Career progression may follow a structured path, from accreditation, to gaining experience in different sectors – such as tax or corporate finance – leading to promotion to management, and eventually, partnership in a firm.

SCHOOL- OR COLLEGE-LEAVER

You may be taken on as a trainee after leaving school or college, working on the job while studying for initial qualifications. Once qualified, you can enter a training programme to become an accredited accountant.

GRADUATE
With a degree in any discipline, you can apply for graduate accountancy training programmes, which are offered by many large accountancy firms, public-sector organizations, and commercial businesses in all sectors of industry.

▼ RELATED CAREERS

▶ **MANAGEMENT CONSULTANT** *see pp. 84–85*

▶ **ACTUARY** *see pp. 104–105*

▶ **ACCOUNTING TECHNICIAN** Assists qualified accountants by preparing accounting figures, tax reports, and helping in all other areas of business finance.

▶ **COMPANY SECRETARY** Works with a company's senior management to ensure that legal, financial, and regulatory requirements are followed.

The Federal Bureau of Investigation (FBI) employs more than 1,500 accountants to solve financial crime.

SKILLS GUIDE

 Excellent numerical skills and the ability to interpret complex financial data.

 Precision and attention to detail in order to perform repetitive calculations accurately.

 Strong communication skills for explaining financial information to clients and senior managers.

 The ability to analyse financial problems and identify the most appropriate solution.

Honesty, integrity, and discretion for dealing with sensitive financial information appropriately.

CORPORATE FINANCE ACCOUNTANT Works in a company's corporate finance division, performing functions such as analysing accounts to identify money that can be used for growing the business, through to acquiring firms or merging existing ones.

 TAX ACCOUNTANT Uses extensive knowledge of tax law for businesses to advise clients on their legal obligations and business affairs.

BUSINESS INSOLVENCY ACCOUNTANT Provides specialist advice to companies in financial trouble, helping them to close their businesses in a controlled manner.

FORENSIC ACCOUNTANT Studies the financial dealings of companies to detect fraud, enabling insurance companies and corporate lawyers to resolve financial disputes.

ACCOUNTANT Once qualified, you will need to study for up to three years to gain accredited status. You can then choose to train further to specialize in one area of accountancy.

AUDITOR Reviews the financial accounts of companies and organizations to ensure that they are valid and that they meet legal guidelines. Auditors also assess the health of clients' businesses and advise on working practices.

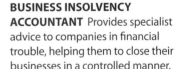

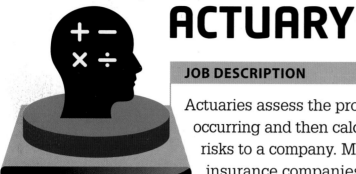

ACTUARY

JOB DESCRIPTION

Actuaries assess the probability of a particular event occurring and then calculate the possible financial risks to a company. Many actuaries work for insurance companies, at which they calculate the likelihood of a loss, such as the chances of a ship sinking at sea, and set the amount to be paid by the ship's owners. Others work in banks, monitoring the levels of risk when buying and selling investments.

SALARY

Graduate trainee ★★★☆☆
Senior director ★★★★★

INDUSTRY PROFILE

Jobs available worldwide, although competition for places is strong • Opportunities within a wide range of businesses and organizations • High salary

AT A GLANCE

 YOUR INTERESTS Mathematics • Statistics • Economics • Risk management • Business studies • Information Technology (IT) • Science

 ENTRY QUALIFICATIONS A degree in a numerate subject – such as mathematics, statistics, or actuarial science – is essential.

 LIFESTYLE Actuaries usually work regular hours, although evening or weekend working may be required to meet deadlines.

 LOCATION Actuarial work is office-based and firms are mostly found in large cities. Business travel to visit clients is occasionally required.

 THE REALITIES This mathematical, intellectually challenging field requires a determined mindset. The exams to achieve accreditation can be gruelling.

▼ RELATED CAREERS

▶ **INVESTMENT ANALYST** see pp. 100–101

▶ **ACCOUNTANT** see pp. 102–103

▶ **AUDITOR** Checks the financial accounts of companies and organizations to ensure that they are accurate and follow legal guidelines. Auditors also assess the health of clients' businesses and advise on ways to avoid risk.

▶ **INSURANCE UNDERWRITER** Works for an insurance company assessing applications for the insurance cover of individuals and businesses. Underwriters decide if insurance cover should be given and set the terms and price of the insurance policy.

In 2013, actuary was rated the best job in the USA, based on salary, prospects, stress levels, and work environment.

CAREER PATHS

Graduates with a degree in a numerate subject can apply to train as an actuary. Training involves up to six years of on-the-job study, during which time trainees need to take a series of exams to gain professional accreditation.

GRADUATE To be taken on as a trainee, you will need a degree in mathematics, statistics, or a similar subject, and will then have to pass a series of selection tests.

POSTGRADUATE You can increase your chances of being taken on by studying actuarial science at postgraduate level, which may also count towards your future accreditation.

SKILLS GUIDE

Strong communication and presentation skills for explaining complex findings to non-experts.

A logical and analytical approach to make sense of complex information.

Advanced numerical skills to analyse and interpret large amounts of data.

A thorough knowledge of issues affecting financial markets when pricing products and services.

Precision and attention to detail to ensure mathematical calculations are correct.

ACTUARY Traditionally employed by insurance firms, actuaries now work for a range of organizations, from health authorities to government departments. After qualifying, you can specialize in a particular sector or work towards senior roles.

CHIEF RISK OFFICER Coordinates a team of actuaries and other professionals who assess and take action to avoid potential risks. This is a senior position in a large company.

INVESTMENT BANK ACTUARY Conducts research to identify the financial costs and potential risks of investment decisions, such as investing in a new business.

CONSULTANT ACTUARY Gives advice on business activities, such as company mergers or acquisitions, usually to large companies or corporations.

LIFE ASSURANCE ACTUARY Analyses statistical information on risk factors – such as existing health conditions – to set the prices that customers pay for their life assurance policies.

ENTERPRISE RISK MANAGER Identifies risks that may affect the operation of a business, and then assesses the impact these risks might have. Also devises strategies to avoid these risks or to minimize their effects on the business.

FINANCIAL ADVISER

JOB DESCRIPTION

Financial advisers help people to plan their financial futures. They meet with clients, usually in person, to provide informed advice on a range of financial products and services, from pensions and investments, to mortgages and tax-efficient savings. Taking into account a client's income and circumstances, they recommend products and strategies to help them meet their financial goals.

SALARY

Trainee financial adviser ★★★★★
Senior financial adviser ★★★★★

INDUSTRY PROFILE

Employers include investment firms, banks, financial-services companies, and insurance companies • Demand for financial advice, particularly on pensions, is growing rapidly

AT A GLANCE

YOUR INTERESTS Economics • Mathematics • Business studies • Law • Accountancy • Information Technology (IT) • Dealing with people

ENTRY QUALIFICATIONS Experience of working in a sales, customer service, or finance role, or a degree or diploma in a related subject are useful.

LIFESTYLE While financial advisers work regular office hours, they may need to meet clients during evenings and weekends.

LOCATION Financial advisers work from an office or from home. Travelling to meet with clients in their homes is a regular feature of the job.

THE REALITIES Dealing with multiple clients can be stressful, especially in hard economic times. It can take years to build a client base.

CAREER PATHS

To enter this career, applicants must pass a series of professional examinations and be registered by a regulatory body that ensures they give high-quality, unbiased advice. Qualified advisers can choose to provide general guidance to their clients or to specialize in one type of product, such as pensions or insurance.

ASSISTANT You can become a financial adviser without a degree by working as an assistant and training on the job. However, prior experience in banking or insurance is beneficial.

GRADUATE You will need a degree, preferably in finance or business management, to apply for graduate training schemes, which are run by some banks and independent financial-advice firms.

▼ RELATED CAREERS

▶ **BANK MANAGER** *see pp. 96–97*

▶ **INSURANCE BROKER** Helps people to decide on the best insurance policy to meet their individual needs, whether they require home, travel, car, or life insurance. Retail insurance brokers arrange cover for individual clients, while commercial insurance brokers provide high-value cover for businesses involved in fields such as air travel, or the oil and gas industries.

▶ **PENSIONS ADMINISTRATOR** Performs administrative tasks relating to a pension scheme, such as dealing with enquiries from scheme members, or calculating pension forecasts. May work for an insurance company, pensions provider, or a public-sector organization.

SKILLS GUIDE

The ability to explain complicated financial matters in simple terms, and to understand a client's needs.

Good interpersonal skills for building relationships and establishing trust with clients.

Sharp analytical skills to analyse financial information to identify the best product for a client.

Determination and self-motivation for maintaining high levels of service and meeting sales targets.

Understanding and awareness of financial markets in order to offer accurate advice to clients.

WEALTH MANAGER
Helps wealthy individuals invest their money to bring as high a return on their investment as possible. Wealth managers also advise on regulatory matters, such as inheritance tax rules.

SPECIALIST FINANCIAL ADVISER
Provides specialist advice in one type of product or to one type of client, for example, property investment or financial planning for farmers.

COMPLIANCE MANAGER Works for a company of financial advisers, inspecting premises and reviewing financial records and policies to ensure legal and industry standards are met. This is a senior role.

FINANCIAL ADVISER While training, you choose between two types of practice: independent (offering unbiased advice on all the products available to a client) and restricted (offering advice on your company's products alone). Financial advisers often specialize in a client group – such as wealthy clients – or a type of product.

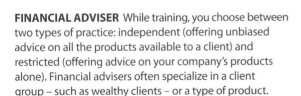

GENERAL MANAGER Supervises the work of financial advisers and oversees areas such as recruitment and training, as well as a firm's marketing strategy. Managers in financial firms are often former financial advisers who have been promoted into the role.

ECONOMIST

JOB DESCRIPTION

Economists research and analyse how people and businesses spend their money and make use of resources, such as labour and energy. They produce reports and forecasts for companies and governments, who use the information in various ways, such as shaping their policies on matters such as wages and taxation, or making them more competitive compared to their rivals.

SALARY

Junior economist ★★★☆☆
Senior economist ★★★★★

INDUSTRY PROFILE

Varied opportunities for employment in sectors such as governments, banks, and other financial companies • Excellent salaries on offer for highly qualified individuals

AT A GLANCE

YOUR INTERESTS Economics • Mathematics • Statistics • Business studies • Information Technology (IT) • Philosophy • Politics • Social science

ENTRY QUALIFICATIONS A relevant university degree is essential. A postgraduate qualification is needed for higher-level positions.

LIFESTYLE Economists typically keep regular office hours, although preparing for conferences or writing for publications may demand extra work.

LOCATION Economists are office-based, but may have to travel to conferences to present findings to clients around the world.

THE REALITIES Economists need to be motivated to carry out independent research and are expected to learn new skills throughout their career.

▼ RELATED CAREERS

▶ **FINANCIAL ADVISER** *see pp. 106–107*

▶ **POLITICIAN** *see pp. 114–115*

▶ **MATHEMATICIAN** Uses advanced mathematics to develop ways of analysing and solving difficult problems in the world. Practical business uses include calculating risks in the insurance industry, analysing statistics to examine the effectiveness of a new drug, or investigating the way that air flows over the wing of an aircraft.

Employment opportunities for economists in the USA are expected to grow 14 per cent by 2022.

CAREER PATHS

All economists require a degree or postgraduate qualification in economics. They continue learning throughout their career, becoming an expert in one or more fields – such as health care or taxation – and publish papers and reports to build their reputation. Many economists also hold teaching or research jobs in universities at some stage of their career.

RESEARCHER With a degree in economics or finance, you may find an entry-level job as a researcher at a financial organization. With experience and higher qualifications, you can progress to more senior roles.

ECONOMIST You work in government or public-sector organizations or in academic, managerial, and various other consultancy roles. In this job you rely increasingly on computerized data analysis and mathematical modelling techniques. With experience, you can become a statistician, a political scientist, an investment banker, or a financial director.

SKILLS GUIDE

A strategic understanding of politics and business to help with leading teams and solving complex issues.

The ability to interpret complex data, identify economic trends, and make accurate forecasts.

Strong mathematical skills for analysing key data and assessing the state of the economy.

A good working knowledge of specialist software programs to conduct statistical analyses.

Sound business knowledge and understanding of financial systems in the public and private sectors.

An eye for detail for interpreting mathematical data and producing accurate reports.

STATISTICIAN Collects, analyses, and interprets statistics. Statisticians work in a number of sectors, including health, education, government, finance, market research, and the environment.

POLITICAL SCIENTIST Works in government, for political parties, or for private research groups, to develop new policies.

INVESTMENT BANKER Raises money from individual and corporate investors on behalf of businesses that need funds to get started, grow, or develop.

FINANCIAL DIRECTOR Oversees the financial activities of a business or other organization. Financial directors are responsible for producing financial statements, monitoring budgets and spending, and developing new business objectives.

SOLICITOR

JOB DESCRIPTION

Solicitors provide legal services and advice to their clients, from drawing up contracts and wills to resolving legal disputes. In this role, you might act on behalf of a client, seek specialist advice from a barrister, or brief a barrister to represent a client in court. Solicitors work for individuals, charities, corporations, or government agencies, and can specialize in a range of legal areas, from family law to corporate mergers.

SALARY

Newly qualified solicitor ★★★★★
Managing partner ★★★★★

INDUSTRY PROFILE

Highly regulated profession • Intense competition for training "contracts" • Private-sector law firms are biggest employers • Global opportunities in multinational businesses of all kinds

CAREER PATHS

Once they have qualified, solicitors can begin practising as an associate, working under the supervision of a senior partner at a law firm. With experience and ability, they can become a partner in the firm. Solicitors can choose from a range of specialisms, such as serving charitable organizations, military services, or dealing with the legal matters of individuals or the government.

PRIVATE PRACTICE SOLICITOR Provides individuals with legal advice on matters such as property sales, wills, divorce, injury, and criminal prosecutions.

NON-LAW GRADUATE You will need to take a law-conversion course at university or law school if you hold a degree in another subject, and then follow the same path as a law graduate.

GRADUATE As a law-degree graduate, you can take a one-year legal practice course at a university or law school, followed by a two-year training "contract" with a firm of solicitors. Upon completion of this contract, you are entitled to join the roll of solicitors.

LEGAL EXECUTIVE You can become a solicitor without a degree by taking a work-based training programme while working as a legal executive. It takes longer to qualify in this way than it would by taking the degree route.

SOLICITOR After you qualify you may start your career at the firm where you completed you training contract or elsewhere. You then continue to learn on the job and can choose from a wide range of career paths.

SKILLS GUIDE

Excellent verbal and written skills and the ability to understand complex legal language.

Strong problem-solving skills for identifying the best course of action for clients.

The ability to follow detailed legal procedures correctly in order to maintain professional integrity.

Sensitivity for dealing with a range of clients, and the ability to explain legal matters to non-experts.

Dedication and perseverance to press your client's interests from start to finish of a legal case.

COMMERCIAL SOLICITOR Works for a business or organization, dealing with areas such as employment law, company mergers, acquisitions, and corporate strategy.

GOVERNMENT SOLICITOR Working in government, develops policies and prosecutes legal cases in areas that include housing, planning, waste disposal, and education.

CHARITY SOLICITOR Represents charitable and non-profit organizations, giving advice on areas such as governance, funding, and operating within government regulations.

MILITARY SOLICITOR Advises and represents members of the armed forces in civil and criminal cases and in military courts.

▼ RELATED CAREERS

▶ **BARRISTER** *see pp. 112–113*

▶ **CORONER** Acting as an independent judicial officer, a coroner investigates deaths from unknown or unnatural causes, and is usually a qualified solicitor, barrister, or legal executive with at least five years' post-qualifying experience.

▶ **PARALEGAL** Works on legal matters, but is not a qualified solicitor. Paralegals prepare reports and research information for solicitors, but with experience can also advise clients and present legal applications to district judges.

▶ **WELFARE RIGHTS ADVISER** Provides free basic legal advice to individuals on issues such as debt, housing, loans, consumer rights, and employment, often working for charities or advice centres.

AT A GLANCE

YOUR INTERESTS Law · Criminology · English · Psychology · Sociology · History · Business studies · Debating · Research and writing

ENTRY QUALIFICATIONS It is possible to qualify without a degree, but graduate entry is the most common, and quickest, route.

LIFESTYLE Solicitors work regular office hours, but evening and weekend work is not uncommon. On-call work can take place any time of day or night.

LOCATION The work is predominantly office-based, but travelling to meet clients, or to attend court cases, is a common feature of the job.

THE REALITIES This profession is intellectually demanding, and involves long working hours. Experienced solicitors are paid well.

BARRISTER

JOB DESCRIPTION

Barristers are highly qualified lawyers who represent their clients in court. They are usually hired by the client's solicitor, and are briefed to present facts and arguments to a judge and jury. They specialize mainly in particular areas of law, such as criminal, employment, or entertainment law, and may represent individuals, organizations, or even governments in court.

SALARY

Newly qualified barrister ★★★★★
Experienced barrister ★★★★★

INDUSTRY PROFILE

Majority of barristers are self-employed • Fiercely competitive • Profession has been affected by competition from solicitors, who can now handle some cases previously restricted to barristers

AT A GLANCE

YOUR INTERESTS Law • Debating • English • History • Psychology • Sociology • Criminology • Research and writing

ENTRY QUALIFICATIONS A degree, preferably in law, is essential. Postgraduate conversion courses are available for non-law graduates.

LIFESTYLE Courts operate during regular office hours, but evening and weekend work is often necessary in order to prepare cases.

LOCATION Preparatory work takes place in an office or "chambers". Barristers need to visit clients and solicitors, and will appear in court.

THE REALITIES The hours can be long and the work intellectually demanding, requiring quick understanding of details. Financial rewards can be high.

CAREER PATHS

Most barristers begin their career as a junior within a practice, or "chambers", located close to law courts. They can choose to remain self-employed or take up salaried jobs, providing specialist advisory services to the government, the armed forces, or charities.

GRADUATE You will need a degree to practise as a barrister. Most barristers have a degree in law, but conversion courses are available for graduates of other subjects. This is followed by a one-year professional training course and a "pupillage" year – working under an experienced barrister.

Barristers are often required to juggle up to 25 different legal cases at once.

▼ RELATED CAREERS

▶ **SOLICITOR** *see pp. 110–111*

▶ **COMPANY SECRETARY** Oversees the legal and financial affairs of a large company, working closely with lawyers and accountants, as well as with senior strategic managers.

▶ **CORONER** Works as an independent judicial officer who investigates deaths from unknown or unnatural causes. Coroners are usually qualified solicitors, barristers, or legal executives with at least five years' post-qualifying experience.

▶ **PATENT ATTORNEY** Verifies applications for patents – an official document that grants the holder the exclusive right to make or licence an item or process – for inventions and concepts, and investigates cases of patent infringement.

SKILLS GUIDE

 Excellent written and verbal skills and the ability to speak in court while under pressure.

 The ability to understand a client's point of view accurately to represent them in court.

 Highly organized approach and good time-management skills to work on cases simultaneously.

 Keen attention to detail for observing and interpreting facts in order to build a legal case.

 Perseverance, determination, and stamina to prepare cases and attend lengthy court sessions.

COMMERCIAL BARRISTER
Works for a large company or legal practice, specializing in law that is related to business agreements. Commercial barristers may also help a company develop legal strategy, policy, and practice.

 CRIMINAL BARRISTER Represents defendants in criminal cases, spending significant time – up to four days per week – attending trials and hearings.

 MEDIA AND ENTERTAINMENT BARRISTER Takes on copyright infringement or intellectual property rights cases for the music, film, news, and publishing industries.

 FAMILY BARRISTER Specializes in family law, representing clients in court or mediating between parties to reach out-of-court agreements, on matters such as child-protection issues and financial disputes.

BARRISTER Once qualified, you will usually work in chambers – offices shared with other barristers who specialize in a specific legal area, such as company, criminal, or family law. Experienced barristers can move to senior positions, such as being a judge or senior barrister, or diversify into a related field.

 EMPLOYMENT BARRISTER Works on employment law and pension issues, representing clients with complaints such as non-payment of wages or unfair dismissal.

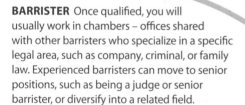

POLITICIAN

JOB DESCRIPTION

Politicians are public servants who are elected by voters to represent their local community in a local, regional, or national parliament. They aim to improve citizens' lives by pressing for changes in society and the laws that govern it. In this role, you will hold face-to-face advice sessions in your local community, debate issues and vote in parliament, and campaign on behalf of your political party.

SALARY

Local councillor ★★★★★
Senior minister ★★★★★

INDUSTRY PROFILE

Entry into politics is competitive • Opportunities to work at a local and/or national level • Career prospects and pay rates vary depending on the role

CAREER PATHS

Entry into – and advancement within – this career is largely down to self-motivation, and career paths will vary according to the type of politician you want to be. Some politicians work in local government, while others represent their voters at regional or national level. Progression may lead to senior roles in party leadership or – if their party is voted into office – government.

RESEARCH ASSISTANT
Working for a politician as a parliamentary research assistant is a good way of gaining work experience in politics.

GRADUATE You can improve your political prospects by studying for a degree-level qualification in a subject such as political science, law, or economics.

LOCAL POLITICAL ACTIVIST
You can demonstrate your commitment to a political career by working as a voluntary campaigner on a local level for your chosen political party.

POLITICIAN After gaining selection to a political party and campaigning for public votes, you will only enter the active phase of your career if you win an election at local or national level. You can choose to specialize in particular areas of policy, and may be promoted to senior roles on merit.

SKILLS GUIDE

Excellent public speaking skills for presenting political arguments and winning support for policies.

The ability to work as part of a team in order to reach a consensus on legislation and policies.

Interpersonal skills for relating to members of the public and understanding their concerns.

Good problem-solving skills for devising political solutions to economic and social problems.

Perseverance and integrity to press for political change and inspire others to adopt the party's cause.

LOCAL COUNCIL LEADER
Leads a team of local council staff and is responsible for delivering important public services, such as housing, and education.

NATIONAL REPRESENTATIVE
Represents the issues and concerns of their local community – as well as those of their political party – in votes and debates at the national parliament.

GOVERNMENT MINISTER Creates policies and legislation in a specific area of government, such as transport or health. This senior role may involve leading a government department.

PRIME MINISTER Leads a national government, and is responsible for choosing and developing government policies and leading a political party.

▼ RELATED CAREERS

▶ **CHARITY FUNDRAISER** *see pp. 90–91*

▶ **SOLICITOR** *see pp. 110–111*

▶ **TRADE UNION OFFICIAL** Represents trade union members – and gives them advice and support – in disputes with employers over employment issues, such as pay, training, and redundancy.

> Only 22 per cent of politicians in the Houses of Parliament – the UK's national assembly – are female.

AT A GLANCE

YOUR INTERESTS Politics • Debating • Current affairs • Law • Economics • Business studies • Sociology • English • History

ENTRY QUALIFICATIONS No set requirements, but evidence of past political activity is vital. Most politicians have studied to degree level or higher.

LIFESTYLE Long working hours are common. Parliamentary debates and campaigning or networking events are often held during evenings.

LOCATION Politicians work at a local, regional, or national parliament, and also have an office in the community. National and overseas travel is required.

THE REALITIES Time at parliament or on political business, and canvassing during elections require frequent overnight stays away from home.

INFORMATION TECHNOLOGY AND COMPUTING

Today's business world depends on the availability and flow of high-quality data. Information Technology (IT) and computing are key, so the range of careers in this field – from maintaining computer networks to designing websites – is increasing all the time.

SOFTWARE ENGINEER
Page 118

Computerized devices are the tools of the electronic age. Software engineers provide the link between user and machine, writing the code that brings devices to life.

SYSTEMS ANALYST
Page 120

Virtually every business or organization relies upon the efficient flow of data, so the systems analysts who examine and improve IT systems are critical to today's economy.

DATABASE MANAGER
Page 122

Working across every industry and sector, database managers ensure that electronically stored information is accurate, consistent, and protected from hackers.

NETWORK ENGINEER
Page 124

Computer and communications systems rely on electronic networks. Engineers in this field work on a range of computer networks, such as fibre optic or wireless systems.

IT SUPPORT EXECUTIVE
Page 126

Drawing on a detailed knowledge of computer systems and software, IT support executives offer help and advice to users who encounter technological problems.

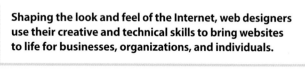

WEB DESIGNER
Page 128

Shaping the look and feel of the Internet, web designers use their creative and technical skills to bring websites to life for businesses, organizations, and individuals.

GAMES DEVELOPER
Page 130

Growing in popularity year by year, the computer gaming industry relies on innovative and creative developers to produce the code that drives games.

CYBER-SECURITY ANALYST
Page 132

As IT security threats become more frequent, cyber-security analysts are the guardians of computer systems, using technical skills to protect against data attacks.

SOFTWARE ENGINEER

JOB DESCRIPTION

Software engineers plan, analyse, design, develop, test, and carry out maintenance work on a wide variety of computer software products. These can range from games, apps, and home entertainment systems, to programs that run a computer's operating system or control network communications between computers.

SALARY

Graduate engineer ★★☆☆☆
Senior engineer ★★★★★

INDUSTRY PROFILE

High demand • Many jobs in Information Technology (IT) consultancies, and software and telecommunication companies • Highly paid contract-based roles available for experienced engineers

AT A GLANCE

YOUR INTERESTS Computer science • IT • Mathematics • Physics • Engineering • New technologies

ENTRY QUALIFICATIONS A degree or a postgraduate qualification in software engineering or related discipline is the best way to get a job.

LIFESTYLE Working hours are flexible, and tight deadlines demand long hours. Software engineers may need to travel to meet clients.

LOCATION Most jobs in this sector are office-based, but some software engineers can also work from home where there is little distraction.

THE REALITIES The market is highly competitive. Junior software engineers can spend a lot of time working on routine tasks, such as computer coding.

CAREER PATHS

Software engineers start their careers supporting a team that is developing or modifying computer code. After gaining experience and knowledge of multiple computer systems and languages, they can progress to lead their own development teams or enter specialist areas of the industry.

GRADUATE You will need a degree in an analytical or technical subject – but not necessarily in computer science or IT – and some experience in computer coding.

POSTGRADUATE If you hold a degree in a non-technical discipline, you may take an IT conversion course at postgraduate level. Many business and management graduates take this route into the industry.

SKILLS GUIDE

 Good team-working skills and the ability to work with people from all over the globe.

 Strong analytical and problem-solving skills to work through the many challenges of a project.

 A creative approach to solving what can often be extremely complex problems.

 Excellent IT skills and the resourcefulness to stay up to date with new technologies.

 Attention to detail and the patience to code and test new software products.

▼ RELATED CAREERS

▶ **SYSTEMS ANALYST** *see pp. 120–121*

▶ **DATABASE MANAGER** *see pp. 122–123*

▶ **WEB DESIGNER** *see pp. 128–129*

▶ **DATA ANALYST** Analyses and interprets massive amounts of data for clients. This information, usually in the form of charts, diagrams, tables, or reports, helps companies to identify patterns and trends in order to make better commercial decisions.

> Employment in this field is expected to grow by 22 per cent by 2020.

LEAD SOFTWARE ENGINEER Runs their own team, setting out the specific requirements of individual projects. This role requires experience in order to mentor new recruits, and manage the development of their technical skills.

QUALITY ASSURANCE TESTER Tests software to understand the quality of a potential product. This requires an inquisitive mind that can identify the various ways in which a piece of new software can fail.

GAMES DEVELOPER Writes and tests the code used to run games on computers, consoles, and hand-held devices such as tablets and mobile phones.

SOFTWARE ENGINEER Experienced software engineers have numerous options for career development. You can progress to a lead engineer or specialize in a variety of areas.

SOFTWARE RESEARCHER Conceives new ideas – individually or for a company – and develops them as software prototypes. Coding skills are essential for this role.

SYSTEMS ANALYST

JOB DESCRIPTION

Information Technology (IT) lies at the heart of most businesses and organizations, so a poorly designed computer system can make a company less efficient. Systems analysts identify potential problems in a computer system by working closely with its users and programmers. They provide recommendations as to how the system may be redesigned, and plan and manage ways of achieving these goals.

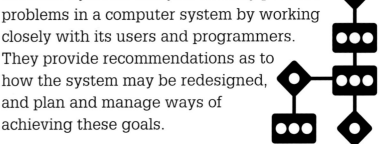

SALARY

Junior systems analyst ★★★★★
Senior systems analyst ★★★★★

INDUSTRY PROFILE

Healthy job market • Employers range from large corporations to small enterprises • Growth in employment in the public and financial services sectors

AT A GLANCE

YOUR INTERESTS IT • Computer science • Business information technology • Electronic engineering • Mathematics

ENTRY QUALIFICATIONS A degree in a computing-based subject is essential. A postgraduate qualification in business administration is desirable.

LIFESTYLE Systems analysts usually work regular hours, but they may have to work overtime to meet project deadlines.

LOCATION The work is usually office-based, but sometimes projects can be done remotely from home. Travel to visit clients may be required.

THE REALITIES The fast-paced nature of work and tight deadlines can be stressful. Systems analysts need to keep up to date with fast-evolving technology.

▼ RELATED CAREERS

▶ **SOFTWARE ENGINEER** *see pp. 118–119*

▶ **DATABASE MANAGER** *see pp. 122–123*

▶ **NETWORK ENGINEER** *see pp. 124–125*

▶ **DATA ANALYST** Analyses the huge volume of computer data companies collect to identify patterns that may help to make a business more profitable. Data analysts then present these findings to senior management.

▶ **IT RISK MANAGER** Scrutinizes a company's IT systems, and identifies and fixes security weaknesses that could lead to the theft or damage of computer-based information.

In its list of "Best Jobs in 2014", *US News* listed systems analyst at number two.

CAREER PATHS

Once qualified, systems analysts can specialize in a particular type of computer system, such as an accounting or health care system. If they work for a big company, they may be able to move into management or a strategic planning role.

SKILLS GUIDE

The ability to work in a team made up of people from diverse backgrounds.

Strong leadership skills to motivate technicians, instruct developers, and influence managers.

An analytical and logical approach to designing and testing complex systems.

Highly developed IT skills across a wide range of hardware, software, and networks.

Sound commercial awareness to provide clients with cost-effective system solutions.

TRAINEE After leaving school, you can become a trainee IT technician and then study part-time or via distance learning for a relevant degree.

GRADUATE To become a systems analyst, you need a degree in computer science, mathematics, business studies, or a related area.

SYSTEMS ANALYST Analysts work closely with business managers to develop effective IT systems. As an analyst, you may recommend and install new hardware or software, test the system, and teach staff how to use it. With experience, you may choose to specialize.

SENIOR ANALYST Heads up a team of IT professionals, or takes on a management role, advising the directors of a company on IT strategy, such as implementing the use of databases.

TECHNICAL ARCHITECT Makes decisions about the types of hardware and software products to be used. A technical architect is sometimes called a systems designer.

IT SYSTEMS PROJECT MANAGER Oversees an IT project from start to finish. Project managers develop plans, manage teams, study risks, and track project budgets.

SOFTWARE ANALYST Diagnoses problems with business software, and may develop and write code for new applications when necessary.

IT CONSULTANT Provides advice on IT matters to a range of businesses and government bodies for a management consultancy firm.

DATABASE MANAGER

010101

JOB DESCRIPTION

Companies in almost every sector, from engineering to marketing, rely on accurate data to make key business decisions. Database managers store and organize data in databases that recognize patterns in the information. They ensure that the databases run efficiently, providing users with data when they need it.

SALARY

Graduate ★★☆☆☆
Experienced manager ★★★★★

INDUSTRY PROFILE

Worldwide job opportunities •
Possibility of working in a variety of
sectors, from publishing to finance

SKILLS GUIDE

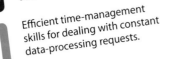

Good communication skills to understand and supply accurate data as it is requested.

Efficient time-management skills for dealing with constant data-processing requests.

Problem-solving skills to ensure that data is backed up reliably, easy to retrieve, and secure.

A keen interest in, and a good understanding of, software and coding.

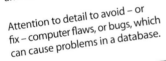

Attention to detail to avoid – or fix – computer flaws, or bugs, which can cause problems in a database.

▼ RELATED CAREERS

▶ **SOFTWARE ENGINEER** *see pp. 118–119*

▶ **SYSTEMS ANALYST** *see pp. 120–121*

▶ **NETWORK ENGINEER** *see pp. 124–125*

▶ **WEB DESIGNER** *see pp. 128–129*

▶ **FINANCIAL PROGRAMMER** Works with modern programming languages to write software used by financial institutions, such as banks.

▶ **INFORMATION SCIENTIST** Manages an organization's information resources, such as databases, online services, books, and paper-based records.

▶ **INFORMATION TECHNOLOGY CONSULTANT** Advises a business on how to improve its Information Technology (IT) infrastructure. Must have a good knowledge of databases, networks, and different kinds of software.

AT A GLANCE

YOUR INTERESTS Computer science • Coding • IT • New technologies • Data security • Mathematics

LOCATION The work is office-based, although managers may be able to work from home, even though they deal with staff from all parts of a company.

ENTRY QUALIFICATIONS A technical degree, such as in software engineering, computer science, or mathematics, is desirable but not essential.

THE REALITIES A database manager is a high-pressure role. They are expected to respond quickly and accurately to problems. Working on screen can be tiring.

LIFESTYLE Working out-of-hours is likely. Round-the-clock requests from members of the company are common.

Security and data recovery are important aspects of this job.

CAREER PATHS

Large companies with complex data requirements provide the best opportunities for career progression. Database managers can specialize in one area of technology.

TRAINEE If you have a keen interest in IT, you may be able to train on the job within a company's IT department.

DATABASE MANAGER Increasing data needs and advances in technology mean that you will have several potential options for career development in this field.

GRADUATE Graduates with degrees in IT or another related technical subject can join schemes run by companies.

NETWORK MANAGER Ensures that networks are secure and synchronized across the globe, and also implements the latest technologies.

PROJECT MANAGER Oversees a project from start to finish, liaising with a range of people across the business.

DATABASE ARCHITECT Designs the underlying structure of a database, based on the client's needs and aim.

DATA WAREHOUSE SPECIALIST Manages and analyses data (both current and historical) collected from different parts of an organization.

NETWORK ENGINEER

JOB DESCRIPTION

Network engineers set up and maintain the networks that carry information between computers. These networks may connect computers located either in a single office or computers separated by huge distances, and use a range of technologies to work. Network engineers also diagnose and fix problems with network software, and check the cables, radio links, and even satellites that carry the information. They also provide on-site help to a company's staff.

SALARY

Junior network engineer ★★☆☆☆
Senior network engineer ★★★★☆

INDUSTRY PROFILE

Growing job market • Opportunities available in almost every area of business or industry • Can work in-house or on a freelance basis for external consultancies

CAREER PATHS

Career progress as a network engineer depends on the type and size of the company you work for. If that company is small, you will be called upon to deal with a variety of computer issues, from slow Internet speeds to virus infections. However, if you work for a large global company, you are more likely to specialize in one particular area, such as network architecture or cyber security.

NETWORK ARCHITECT Designs an organization's computer network. This involves analysing how the business works and planning a network that can meet its needs, both now and in the future.

TRAINEE Leaving school with a good general education and strong Information Technology (IT) skills may help you find work as a trainee technician. On-the-job learning and taking courses at college may put you on the path to becoming a network engineer.

GRADUATE If you have a graduate or postgraduate degree in computer science or systems engineering, you can find work with companies that run large and complex networks.

NETWORK ENGINEER The role requires continual learning to keep up to date with ever-changing technologies. You usually specialize in one or more networking systems made by different manufacturers. With experience, you can move into a number of different roles.

SKILLS GUIDE

 Excellent communication skills to be able to work with non-technical staff in an organization.

 The ability to work as part of a team of software developers, and other IT professionals.

 The efficient management of IT technicians and an ability to support senior managers.

 The ability to identify and solve technical problems within urgent time frames.

 Patience and perseverance to resolve problems and restore a company's network function.

 Knowledge and expertise across a wide range of IT software, hardware, and networks.

AT A GLANCE

 YOUR INTERESTS IT • Computer science • Electronic or electrical engineering • Computer networks • Mathematics

 ENTRY QUALIFICATIONS A technical degree in computer-systems engineering or another related subject is useful but not essential.

 LIFESTYLE Network engineers work shifts or are on call to resolve issues outside normal hours, as companies rely on their networks 24 hours a day.

 LOCATION Much of the work is office-based, but some network engineers operate remotely from home, depending on the type of project.

 THE REALITIES Technological advances mean this is a growth area with many new fields of work opening up. Skills need to be regularly updated.

 NETWORK CONTROLLER Manages the staff who maintain the network, and ensures that the network operates reliably.

 IT CONSULTANT Works for an IT consultancy or sets up their own business to provide networking advice and services to a range of clients.

 **HELPDESK PROFESSIONAL** Provides telephone and online support and advice to a company's network users.

▼ RELATED CAREERS

▶ **SOFTWARE ENGINEER** *see pp. 118–119*

▶ **SYSTEMS ANALYST** *see pp. 120–121*

▶ **DATABASE MANAGER** *see pp. 122–123*

▶ **CYBER-SECURITY ANALYST** *see pp. 132–133*

> The US Bureau of Labor Statistics predicts that the number of job opportunities for network engineers will grow 18 per cent by 2018.

IT SUPPORT EXECUTIVE

JOB DESCRIPTION

Information Technology (IT) support executives provide technical assistance or help to computer users in an organization. They aim to solve common problems, such as forgotten passwords or lost data, and maintaining computer hardware and networks to ensure that they work efficiently and function continuously.

SALARY

Newly qualified executive ★★★★★
Experienced executive ★★★★★

INDUSTRY PROFILE

Varied opportunities with a wide range of employers, from large corporations to small firms • Growing demand for IT support in public and financial services sectors

AT A GLANCE

YOUR INTERESTS IT • Mathematics • Physics • Business studies • Business information technology • English • Computer programming

ENTRY QUALIFICATIONS A degree in an IT-related subject is desirable, but entry with suitable vocational training is also possible.

LIFESTYLE Most IT support companies operate 24 hours a day, so shift work is common. Part-time opportunities are offered by many employers.

LOCATION The work is office-based and involves visiting individual workstations, or offering advice by phone or email. Travel to other work sites is common.

THE REALITIES This work can be fast-paced and target-driven, with pressure to resolve calls quickly. Dealing with clients can be stressful.

CAREER PATHS

IT support jobs are found across a wide range of industries, in public sector organizations, and in IT consultancies providing support services to clients. Support executives are computer "all-rounders" with a good knowledge of hardware and software, and so may move into related IT jobs, such as network engineering or database management.

SCHOOL- OR COLLEGE-LEAVER
You can enter IT support by studying for qualifications from technology firms such as Microsoft, Linux, or CISCO. This will qualify you to maintain their systems or software products.

GRADUATE
You need a degree in a subject such as business information technology, systems engineering, or software engineering to apply for graduate IT support jobs.

▼ RELATED CAREERS

▶ **PROJECT MANAGER** *see pp. 82–83*

▶ **SYSTEMS ANALYST** *see pp. 120–121*

▶ **DATABASE MANAGER** *see pp. 122–123*

▶ **NETWORK ENGINEER** *see pp. 124–125*

▶ **CALL CENTRE MANAGER** Manages the daily operation of telephone call-centre staff, who deal with client and customer queries and complaints, and sell products or services over the telephone. There is strong demand for call-centre managers in industries such as IT and mobile telephony, and financial services, such as banking and insurance.

SKILLS GUIDE

 Excellent communication skills to ensure problems are understood and resolved efficiently.

 The capacity to work well in a team and identify serious issues for managers and IT specialists.

 Good management skills to guide IT support staff, and the ability to influence senior managers.

 The application of technical skills and a logical approach for effective problem-solving.

 Expertise in IT programs, systems, and networks, and the capacity to learn quickly on the job.

NETWORK SUPPORT ENGINEER Provides hardware and software support for users of telephone and computer networks, both in person and on the telephone.

DESKTOP SUPPORT EXECUTIVE Delivers IT user support across a particular business area, such as retail or banking, to resolve systems faults and user problems.

WEBSITE HOSTING EXECUTIVE Works for a website hosting firm, providing 24-hour IT support for users who have purchased server space from the company for their website or email services.

 **IT SUPPORT EXECUTIVE** Working in this role will give you an insight into all the IT functions of an organization, so sideways moves into related IT jobs are common. You can also specialize in a technical area, such as network support, or industry.

SERVICE DESK MANAGER Manages a team of staff who are responsible for delivering support for IT applications and business services, ensuring that targets and client expectations are met or exceeded.

WEB DESIGNER

JOB DESCRIPTION

Building an effective website requires a blend of technical and creative skills. Web designers take into account the appearance and usability of the website as well as its back-end – the software that delivers the information to the user and makes the site run smoothly. Web designers usually have a strong technical and programming background, and a keen eye for detail.

SALARY

Junior web designer ★★★★★
Experienced web designer ★★★★★

INDUSTRY PROFILE

Fast-moving environment •
Opportunities in small or large design agencies • Freelancing common •
Huge global market

CAREER PATHS

Web designers typically work as part of a team, developing or testing a website. With experience, they may progress to leading a development team or working with clients at a web-design agency.

WEB PROGRAMMER
Specializes in writing the code that makes a website work. Code is written using languages such as HTML, Javascript, and PHP.

ASSISTANT If you have strong Information Technology (IT) skills, you may be able to find work with an agency as a design assistant. You will need to prove yourself on the job to progress.

GRADUATE You can become a web designer if you have a degree or postgraduate qualification in IT or web design, along with a good knowledge of current web technologies.

WEB DESIGNER
Throughout your career you will continue to acquire new skills. You can specialize in various technical areas from web programming to graphic design.

SKILLS GUIDE

 Creativity and innovation to stay ahead in the competitive world of website design.

 Clarity of thought and strong analytical skills to handle complexities in the design.

 The ability to analyse the design of a website, then identify and solve problems in it.

 Confidence with technology and a willingness to keep up to date with new software developments.

 An eye for detail when planning and designing the content of complex websites.

 GRAPHIC DESIGNER Uses images, colours, and type, to create layouts to express information and messages for print or electronic media in a visual way.

 USER-EXPERIENCE DESIGNER Specializes in improving the function and layout of a website to make it as user-friendly as possible.

 **CREATIVE DIRECTOR** Combines extensive design experience – using computer programs such as Photoshop and Illustrator – with managing a team. Excellent organizational skills are essential.

▼ RELATED CAREERS

▶ **ILLUSTRATOR** *see pp. 26–27*

▶ **SOFTWARE ENGINEER** *see pp. 118–119*

▶ **GAMES DEVELOPER** *see pp. 130–131*

▶ **MULTIMEDIA PROGRAMMER** Creates interactive features for products such as DVDs, websites, and applications using a range of exciting photographs, animation clips, sounds, and text.

▶ **PEN TESTER** Employed by a company to hack into its websites to test their effectiveness against potential external cyber attacks.

▶ **WEB MARKETING DESIGNER** Comes up with a strategy to direct Internet traffic to websites, typically through email campaigns and online advertisements.

AT A GLANCE

 YOUR INTERESTS IT • Computer science • Design • Internet security • New technologies • Multimedia • Graphics

 ENTRY QUALIFICATIONS A qualification in software engineering or graphic design is useful, but many web designers are self-taught.

 LIFESTYLE Working hours are flexible, but tight deadlines often mean working into the evening or weekend. Freelance contracts are common.

 LOCATION The work can be done either in an office or remotely from home. Some travel might be required to meet clients.

 THE REALITIES A web designer's reputation is the key to success. It is essential to ensure you keep up to date with regularly changing technologies.

GAMES DEVELOPER

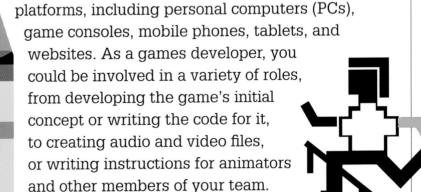

JOB DESCRIPTION

A games developer produces games for different platforms, including personal computers (PCs), game consoles, mobile phones, tablets, and websites. As a games developer, you could be involved in a variety of roles, from developing the game's initial concept or writing the code for it, to creating audio and video files, or writing instructions for animators and other members of your team.

SALARY

Junior developer ★★☆☆☆
Lead developer ★★★★☆

INDUSTRY PROFILE

Massive expansion in recent years, and set to grow further • Many freelance contracts available • Smaller companies with fewer than 50 employees common

AT A GLANCE

YOUR INTERESTS Computer science • Graphics • 3-D design • Animation and illustration • Gaming • Coding • Physics • Mathematics • Information Technology (IT)

ENTRY QUALIFICATIONS A degree in computer science or a media-related discipline is useful although not essential to becoming a developer.

LIFESTYLE Teams are close-knit and may work extra hours to prepare a new game for a set launch date. Most developers are in their 20s or 30s.

LOCATION Games developers work mainly on a computer in an office. The atmosphere is informal and creative, with people from many disciplines.

THE REALITIES Entry to the field is highly competitive. Strict deadlines drive the work and spending long periods on a computer can be tiring.

CAREER PATHS

There is no formal career structure for games developers. Progress depends largely on which specialist path is taken – for example, focusing on programming graphics or the user interface. In this young and dynamic industry, success depends on performance, and on the sales and critical acclaim of the games.

PLAY TESTER If you have excellent IT skills, you may be able to find work with a games company, testing their products for playability and flaws (bugs). This can provide a route into the industry.

GRADUATE Taking a degree in computer science gives you the best chance of employment. Some colleges offer specialist games-programming courses or modules.

▼ RELATED CAREERS

▶ **SOFTWARE ENGINEER** *see pp. 118–119*

▶ **WEB DESIGNER** *see pp. 128–129*

▶ **ANIMATOR** Brings to life characters or objects in cartoons, advertisements, and video games by modelling their movement on screen. An animator needs good artistic and design skills.

▶ **FORENSIC COMPUTER ANALYST** Investigates computer hacking and other illegal computer-related activities. Forensic computer analysts may be hired by the police or large companies.

▶ **STORYBOARD ARTIST** Illustrates how a character progresses in a computer game using a series of drawings or animations. Storyboard artists have good story-telling and drawing skills.

SKILLS GUIDE

Good team-working skills to work smoothly with people from a wide range of educational backgrounds.

Imagination to develop new skills, and the flexibility to handle a wide range of tasks.

A logical approach to problem-solving and strong mathematical and analytical skills.

An in-depth knowledge of computer games and excellent IT skills.

Attention to detail to ensure bug-free codes; the ability to work under pressure and meet deadlines.

SENIOR DEVELOPER Leads a team of specialists to complete an entire game or part of a larger digital product. This role could go to a person with either a programming, or artistic and design, background.

PRODUCER Oversees a project, ensuring that all of the resources and personnel required to complete the work on time are in place.

GAMES DEVELOPER
You may follow one of two routes: a programmer, who builds the game, or a designer, who creates the graphics.

GAMES DESIGNER
Devises the look of the characters, levels, and the game's storyline. May have a programming background, but many games designers come from a design discipline.

In 2012, the games industry generated US$ 20.77 billion in the USA.

CYBER-SECURITY ANALYST

JOB DESCRIPTION

The computerized data a company or a government holds is a valuable asset that needs constant protection. With a high-level knowledge of computing and networks, cyber-security analysts work towards preventing counter-security breaches by identifying and fixing weaknesses in the computer code and hardware of an organization.

SALARY

Newly qualified analyst ★★★★☆
Senior consultant ★★★★★

INDUSTRY PROFILE

Increased reliance on computer systems has seen a growing demand for skilled cyber-security analysts • Better paid sector than other areas of Information Technology (IT)

AT A GLANCE

YOUR INTERESTS IT • Software engineering • Database design • Computer networks • Mathematics • Physics • Law

ENTRY QUALIFICATIONS A degree in software engineering or computer science is essential. A higher qualification in cyber security is useful.

LIFESTYLE Regular office hours are the norm, but cyber-security analysts may be expected to work extra hours if there is a threat to their employer's system.

LOCATION This job is normally office-based, but working remotely from home is possible in some jobs. Some travel to visit clients is required.

THE REALITIES Cyber-security analysts must keep up to date with new systems, technologies, and threats. The high level of responsibility can be stressful.

▼ RELATED CAREERS

▶ **SOFTWARE ENGINEER** see pp. 118–119

▶ **NETWORK ENGINEER** see pp. 124–125

▶ **POLICE OFFICER** see pp. 240–241

▶ **CYBER-CRIME LAWYER** Specializes in the legal aspects of data security and online crime.

▶ **IT CONSULTANT** Advises businesses on how to improve their IT infrastructure. An IT consultant needs an extensive knowledge of databases, IT networks, and software.

More than 10 million cyber attacks are reported every day, and the number is growing.

CAREER PATHS

Most entrants have a relevant computing degree. With experience, cyber-security analysts can move into a management role or choose to specialize in areas such as research into new threats or computer forensics.

SCHOOL-LEAVER If you are a computing enthusiast with good IT skills, you may be able to find work as an IT technician. You can then study for a relevant degree on the job.

GRADUATE You will usually need at least a first degree in a computing or mathematical subject to be considered. Certain roles also require a certificate from a professional body.

SKILLS GUIDE

Creative thinking to spot new ways in which systems could be attacked.

Logical and analytical skills to understand how systems have been put together.

The ability to think quickly and to respond to threats to avert any potential damage.

A good knowledge of a variety of computer-programming languages, networks, and areas of vulnerability.

Attention to detail when checking for fraud and while conducting research.

CYBER-SECURITY ANALYST
Working under a company's IT manager, you will check systems for weaknesses, monitor unusual activity on networks, install security software, and take other measures to neutralize the threats of a cyber attack. Experienced cyber-security analysts have a number of career options.

SECURITY TRAINER Trains staff and network users on how to keep valuable electronically-stored data secure and confidential.

FORENSIC ANALYST
Examines computers, smartphones, and other digital devices to identify and investigate their contents for illegal material. Forensic analysts typically work with the police and other law-enforcement agencies.

RISK MANAGER Analyses security risks that could potentially affect an organization's IT systems. Risk managers also work with senior management to update and organize systems to ensure their reliability.

SECURITY INVESTIGATOR
Conducts research to identify the location, motives, and methods of cyber criminals, often working with the authorities to prevent illegal activities and provide evidence in prosecutions.

PEN TESTER Tests the resistance of computer networks by attempting to penetrate their defences. Identifying gaps in security that could be exploited by malicious computer hackers and ensuring that these gaps are closed are important parts of the job.

SCIENCE AND RESEARCH

The scientific sector comprises a broad range of specialisms, all of which are suited to people with an enquiring mind, an analytical approach, and an excitement for making new discoveries. In these fields, you could be developing vaccines, discovering marine life, or launching satellites into space.

BIOTECHNOLOGIST
Page 136

Biotechnologists use scientific methods – from genetics to biochemistry – to develop new materials, organisms, and products for use in a range of sectors, such as agriculture.

MICROBIOLOGIST
Page 138

Research carried out by microbiologists into viruses, bacteria, and other microorganisms is critical in preventing infectious diseases and protecting public health.

PHARMACOLOGIST
Page 140

Conducting research into new drugs, existing medicines, and other chemical substances, pharmacologists use their scientific knowledge to improve human health.

FOOD SCIENTIST
Page 142

Employed by regulatory bodies and the food and drink industry, food scientists develop new products, and check the health and safety effects of existing products.

MARINE BIOLOGIST
Page 144

Marine biologists study sea life, find new species, and analyse the effects of human activity and climate change on ocean ecosystems.

FORENSIC SCIENTIST
Page 146

Conducting scientific analysis of crime scenes and gathering evidence for criminal cases, forensic scientists help to solve crimes by bringing hidden facts to light.

GEOSCIENTIST
Page 148

Exploring the natural riches of Earth through fieldwork and research, geoscientists enhance our knowledge of the oil, gas, and mineral resources that lie beneath the ground.

MATERIALS SCIENTIST
Page 150

At the forefront of technology, materials scientists create the substances of tomorrow by researching the properties and behaviours of natural and human-made materials.

METEOROLOGIST
Page 152

Conducting climate research, and creating and presenting weather forecasts, meteorologists study and interpret the atmospheric conditions that shape the world around us.

ASTRONOMER
Page 154

Studying the stars, planets, and space through observation and research, astronomers work in an academic discipline to help us understand the Universe.

ASTRONAUT
Page 156

Space science is a niche discipline that contributes greatly to scientific understanding. Astronauts are the celestial explorers who conduct research in outer space.

BIOTECHNOLOGIST

JOB DESCRIPTION

At the cutting edge of science, biotechnologists use their knowledge of how living organisms function to find solutions to problems and develop new products. Their work includes developing new vaccines against diseases, improving animal feed, growing crops that are more resistant to drought and pests, and improving everyday products, such as cheese and bread.

SALARY

Biotechnologist ★★☆☆☆
Senior biotechnologist ★★★★☆

INDUSTRY PROFILE

Many global opportunities •
Wide range of potential employers •
Best job prospects in industrial and medical specialisms

AT A GLANCE

 YOUR INTERESTS Laboratory work • Scientific investigation • Biology • Chemistry • Physics • Mathematics • Engineering

 ENTRY QUALIFICATIONS A degree or postgraduate qualification in a biology- or chemistry-related discipline is essential.

 LIFESTYLE Work hours are regular, but biotechnologists may have to work in the evenings, on weekends, or in shifts to check on research experiments.

 LOCATION For the most part, biotechnologists of all levels work in sterilized laboratories in research or industrial buildings.

 THE REALITIES Ground-breaking discoveries can be exciting, but the work can also be repetitive and frustrating. Many hours are spent in the laboratory.

▼ RELATED CAREERS

▶ **MICROBIOLOGIST** *see pp. 138–139*

▶ **FOOD SCIENTIST** *see pp. 142–143*

▶ **CHEMICAL ENGINEER** *see pp. 180–181*

▶ **BIOCHEMIST** Conducts scientific research into chemical reactions that take place in living organisms. Biochemists analyse the effects of drugs, foods, allergies, and disease on cells, proteins, and DNA.

▶ **BIOMEDICAL RESEARCH SCIENTIST** Performs clinical trials and laboratory tests to research methods of treating disease and other health-related conditions.

In Europe, more than 325 million people have benefitted from drugs manufactured through biotechnology.

CAREER PATHS

Biotechnologist is a broad term that encompasses many roles, from high-level research to manufacturing. To work in research, you will need a relevant degree. After specializing in one field, you may find it difficult to move into another.

TECHNICIAN If you are a school-leaver, you can begin as a trainee laboratory technician and study part-time for a degree or industry qualification.

GRADUATE A degree in biology, chemistry, plant sciences, or biochemistry is essential if you want to become a biotechnologist.

SKILLS GUIDE

 Innovation and a willingness to learn new technologies as they emerge.

 A logical and analytical approach for performing experiments and conducting research.

 Problem-solving skills and the ability to formulate ideas, plan experiments, and interpret results.

 Good computer skills to record and analyse experimental and product data.

 The perseverance and motivation to rethink and restart experiments that may not work.

 The ability to handle scientific equipment and take measurements very carefully.

BIOTECHNOLOGIST There are various opportunities to specialize, but each of these strands of biotechnology require further (specialist) study.

BREWING BIOTECHNOLOGIST Develops new and better methods of brewing and storing beer, lager, and other fermented products.

BIOPHARMACEUTICAL ANALYST Applies advanced techniques, such as genetic engineering, to develop new drugs used for treating diseases, such as arthritis and high blood pressure.

CLINICAL SCIENTIST Works in a hospital carrying out clinical studies and analysing data to develop new therapies or providing diagnoses for medical staff.

FUELS AND CHEMICALS BIOTECHNOLOGIST Conducts research into the manufacture of cleaner fuels, such as bioethanol, or novel materials, such as biodegradable plastics, which are far more eco-friendly than many of the current products in use.

MICROBIOLOGIST

JOB DESCRIPTION

Microbiologists study tiny organisms, such as bacteria and viruses, which can cause disease, pollution, and crop destruction, but which may also be used to produce vaccines to prevent diseases. They collect organisms from the environment or from patients, and study and conduct experiments on them. Their work benefits a number of sectors, from medicine to agriculture.

SALARY

Junior microbiologist ★★☆☆☆
Senior consultant ★★★★★

INDUSTRY PROFILE

A fast-growing sector • Opportunities in research, production, quality control, and in government • Some research studies at the cutting edge of science

AT A GLANCE

YOUR INTERESTS Laboratory work • Health and medicine • Research and development • Food technology • Biology • Physics • Chemistry

ENTRY QUALIFICATIONS A degree in microbiology or a related subject is essential. Many employers require a PhD and academic research experience.

LIFESTYLE Most microbiologists work regular hours, but they may need to supervise laboratory experiments during evenings and weekends.

LOCATION Much of the work is laboratory-based, although experienced microbiologists may need to gather samples at a variety of locations.

THE REALITIES Laboratory work can be repetitive, especially for junior microbiologists. Competition for senior roles is intense.

CAREER PATHS

Qualified microbiologists can find jobs in many areas, including the health care, pharmaceutical, food, water, and agricultural industries. They will be expected to publish research papers to build their academic reputation and gain promotion.

LABORATORY TECHNICIAN After leaving school, you can start working as a laboratory technician, while studying for a degree part-time.

GRADUATE You will need a degree in life sciences, such as microbiology, applied biology, biomedical science, or molecular biology. A postgraduate-level degree will help you to progress to more responsible positions.

▼ RELATED CAREERS

▶ **BIOTECHNOLOGIST** *see pp. 136–137*

▶ **PHARMACOLOGIST** *see pp. 140–141*

▶ **CLINICAL BIOCHEMIST** Carries out complex experiments to analyse samples of blood, urine, and body tissue. Clinical biochemists use their findings to make recommendations about new treatments and further research.

▶ **IMMUNOLOGIST** Studies the immune system and helps devise new diagnostic tools, therapies, as well as treatments. Opportunities exist in research centres, hospitals, and in pharmaceutical companies.

▶ **TOXICOLOGIST** Conducts experiments to find out the impact of toxic and radioactive materials on people, animals, and the environment.

SKILLS GUIDE

 Good team-working skills for collaborating with other scientists and manufacturers.

 An innovative approach to scientific experiments; a desire to challenge existing ideas.

 Good organizational skills for managing complex experiments and large amounts of data.

 The ability to solve difficult problems using logic and a sound experimental approach.

 The perseverance to continue searching for solutions, even in the face of repeated failures.

Attention to detail when taking measurements, making calculations, or studying data.

RESEARCH MICROBIOLOGIST Studies the effects and uses of microorganisms in a wide range of areas. Usually combines research with teaching undergraduates.

CLINICAL MICROBIOLOGIST Works on identifying disease-causing microbes and developing ways to treat disease and prevent its spread. Usually based at a hospital or clinic.

PATENT EXAMINER Assesses applications for patents, which are granted to inventors to give them the right to prevent other people from using, selling, or making their inventions.

MICROBIOLOGIST You conduct experiments on microorganisms to enhance your understanding of why they can be harmful to humans and crops and to see whether they can be used for human benefit. With experience, you can specialize in a number of areas.

PHARMACEUTICAL SALESPERSON Uses a specialist knowledge to work in sales for pharmaceutical companies. Sells their products to doctors, researchers, and other companies in the medical field.

PHARMACOLOGIST

JOB DESCRIPTION

Pharmacologists conduct experiments on chemicals that have medicinal properties in order to research their effects on people, animals, and the environment. Working for pharmaceutical companies, universities, hospitals, or government laboratories, they study the beneficial and possible harmful effects of these substances, using their data to develop new drugs and treatments that are safe to use.

SALARY

Junior pharmacologist ★★☆☆☆
Senior pharmacologist ★★★★★

INDUSTRY PROFILE

Highly competitive field • Growing sector due to advances in research and increased human life expectancy • Opportunities in pharmaceutical industry, hospitals, and universities

CAREER PATHS

A degree in pharmacology is essential to enter this scientific profession; many senior researchers hold a PhD and have experience of conducting related research at university level. Pharmacologists usually specialize in developing drugs in a specific area, such as those that work on the heart, or the nervous or digestive systems.

TOXICOLOGIST Carries out clinical and laboratory studies to identify toxic chemicals and substances for a range of purposes, such as new product development in the pharmaceutical or petrochemical industries.

GRADUATE While having a degree in pharmacology is preferable, other subjects such as biochemistry, biomedical sciences, physiology, and toxicology can provide an entry into this career. Work experience with a pharmaceutical company during your studies is also an advantage.

POSTGRADUATE A master's degree or PhD in a relevant science subject will allow you to enter this profession at a higher level.

PHARMACOLOGIST As a pharmacologist, you might be involved in non-laboratory work, such as sales and marketing or product licensing for new drugs. With experience, you can expect to move into more senior roles with increased managerial responsibilities.

SKILLS GUIDE

Good communication skills for preparing reports and presenting the results of experiments.

The ability to lead and motivate others in a team, and supervise or train junior team members.

Sharp analytical skills to interpret data from experiments and peer-reviewed publications.

Strong problem-solving skills for improving medicines during the drug-development phase.

Excellent computer skills to record test results and analyse complex data.

Acute observational skills and attention to detail in carrying out precise scientific work.

NEUROPHARMACOLOGIST Studies how nerve cells and human behaviour are affected by drugs, and develops new medicines to treat conditions such as depression and bipolar disorder.

CLINICAL PHARMACOLOGIST Drafts guidelines for how and when medicines should be prescribed, runs clinical trials of new drugs, and monitors the effectiveness and possible side-effects of medicines.

UNIVERSITY RESEARCHER Works in a university pharmacology department, leading teams undertaking research projects and experiments, teaching and supervising students, and performing administrative and management tasks.

▼ RELATED CAREERS

▶ **MICROBIOLOGIST** *see pp. 138–139*

▶ **FORENSIC SCIENTIST** *see pp. 146–147*

▶ **DOCTOR** *see pp. 276–277*

▶ **PHARMACIST** *see pp. 284–285*

▶ **BIOCHEMIST** Conducts scientific research into chemical reactions that take place inside living organisms. Biochemists study DNA, proteins, and cells to observe the effects of drugs, foods, allergies, and disease.

▶ **BIOMEDICAL RESEARCH SCIENTIST** Performs clinical trials and laboratory tests to research new treatments for diseases and other health issues.

AT A GLANCE

YOUR INTERESTS Chemistry • Biology • Physics • Mathematics • Information Technology (IT) • Health and medicine

ENTRY QUALIFICATIONS A degree in a science-related subject is necessary. A postgraduate degree is demanded by some employers.

LIFESTYLE Working hours are regular, but weekend or shift work may be required to monitor experiments. Part-time hours may be available.

LOCATION Pharmacological work is primarily laboratory- or office-based, but travelling to scientific conferences is a common part of the job.

THE REALITIES Laboratory analysis may be repetitive and involve working with hazardous chemicals. Some roles involve animal testing.

FOOD SCIENTIST

JOB DESCRIPTION

Food scientists research and develop a wide range of food-related products, making sure they are safe and palatable for consumption. They develop new ingredients, test the quality of food items, check labelling for accurate nutritional information, and design or improve food manufacturing machinery to find ways of producing food more quickly and safely.

SALARY

Newly qualified scientist ★★★★★
Experienced scientist ★★★★★

INDUSTRY PROFILE

Many job opportunities worldwide • Primary employers include food manufacturers, retailers and supermarket chains, and government research establishments

CAREER PATHS

A food scientist may find work with large food- and drinks-manufacturing companies, retail chains, government food-inspection departments, public health laboratories, and academic research organizations. To gain seniority and responsibility, you can advance within large companies or move between organizations.

FOOD DEVELOPMENT TECHNOLOGIST
Specializes in creating and developing new food products for manufacturing companies, supermarkets, and other food retailers.

LABORATORY TECHNICIAN
You can start your career as a laboratory technician and train on the job while studying for a part-time degree in a relevant subject.

GRADUATE To become a food scientist, you need an undergraduate or postgraduate degree in food science, food technology, or another related science subject.

FOOD SCIENTIST Once qualified as a food scientist at degree level, you can move into many different areas, such as food production, research, quality, and environmental health.

SKILLS GUIDE

An innovative approach to researching new food products and production techniques.

Good analytical skills to assess products for quality and to develop new processes.

Strong computer skills for recording and analysing research and development.

The perseverance to conduct multiple experiments and produce numerous sample products.

Attention to detail and precision in handling tasks, such as food labelling and checking hygiene.

AT A GLANCE

YOUR INTERESTS Food science and technology • Food production • Consumer research • Engineering • Chemistry • Biology

ENTRY QUALIFICATIONS A degree in a food-related subject, such as food technology, biology, or chemistry, is essential.

LIFESTYLE Food scientists usually work normal hours, but they may also work shifts to check food manufacturing production lines.

LOCATION As well as working in laboratories, food scientists may have to travel to factories and production lines, and to meet suppliers.

THE REALITIES As the work involves repetitive quality checks and experiments, food scientists spend many hours in a laboratory.

FOOD PRODUCTION MANAGER
Sets and monitors quality standards in processed food and oversees food production, ensuring that the items leaving a factory or processing plant meet the appropriate standards.

FOOD MARKETING MANAGER
Presents and markets food products to the public. The job involves close collaboration with market researchers, packaging designers, and advertising teams.

ACADEMIC FOOD RESEARCHER
Conducts research into areas such as food production, storage, and processing. Academic food researchers may also teach university students.

▼ RELATED CAREERS

▶ **BIOTECHNOLOGIST** *see pp. 136–137*

▶ **MICROBIOLOGIST** *see pp. 138–139*

▶ **BIOCHEMIST** Conducts scientific research into chemical reactions in living organisms in order to study the effects of drugs, foods, allergies, and disease on cells, protein, and DNA.

▶ **CONSUMER SCIENTIST** Conducts research and advises companies on consumer preferences. Consumer scientists work with industries dealing in food, marketing, advertising, and publishing, and also with government departments.

▶ **DIETICIAN** Diagnoses and treats diet-related health problems, advising on nutrition, weight loss or gain, and general eating habits.

MARINE BIOLOGIST

JOB DESCRIPTION

Marine biologists study life within the world's seas and oceans, conducting research in both the water and in the laboratory to analyse how plants and animals are affected by changes in the environment, some of which are caused by human activities. They often specialize in studying one species of animal or plant, and may travel the world to study its habitats and feeding patterns.

SALARY

Junior marine biologist ★★★★★
Senior marine biologist ★★★★★

INDUSTRY PROFILE

Growth opportunities in sectors including pollution control, biotechnology, and aquaculture • Work available across the world • Competitive job market

▼ RELATED CAREERS

▶ **MICROBIOLOGIST** see pp. 138–139

▶ **ECOLOGIST** see pp. 172–173

▶ **BIOCHEMIST** Investigates chemical reactions that take place in living organisms. Areas of research include DNA, proteins, drugs, allergies, and disease.

▶ **ENVIRONMENTAL CONSERVATIONIST** Works to protect and manage the natural environment in locations such as forests, deserts, and coastal areas.

▶ **OCEANOGRAPHER** Conducts scientific research related to the oceans and seas, and how they interact with rivers, glaciers, and the atmosphere. Oceanographers work in waste management, offshore wind farms, coastal construction, and for oil and water companies.

Oceans cover 71 per cent of Earth's surface, but we have explored only 10 per cent of them.

AT A GLANCE

YOUR INTERESTS Marine life • Palaeontology • Oceanography • Conservation • Biology • Geography • Geology • Chemistry

ENTRY QUALIFICATIONS A degree in a relevant subject, such as marine biology, zoology, or oceanography, is essential.

LIFESTYLE Work hours are often irregular. Field trips are commonplace, and may require long-distance travel, often at short notice.

LOCATION Long days at sea are normal when collecting data on field trips, but much of the work is based in a laboratory or an office.

THE REALITIES Activities such as diving and working on board a ship are exciting but also physically demanding, and may be dangerous at times.

CAREER PATHS

Many marine biologists aspire to work in the conservation of species and ecosystems, but employment in this area is scarce. You are more likely to find work with government agencies or industries concerned with pollution control, fisheries management, and environmental monitoring.

SKILLS GUIDE

 The ability to work well in a team, especially when spending long periods away at sea.

 Good flexibility, as a variety of tasks are involved, from setting up experiments to planning trips.

 Good organizational skills for coordinating research and experiments effectively.

 The motivation and perseverance to continue research in difficult and challenging conditions.

 Physical endurance, resilience, and stamina while undertaking work in the oceans.

 Attention to detail, as the results of oceanic experiments must be reported accurately.

GRADUATE You will need a degree and usually a postgraduate qualification to become a marine biologist. Following your degree, you can improve your job prospects by working as an intern in marine research or conservation.

MARINE BIOLOGIST The job of a marine biologist is varied. Early in your career, you may spend time collecting samples, analysing data in a laboratory, and writing reports. With experience, you may lead a research team or give advice to government or industry.

MARINE CONSERVATIONIST Specializes in protecting animals, plants, and the oceans from harmful pollutants, over-fishing, and other human-made changes to biodiversity.

MARINE BIOTECHNOLOGIST Investigates marine animals and plants, which contain chemicals that can be developed into drugs or other useful products.

FISHERIES AND AQUACULTURE SCIENTIST Works to increase fish production and improve the health of marine life at commercial fish farms or in the wild, using their in-depth knowledge of fish and crustacean biology.

RESEARCHER AND LECTURER Researches marine biology at university. This can be purely scientific or applied to real-world problems. This role also involves teaching students marine-related subjects.

FORENSIC SCIENTIST

JOB DESCRIPTION

Forensic scientists work with the police and other law enforcement agencies to help solve crimes. Collecting samples, such as body fluids, hair, fibres, or fragments from the scene of a crime, they then examine the samples for evidence that may help in the identification of a suspect or victim, or provide other valuable information about the incident.

SALARY

Assistant forensic scientist ★★★★★
Senior forensic scientist ★★★★★

INDUSTRY PROFILE

New techniques in forensics, such as DNA fingerprinting, have opened specialist job opportunities • Fierce competition for jobs

CAREER PATHS

A degree in a scientific subject is the first step in this career. You begin as a trainee, visiting crime scenes to collect evidence for laboratories. With experience, you can go on to manage teams of scientists, or move into private consultancy, where you may investigate the causes of industrial fires or accidents.

DNA ANALYST Analyses human genetic material, DNA. This lab-based job in a fast-growing, cutting-edge specialism of forensics demands an in-depth knowledge of DNA sequencing techniques and how to interpret genetic data.

GRADUATE You will need a degree to enter the profession. Graduates in chemistry, biology, biochemistry, or medical science are the usual recruits, but opportunities are also available for graduates in computer science. This is because recovering electronic data from computers and phones is a growing field in forensics.

POSTGRADUATE You may stand a better chance of getting a job with a postgraduate qualification in a specialism such as ballistics (firearms) or forensic chemistry.

FORENSIC SCIENTIST Most of your training will be on the job. After a few years' experience, you may be called as an "expert witness" to give evidence in court. Alternatively, you can apply for management positions or enter private consultancy.

SKILLS GUIDE

Good communication skills for presenting complex scientific evidence to legal experts.

The ability to work as part of an investigative team made up of scientists and police.

Excellent analytical skills and absolute attention to detail when examining evidence.

A logical and methodical approach to build a probable sequence of events in a crime case.

▼ RELATED CAREERS

▶ **INTELLIGENCE OFFICER** *see pp. 246–247*

▶ **BIOCHEMIST** Investigates chemical reactions that take place inside living organisms. Research areas include DNA, proteins, drugs, and disease.

▶ **LABORATORY TECHNICIAN** Supports scientists during laboratory investigations. Prepares samples for analysis, carries out experiments, and maintains laboratory equipment and supplies.

▶ **PATHOLOGY TECHNICIAN** Supports doctors during post-mortem examinations to identify the cause of a person's death.

▶ **TOXICOLOGIST** Conducts experiments to determine the impact of toxic and radioactive materials on people, animals, and the environment.

PUBLIC HEALTH FORENSIC SCIENTIST Works with health or government organizations to locate the sources of environmental contamination or investigate the causes of disease epidemics.

FORENSIC EXPLOSIVES SPECIALIST Uses chemical analysis to establish both the cause of an explosion and the origin of the chemicals involved in it.

Fingerprint evidence has been used to catch criminals since 1902.

AT A GLANCE

YOUR INTERESTS Chemistry • Biology • Mathematics • Physics • Information Technology (IT) • Research and laboratory work

ENTRY QUALIFICATIONS A degree in a relevant science subject is essential, while a postgraduate qualification in forensic science is useful.

LIFESTYLE Hours of work are variable because call-outs to crime scenes can come at any time, including evenings and weekends.

LOCATION Most work is carried out in a laboratory, although visits to crime scenes and courts to present evidence are also a crucial part of the role.

THE REALITIES Visiting accident or crime scenes can be distressing. Forensic scientists have to keep up to date with changing technology.

GEOSCIENTIST

JOB DESCRIPTION

This is the perfect career for those who love to study Earth, its structure, and how it interacts with the oceans, atmosphere, and living things. Geoscientists use their knowledge of physics, chemistry, and mathematics to study a variety of issues in the world – from predicting volcanic activity, to ensuring clean water supplies, and finding the best way to extract natural resources (such as oil and gas) from the ground.

SALARY

Newly qualified geoscientist ★★☆☆☆
Consultant geoscientist ★★★★☆

INDUSTRY PROFILE

Job opportunities worldwide • Industry demands highly technical skills • Higher salaries offered by oil and gas companies

AT A GLANCE

YOUR INTERESTS Geology • Physics • Scientific exploration • Mathematics • Engineering • Chemistry • Biology • Information Technology (IT)

ENTRY QUALIFICATIONS A degree is essential but, increasingly, a postgraduate qualification in geology, geophysics, or Earth science is also required.

LIFESTYLE Geoscientists usually work regular hours in an office, but they also have to carry out field work, which can lead to longer hours.

LOCATION When not in the office, geoscientists may work from various locations, such as oil rigs, earthquake zones, quarries, and nuclear waste sites.

THE REALITIES Travelling to sites across the world and working with equipment, such as drilling machines, can be physically demanding.

CAREER PATHS

Geoscientists are employed in a wide range of fields. They may find work in research, investigating issues such as earthquakes or climate change, or in government, advising on policy. Most opportunities exist in either the mineral and extraction industries or in consultancies that advise on the impact of developments, such as dams, tunnels, and waste-treatment projects.

GRADUATE A degree in geoscience or a related subject is essential to become a geoscientist. Accreditation from a professional body may be required to work in some parts of the world.

POSTGRADUATE Most employers expect you to have a master's degree or PhD, combined with some academic research experience.

▼ RELATED CAREERS

▶ **METEOROLOGIST** *see pp. 152–153*

▶ **ARCHAEOLOGIST** Excavates and explores ancient sites. The role may involve working in museums or research organizations, and specializing in particular fields, such as historical periods or geographic locations.

▶ **CARTOGRAPHER** Studies and produces maps and geographical charts. Using the latest technology, cartographers produce maps for the public and the military, as well as for surveying purposes.

▶ **HYDROLOGIST** Studies the movement, distribution, and quality of water on Earth. May look at rainfall patterns or the issue of melting icecaps and its effect on the environment.

SKILLS GUIDE

 The ability to communicate effectively, and use diplomacy to address sensitive issues.

 A logical, methodical, and organized approach to solving problems.

 Knowledge of mathematics and statistics to handle detailed measurements and calculations.

 Competence in IT to work with scientific equipment and interpret results.

 Attention to detail for precise measurements and making accurate calculations.

MINING GEOSCIENTIST
Works for mining companies, exploring and evaluating production sites and making recommendations about extraction techniques.

PETROLEUM GEOSCIENTIST
Specializes in the exploration and extraction of oil and gas, usually working for large multinational petrochemical companies.

GEOSCIENTIST You will specialize in a specific area once you are qualified. Areas include geology, mining, petroleum, and energy resources.

ENVIRONMENTAL GEOSCIENTIST
Applies scientific knowledge to environmental issues, such as pollution and waste disposal, and to issues concerned with large-scale construction projects.

The best-paid geoscientists work in the oil industry.

MATERIALS SCIENTIST

JOB DESCRIPTION

Materials scientists study the composition and structure of matter at a microscopic level. Using this specialist knowledge, they develop materials with new properties. The silicon chips used in computers, the carbon fibre frames of racing bikes, and the concrete used in skyscrapers have all been developed and tested by materials scientists.

SALARY

Newly qualified scientist ★★☆☆☆
Senior materials scientist ★★★★☆

INDUSTRY PROFILE

Good opportunities across a wide range of industries • Industry currently facing a skills shortage • Most jobs with large companies with more than 1,000 employees

CAREER PATHS

Materials scientists usually specialize in working with one type of material and this will govern their career direction. You could, for example, develop lightweight metals for the aerospace industry or environmentally-friendly plastics for use in food packaging. You can usually opt to focus on research or manufacture, or move into a management role later in your career.

RESEARCH ENGINEER
Uses an advanced knowledge of physics and chemistry to study the structure of solids, and to design, produce, and test new materials.

MATERIALS TECHNICIAN With a set of good school qualifications in science and mathematics, you may find work as a materials technician with a large company. You can then study for a degree-level qualification while on the job.

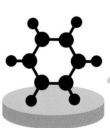

GRADUATE You will need a degree in a relevant subject, such as chemistry, physics, or materials engineering. Some employers will expect a higher degree in your chosen area of specialism.

MATERIALS SCIENTIST As a qualified materials scientist, you can work in diverse industries, from metal foundries to nanotechnology – the design and engineering of machines on a microscopic scale. Many go on to become production specialists, research engineers, or project managers.

SKILLS GUIDE

 Strong communication skills to articulate new ideas and proposals, and to report findings.

 An ability to collaborate with scientists and engineers of various disciplines.

 Strong analytical skills to investigate the properties of materials in the laboratory.

 Mathematical and Information Technology (IT) skills to develop materials.

 Practical problem-solving skills to address engineering and manufacturing issues.

 PROJECT MANAGER Leads a team of scientists and engineers to develop new materials or the processes for their manufacture. Project managers also monitor progress, assign resources, and liaise with the client.

 PRODUCTION SPECIALIST Ensures that materials are made to agreed quality and safety standards at manufacturing plants, and resolves any production problems on site.

 Manufacturing companies employ about 41 per cent of all materials scientists.

▼ RELATED CAREERS

▶ **GEOSCIENTIST** *see pp. 148–149*

▶ **CHEMICAL ENGINEER** *see pp. 180–181*

▶ **AEROSPACE ENGINEER** *see pp. 190–191*

▶ **ENVIRONMENTAL SCIENTIST** Researches ways of protecting the environment, and reducing pollution and waste.

▶ **INDUSTRIAL ENGINEER** Devises efficient ways of making a product through the best use of materials, machines, workers, and energy resources.

▶ **METALLURGIST** Studies the chemical and physical behaviour of metals under different conditions. Metallurgists help to test existing products and develop new technologies.

AT A GLANCE

 YOUR INTERESTS Engineering • Mineralogy • Geology • Physics • Chemistry • Mathematics • IT

 ENTRY QUALIFICATIONS A degree-level qualification in a subject such as materials science or applied chemistry is essential.

 LIFESTYLE Researchers work normal office hours; production staff may need to work shifts to supervise costly manufacturing processes.

 LOCATION Materials scientists may work in a laboratory, an office, or at an industrial plant. They may also have to travel to visit clients.

 THE REALITIES Degree programmes are demanding and ongoing study is required to keep up with fast-changing technologies.

METEOROLOGIST

JOB DESCRIPTION

Meteorologists study Earth's weather, climate, and atmospheric conditions. In this role, you will use weather data from observation stations, satellite images, and radar to produce short- and long-range weather forecasts for the general public, commercial clients, government agencies, or the military. Meteorologists also play a key role in research into global climate change.

SALARY

Junior meteorologist ★★★★★
Senior meteorologist ★★★★★

INDUSTRY PROFILE

Competitive field • Employers include national weather services, the armed forces, and media and research organizations • Predicted growth in private-sector weather services

▼ RELATED CAREERS

▶ **HYDROLOGIST** Monitors, studies, and promotes the sustainable management of water resources, such as lakes, reservoirs, and domestic pipelines. Works for utility firms, government agencies, universities, and environmental consultancies.

▶ **OCEANOGRAPHER** Conducts scientific research into the ocean environment, studying how the seas interact with rivers, ice sheets, and the atmosphere. Also provides advice on subjects including currents and tides, marine pollution, and underwater mineral resources to clients such as oil companies and coastal construction firms.

Accurate forecasting relies on the fastest supercomputers in the world, which perform millions of calculations per second to model weather data.

AT A GLANCE

 YOUR INTERESTS Earth sciences • Geography • Mathematics • Physics • Chemistry • Biology • Information Technology (IT)

 ENTRY QUALIFICATIONS A relevant degree is needed to enter the field, while a postgraduate qualification is necessary to conduct research.

 LIFESTYLE Forecasters work in shifts to provide 24-hour cover. Researchers work regular hours, with occasional overtime if necessary.

 LOCATION A meteorologist is based in an office at a regional weather station or commercial weather-service provider, at a television studio, or on a military base.

 THE REALITIES Meteorologists have a responsibility for accurate forecasting, particularly when severe weather threatens property or lives.

CAREER PATHS

National weather services are the largest employers of meteorologists, but there are also recruitment opportunities with private-sector firms, research institutes, environmental consultancies, and utility companies.

GRADUATE To enter this profession you will need a degree in meteorology, environmental science, physics, mathematics, or a related subject.

POSTGRADUATE If you have a postgraduate degree in a related subject, you can apply for research posts. A degree will also help if you are applying for forecasting jobs.

METEOROLOGIST You will need to stay up to date with scientific and technological advances throughout your career, in areas such as climate change or mathematical modelling. You can move between a variety of roles, including research, forecasting, training, and consultancy.

SKILLS GUIDE

 Effective verbal and written communication skills to explain weather forecasts clearly.

 Good team-working skills to interact with groups, from the general public to technical staff.

 Strong analytical skills for studying and interpreting complex meteorological data.

 Excellent numeracy for using advanced mathematical models to process weather data.

 Advanced computer skills to use modelling software for simulating weather scenarios.

 Attention to detail to spot unexpected weather events so that future forecasts can be revised.

FORECAST METEOROLOGIST Prepares weather forecasts using real-time observations and data from computerized models. Forecasters also compile rolling weather reports that are shared with international weather organizations.

BROADCAST METEOROLOGIST Presents forecasts that are televised, broadcast on radio stations, or accessed via the Internet, using maps to show aspects such as temperature and rainfall.

FORENSIC METEOROLOGIST Usually works in a consultancy capacity, analysing and reconstructing past weather events to help insurance companies or lawyers determine the impact of the weather conditions on a particular claim or legal case.

ENVIRONMENTAL METEOROLOGIST Conducts research into areas including severe weather patterns, air pollution, or how weather affects the spread of disease.

ASTRONOMER

JOB DESCRIPTION

Astronomers are scientists who study the Universe. They rely on ground- or space-based telescopes, spacecraft, and other advanced instruments to make their observations. Using mathematical techniques to interpret data, they investigate the properties and behaviour of planets, stars, and galaxies, and then propose and test theories about the nature and make-up of the Universe.

SALARY

Postgraduate student ★★★★★
Astronomy professor ★★★★★

INDUSTRY PROFILE

Academic profession with few employment opportunities • Entry to research posts is competitive • Jobs found in government departments, laboratories, and observatories

AT A GLANCE

YOUR INTERESTS Astronomy • Mathematics • Physics • Chemistry • Geology • Engineering • Information Technology (IT) • Exploration

ENTRY QUALIFICATIONS Entrants to this profession usually hold a postgraduate degree in astronomy, space science, astrophysics, or geophysics.

LIFESTYLE Studying the sky and collecting data can involve long, irregular hours. Weekend and evening work is a crucial part of the job.

LOCATION Astronomers work mainly in space laboratories, observatories, and research departments. They may travel overseas for meetings and conferences.

THE REALITIES This is a highly demanding, theoretical field. Entry is competitive, and many graduates are not able to find work as astronomers.

CAREER PATHS

Because astronomy is a highly academic field, aspiring astronomers need a degree in physics or astronomy and usually a PhD to progress. Most professional astronomers carry out research and hold teaching posts at universities, but some move into related fields, such as instrument engineering, computer programming, or space science, where they provide support for space missions.

UNDERGRADUATE If you have an astronomy degree, you can apply for support roles in planetariums, research laboratories, and science museums. You can also gain relevant work experience before moving to postgraduate study.

POSTGRADUATE You will require the highest level of academic qualifications to progress in this field: a master's or PhD in astronomy will improve your prospects.

▼ RELATED CAREERS

▶ **SOFTWARE ENGINEER** *see pp. 118–119*

▶ **ELECTRONICS ENGINEER** Designs and creates electronic equipment for use in industry – from telecommunications to manufacturing.

▶ **GEOPHYSICIST** Studies physical aspects of Earth, analysing data on phenomena such as earthquakes, volcanoes, and the water cycle.

▶ **RESEARCH PHYSICIST** Investigates and proposes theories about the nature and properties of matter and energy. Physicists may work in academic or industrial research, or in government laboratories.

▶ **SATELLITE SYSTEMS ENGINEER** Uses a knowledge of electronics, computer science, and astronomy to design and build space satellites.

SKILLS GUIDE

 A logical approach to solving complex problems and analysing abstract astronomical ideas.

 Advanced mathematical skills for aiding in computer modelling and conducting theoretical research.

 Excellent computer skills for generating theoretical models and interpreting observational data.

 Perseverance to study infrequent and slowly occurring astronomical phenomena patiently.

 Attention to detail and the ability to make precise measurements and keep meticulous records.

THEORETICAL ASTRONOMER Creates complex computer models to develop and test theories, and presents findings in reports, scientific journals, and at conferences around the world.

OBSERVATIONAL ASTRONOMER Uses radio, infrared, and optical telescopes to gather data from spacecraft and satellites, then records and analyses that data to test theories and predictions.

PLANETARIUM DIRECTOR Develops exhibitions and film shows on the subject of planetary science to educate and entertain visitors, and hosts and liaises with different visitor groups, from tourists to school parties.

ASTRONOMER This is an inherently academic career, so you will be expected to carry out original research, publish papers, and continue learning, as well as teaching others.

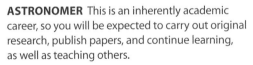

ASTRONOMY LECTURER Teaches astronomy at undergraduate and postgraduate levels, and conducts research to contribute to our understanding of the Universe.

ASTRONAUT

JOB DESCRIPTION

Astronauts are highly trained individuals who pilot spacecraft or carry out specialist missions in space. These may include launching or repairing satellites, or carrying out scientific experiments in low-gravity conditions. Astronauts are employed by national space agencies, and only a select few ever end up actually travelling into space, making this one of the world's most exclusive careers.

SALARY

Astronaut ★★★★★

INDUSTRY PROFILE

Very few openings – there have been slightly more than 500 astronauts in total since space flight began • Highly competitive selection process • Many other opportunities in the growing space industry

CAREER PATHS

To be selected as an astronaut, you usually need to be a citizen of the country running a manned space programme. You must be physically fit, and meet the space agency's height, weight, and age criteria. Almost all astronauts also hold degrees or higher qualifications in science or engineering, or are skilled and experienced jet pilots. You will undergo multiple rounds of interviews to determine if you are physically and psychologically suited to the role.

INSTRUCTOR Provides training in the skills required to fly and maintain a spacecraft. Uses flight simulators to teach new astronauts how to deal with routine operations and potential emergencies.

JET PILOT You could begin your career by joining your country's air force and specializing as a test pilot. You may then be able to apply to join a space programme. Most space agencies will require you to hold a degree as a minimum qualification.

SCIENTIST OR ENGINEER You can apply to train as an astronaut if you have a degree – and preferably a postgraduate qualification – in science or engineering, plus flight-related work experience.

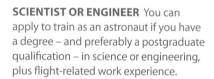

ASTRONAUT Basic astronaut training takes about two years. If selected for a flight, you have a choice of roles, from fixing equipment in Earth's orbit to conducting research on a space station.

SKILLS GUIDE

 The ability to work well with crew members and the many staff who support missions on the ground.

 Creativity for solving unexpected and complex problems using limited resources.

 The flexibility to adapt to extreme environments and to deal with difficult living conditions.

 A logical and analytical approach when handling critical and challenging situations.

 Physical endurance to train for live missions, which can be hugely demanding.

 An eye for detail and constant vigilance to complete missions in space successfully.

AT A GLANCE

 YOUR INTERESTS Space • Flight • Mathematics • Physics • Mechanical engineering • Electrical engineering • Materials science

 ENTRY QUALIFICATIONS As a minimum, you need at least a first degree in science or engineering, or extensive experience in flying fast jets.

 LIFESTYLE Working hours are irregular. Training missions involve long periods away from home and space flights can last many months.

 LOCATION Astronauts often work in remote, high-security locations, and may have to travel widely for training purposes.

 THE REALITIES Working hours are long and conditions are tough and dangerous. Extensive training is both physically and mentally challenging.

 COMMANDER OR PILOT Takes responsibility for the flight of the spacecraft, as well as the safety of the crew, and the overall success of a mission. May also carry out other duties, such as helping with onboard experiments or carrying out extravehicular activity, or space walks.

 MISSION OR PAYLOAD SPECIALIST Conducts scientific experiments under low-gravity conditions, is responsible for looking after the crew, and handles and launches specialist equipment, such as probes or satellites.

▼ RELATED CAREERS

▶ **MECHANICAL ENGINEER** *see pp. 182–183*

▶ **ELECTRICAL ENGINEER** *see pp. 186–187*

▶ **ARMED FORCES PILOT** *see pp. 232–233*

▶ **ASTROPHYSICIST** Studies the Universe using sophisticated equipment, such as satellites and telescopes. Studies planets, stars, and other space phenomena to build and test theories about the origins and workings of the Universe.

▶ **SATELLITE ENGINEER** Designs and builds space satellites used for relaying electronic communication, monitoring Earth, or studying the Universe. Also develops scientific instruments for satellites and other associated equipment needed on the ground.

ANIMALS, FARMING, AND THE ENVIRONMENT

If you enjoy working with animals, plants, or on the land, you could consider some of the careers in this sector. From grooming horses and caring for sick animals to researching crop-cultivation techniques, the number of available career options is growing all the time.

VET
Page 160

Protecting the health of animals in zoos, farms, and homes, vets use their knowledge of physiology and anatomy to treat sick and injured animals.

ANIMAL CARE WORKER
Page 162

Providing hands-on care in a range of locations – from rescue centres to pet shops – animal care workers clean, feed, and look after the animals in their care.

ZOOKEEPER
Page 164

Working in zoos and wildlife parks, zookeepers ensure that the animals under their care are well looked after and have a suitable living environment.

FARM MANAGER
Page 166

Modern-day agriculture makes use of large machinery, scientific methods, and biotechnology, so farmers are skilled in both farming and business management.

HORTICULTURAL WORKER
Page 168

Horticulture is a growing industry. Workers in this area may be responsible for planting seeds, taking cuttings, pruning plants, and preventing disease.

LANDSCAPE ARCHITECT
Page 170

With a passion for designing outdoor spaces, landscape architects use their creative skills to produce visually stunning yet practical designs for their clients.

ECOLOGIST
Page 172

Working in universities, government departments, and field stations, ecologists help us to understand living things and the environments in which they live.

VET

JOB DESCRIPTION

Veterinary surgeons, commonly known as vets, treat and operate on sick or injured animals. They train to work with many species, including animals in zoos and in the wild, but in general practice vets focus mostly on domestic and farm animals. As a vet, you may control standards of care and hygiene in animal care environments, such as veterinary hospitals, and also research the diagnosis as well as prevention of animal diseases.

SALARY

Newly qualified vet ★★★☆☆
Senior practitioner ★★★★★

INDUSTRY PROFILE

Nearly half of vets self-employed in general practice • Many opportunities in public health departments, zoos, animal charities, and hospitals

CAREER PATHS

After qualifying, most vets begin their careers as employees in a general veterinary practice. With experience and further study, they can specialize in a wide range of fields, such as surgery, nutrition, or parasitology (the study of parasites). Some go on to start their own practices, or work in research or for the government.

DOMESTIC ANIMAL VET
Works in a veterinary practice that deals with domestic animals, such as cats, dogs, gerbils, rabbits, and caged birds.

GRADUATE You will need a degree in veterinary science accredited by a professional body. Courses take between four and six years, depending on where you study.

VET In this role, you provide general health care treatment to animals. As an experienced vet, you can undertake diploma study to specialize, and gain consultant status in your chosen field.

The word veterinarian comes from the Latin "veterinae", meaning "working animals".

SKILLS GUIDE

Excellent verbal and written communication skills to advise owners on the best care practices for their animals.

Good team-working skills in order to work closely with practice support staff to ensure animals receive the best health care.

Strong organizational skills, particularly when running a practice, which involves accurate billing and record-keeping.

The ability to solve problems quickly, make difficult decisions, and take prompt action when treating ill or injured animals.

AT A GLANCE

YOUR INTERESTS Animal welfare • Biology • Chemistry • Zoology (animal science) • Scientific research • Mathematics

ENTRY QUALIFICATIONS Vets need to complete a degree at a veterinary college. Entry to courses is competitive.

LIFESTYLE The job involves long hours and answering call-outs at odd hours. Vets often work outdoors and in all kinds of weather.

LOCATION Vets usually work in surgeries, but also visit farms, zoos, stables, and wildlife hospitals to treat sick animals.

THE REALITIES The job can be physically and emotionally stressful, and requires assertiveness yet sensitivity when making decisions.

FARM VET Works with animals that are reared on farms, such as sheep, pigs, cattle, and chickens. Farm vets spend a lot of their time travelling to farms, checking livestock, and advising farmers.

ZOO VET Works specifically with wild animals that are kept in captivity in zoos and wildlife parks. Can work with some rare and unusual species.

EQUINE VET Specializes in working with horses in riding schools, farms, or polo clubs, and other similar locations. Some equine vets also care for high-value race horses.

▼ RELATED CAREERS

▶ **ANIMAL CARE WORKER** see pp. 162–163

▶ **ZOOKEEPER** see pp. 164–165

▶ **VETERINARY PHYSIOTHERAPIST** Treats dogs and horses, including both pets and "working animals", such as greyhounds and race horses. Veterinary physiotherapists can also work with farm or zoo animals. A degree in veterinary physiotherapy is essential to qualify in this profession. It is also possible to get a degree in human physiotherapy followed by postgraduate training in veterinary physiotherapy.

ANIMAL CARE WORKER

JOB DESCRIPTION

Animal care workers provide the essentials of life – from food and water to exercising, cleaning, grooming, and administering medical care – to ensure that pets or domesticated animals are healthy. They work in a range of places, such as kennels, stables, pet shops, rescue centres, and animal hospitals.

SALARY

Animal care worker ★★★★★
Animal care manager ★★★★★

INDUSTRY PROFILE

Most opportunities in non-profit organizations and welfare charities • New laws governing treatment of domestic and captive animals have tightened welfare standards

AT A GLANCE

YOUR INTERESTS Animal welfare • English • Chemistry • Mathematics • Biology • Physical Education (PE)

ENTRY QUALIFICATIONS Formal qualifications are not always required; some vocational training in animal care is desirable.

LIFESTYLE Since animal care is an all-day job, working hours often involve shifts over evenings, weekends, or holidays.

LOCATION The work is often outdoors, and may involve a range of domesticated or wild animals. Travel is often required, either to move animals or visit sites.

THE REALITIES Salaries are modest and the work often physically exhausting. Some situations can be emotionally upsetting.

▼ RELATED CAREERS

▶ **ZOOKEEPER** *see pp. 164–165*

▶ **ANIMAL TECHNOLOGIST** Cares for laboratory animals used for research in the medical, veterinary, and dental industries. Animal technologists are responsible for the welfare of the animals, and may also administer medication and monitor the animals during testing.

▶ **VETERINARY NURSE** Assists vets in taking care of sick, injured, or hospitalized animals. Veterinary nurses may take X-rays, prepare animals for surgery, administer drugs and treatments, and also keep records. A degree in veterinary nursing is usually needed, but it may be possible to qualify through vocational study and experience.

In the USA, the animal care sector is expected to grow by 20 per cent by 2018.

CAREER PATHS

A formal qualification is not always necessary to enter this career, but a vocational course or experience through volunteering will improve your job prospects. Career progression is usually achieved through specialization.

ASSISTANT If you have prior experience of working with animals, you can apply for work-based trainee jobs straight after leaving school.

GRADUATE You will need an undergraduate degree in animal care management or animal sciences to enter this sector in a professional or managerial role.

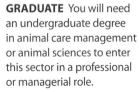

SKILLS GUIDE

 Excellent communication skills for interacting with colleagues, vets, customers, and visitors.

 Keen observation skills to monitor animals for different behavioural patterns and signs of any disease.

 Physical resilience for working outdoors in all weathers and for lifting and carrying sick animals.

 The ability to organize and prioritize routine tasks, and to manage time effectively.

 Good computer skills for maintaining records and accessing the correct information for clients.

ANIMAL CARE WORKER Many animal care workers specialize in a particular type of care, such as rehabilitation through hydrotherapy – exercising animals in a pool of water – or massage. With experience and qualifications, you could move into training or managerial roles.

STABLEHAND Provides daily care for horses at a yard or farm to ensure that they are healthy, happy, and in good condition. Duties include feeding, cleaning, and preparing horses for exercising and events.

ANIMAL TRAINER Trains animals to respond to cues and commands. Trainers work with performing or working animals, such as guide dogs, or with rescue dogs and animals that have behavioural problems.

ANIMAL THERAPIST Treats animals with joint or muscular problems by massaging muscles or flexing and stretching affected areas. Animal therapists need further qualifications for practising.

PET GROOMER Keeps a pet's coat in good condition, advising owners on care of pet hair, grooming, and nutrition. Groomers can be employed by pet salons or may run their own business.

PET SHOP MANAGER Cares for animals, birds, and reptiles prior to their sale as pets, and provides advice to customers on the feeding, housing, exercising, and general welfare of their pets.

ZOOKEEPER

JOB DESCRIPTION

A zookeeper looks after wild, rare, and exotic animals in zoos, animal parks, or aquariums. In this active, often outdoor job, duties range from feeding, washing, and grooming animals, to designing and maintaining enclosures, assisting with the delivery of medical care to animals, and record-keeping. Zookeepers may also guide and educate zoo visitors, and collect data that may be useful in conservation research.

SALARY

Zookeeper ★★★★★
Head keeper ★★★★★

INDUSTRY PROFILE

Strong competition for entry-level positions • More applicants than vacancies • Higher salaries offered in larger zoos

CAREER PATHS

Experience of working with animals is essential to become a zookeeper. Prospective zookeepers can pick up useful skills by joining volunteer programmes, offered by most zoos and animal parks, or through voluntary or paid work in a pet shop, stable, or farm. Senior roles are rare, so progression usually requires moving to another zoo.

GRADUATE You will need a degree in animal management or zoology in order to enter the zookeeping profession at a more senior or specialist level.

VOLUNTEER Although you will not always have direct contact with animals as a volunteer, you can still gain valuable experience of working in a zoo environment. These opportunities are very popular, so you may have to join a waiting list.

COLLEGE-LEAVER You can gain useful experience by taking a related college course or applying for an apprenticeship, both of which may involve direct contact with animals.

ZOOKEEPER Once you have gained experience, you may be able to join – or apply for promotion at – a larger zoo, where there are likely to be good prospects for progression. Opportunities also exist in education and conservation research.

SKILLS GUIDE

 Excellent observational skills for spotting physical and behavioural signs of injury or illness in animals.

 The ability to keep detailed records in a diary or on a computer for monitoring and research purposes.

 Physical strength for lifting and handling equipment and working in wet and dirty conditions.

 Strong team-working skills to interact with other keepers, vets, and animal specialists.

 Good communication skills to give demonstrations and educational talks to visitors.

 SENIOR KEEPER Leads a team of zookeepers and volunteers, overseeing the care and welfare of the animals at the zoo.

 SPECIALIST KEEPER Specializes in the care of one type or group of animals, such as reptiles or primates. Specialist keepers may travel widely, giving advice to zoos and animal collections around the world.

 ANIMAL CURATOR Sources and acquires new animals for zoos to maintain their collections and help with breeding programmes.

 ANIMAL PARK MANAGER Runs the daily operations and services of an animal park. A park manager also guides tourists and is responsible for the care and welfare of the animals.

▼ RELATED CAREERS

▶ **ECOLOGIST** *see pp. 172–173*

▶ **PET SHOP ASSISTANT** Cares for mammals, birds, reptiles, and fish to be sold as pets. Pet shop assistants also sell food, hutches, cages, and equipment, and give advice to customers.

▶ **SAFARI TOUR LEADER** Guides parties of tourists on safari-park tours so that they can see wild animals and birds in their natural habitat. Tour leaders track the animals, transport tourists to them, and ensure the safety of the group.

▶ **WILDLIFE REHABILITATOR** Rescues sick and abandoned wild animals, and nurses them back to health with the ultimate aim of releasing them back into their natural environments.

AT A GLANCE

 YOUR INTERESTS Wildlife and animal behaviour • Biology • Geography • English • Mathematics • Information Technology (IT)

 ENTRY QUALIFICATIONS A good general education, work experience, and commitment are required. A degree is needed for specialist roles.

 LIFESTYLE Shift-work is the norm, but part-time working may be possible. Head keepers will often work evenings while on call.

 LOCATION The job is usually based at public and private zoos, animal parks, or aquariums. Travel may be necessary when transporting animals.

 THE REALITIES Outdoor work in all weathers is often required. Some jobs may aggravate allergies to animals or plants. Some animals pose safety risks.

FARM MANAGER

JOB DESCRIPTION

Farm managers are responsible for ensuring that livestock, dairy, arable, or mixed farms are run smoothly and at a profit. From using machinery and moving animals, to planning crop rotations and managing the business, the job involves a range of duties that varies according to the local climate, soil conditions, the public's demand for produce, and contracts with supermarkets, food companies, and other customers.

SALARY

Assistant farm manager ★★★★★
Experienced farm manager ★★★★★

INDUSTRY PROFILE

Industry is changing due to precision techniques, such as GPS-guided crop sowing • Opportunities with estates, farm-management firms, food companies, and for self-employment

AT A GLANCE

 YOUR INTERESTS Agriculture • Animal welfare • The natural world • Environmental science • Biology • Information Technology (IT)

 ENTRY QUALIFICATIONS Although it is possible to secure work as a farm manager based on experience alone, a degree in a related subject is preferred.

 LIFESTYLE Work patterns are seasonal and farm managers are expected to put in very long hours at harvest or lambing times, for example.

 LOCATION Managers carry out practical work on a farm and administrative tasks in an office. Travel to other sites or to agricultural shows is common.

 THE REALITIES The work can be relentless during busy times of the year. Profitability may be affected by external factors, such as poor weather.

CAREER PATHS

Farming is a diverse industry that offers good career prospects. Farm managers may be employed by landowners or work their own land. Many farms specialize in a single type of farming, so it may be necessary to move to broaden your experience.

FARM ASSISTANT You can work as a farm assistant straight from school or college, gaining the necessary practical experience to apply for management training.

TRAINEE MANAGER You must have some prior experience of agricultural work to join a management-training scheme.

GRADUATE You can join a graduate management-training scheme with a degree in agriculture or farm business management. You also need prior experience of farm work.

▼ RELATED CAREERS

▶ **FISH FARMER** Breeds and rears fish and shellfish for profit, for the food industry, for recreational angling, or as stock for ornamental pools. Fish farmers rear fish from eggs or buy them as young fish and then raise them before selling them on.

▶ **FOREST OFFICER** Supervises activities that develop and protect forest environments. Forest officers also oversee the ecological conservation and recreational use of forests, as well as managing commercial aspects of forestry.

▶ **PARKS OFFICER** Manages parks and open and green spaces for the benefit of local residents and visitors. Park officers supervise and allocate work to teams of park rangers, gardeners, and landscaping staff.

SKILLS GUIDE

 High levels of stamina and resilience to meet the physical demands of the job.

 Good organizational skills for arranging the operation and business management of the farm.

 Keen IT skills for monitoring supply levels and keeping accurate records.

 The ability to form an effective team of farm workers, and to oversee the activities of trainees.

 Business expertise to manage finances, plan budgets, and ensure that production targets are met.

ESTATE MANAGER Supervises and manages the maintenance of grounds and outbuildings, as well as overseeing the financial and legal affairs of farms and country estates.

 AGRONOMIST Carries out field research into the breeding, physiology, production, yield, and management of crops and agricultural plants.

 AGRICULTURAL CONSULTANT Solves agricultural problems and provides technical advice and support to farmers, growers, and government agencies.

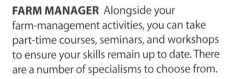 **AGRICULTURAL SALES EXECUTIVE** Sells, promotes, and sometimes trains farmers in the use of agricultural products, such as machinery or fertilizers. Practical experience of farming is useful.

 **FARM MANAGER** Alongside your farm-management activities, you can take part-time courses, seminars, and workshops to ensure your skills remain up to date. There are a number of specialisms to choose from.

HORTICULTURAL WORKER

JOB DESCRIPTION

If you enjoy working outdoors, you may want to explore opportunities in horticulture – the business of growing, harvesting, and selling flowers, plants, shrubs, and trees. You can find work in nurseries, botanical gardens, landscaping companies, and with the authorities who maintain green spaces in towns and cities.

SALARY

Horticultural worker ★★★★★
Horticulturist ★★★★★

INDUSTRY PROFILE

Majority of work in the production of high-value crops • Diverse industry dominated by small- to medium-sized companies

CAREER PATHS

Entry-level jobs in horticulture require only a basic school education. You may need a degree or vocational training to progress into managerial roles, or find jobs in landscape design or horticultural science as a botanist, plant breeder, or soil scientist.

ASSISTANT You can begin your career as an assistant, learning on the job as you work within a team at a plant nursery or in gardens.

COLLEGE-LEAVER Some colleges offer courses in gardening and horticultural skills. Although not essential for entry into this career, an official qualification will help you in the job market.

▼ RELATED CAREERS

▶ **ARBORICULTURALIST** Cultivates, manages, and protects trees, hedgerows, and large shrubs. Arboriculturalists also provide information and advice on tree-related issues.

▶ **FLORIST** Cuts, arranges, and dries flowers to create pleasing visual displays for gifts, weddings, and funerals. Florists may work in a shop or from home.

HORTICULTURAL WORKER In this role, you carry out gardening duties, including plant care, and looking after playing fields or golf courses. You can choose to specialize in working with food crops or ornamental plants in nurseries or farms, or sell plants and advise on plant care.

AT A GLANCE

 YOUR INTERESTS Gardening • Botany (plant science) • Plants and natural history • Biology • Chemistry • Health and fitness • Geography

 ENTRY QUALIFICATIONS A basic school education is required; a degree or higher is needed for more specialist roles.

 LIFESTYLE The hours are generally regular, but shift-work may be required at some nurseries where delicate plants are grown under intensive conditions.

 LOCATION Working bases may be plant nurseries, greenhouse complexes, garden centres, public or private parks, or open spaces in towns or cities.

 THE REALITIES The work can be repetitive and uncomfortable in poor weather. There is little rest, so physical stamina is necessary.

SKILLS GUIDE

 Physical strength and stamina for labour-intensive outdoor work, sometimes in bad weather.

 Manual dexterity for planting seedlings and handling gardening equipment.

 Organizational skills for planning tasks, including unloading supplies, digging soil, and pruning plants.

 Problem-solving skills to examine and care for plants and flowers that need specific treatments to thrive.

 Creativity and imagination to make town spaces, gardens, and nurseries look vibrant and appealing.

 LANDSCAPE DESIGNER Uses a detailed knowledge of plants and horticulture to plan, plant, and maintain gardens and landscapes surrounding homes and businesses.

 BOTANIST Studies plant life and its interactions with soils, the atmosphere, and other living things. Botanists hold degrees, and may work on plant cultivation and growth, and document diverse and exotic plant species.

 HORTICULTURAL TECHNICIAN Specializes in technical areas of horticulture, such as installing irrigation systems, pest control in greenhouses, or laboratory work.

 **HORTICULTURIST** Studies plant disease, genetics, and nutrition in order to improve the quality and productivity of commercial crops.

 HORTICULTURAL THERAPIST Uses practical gardening to promote wellbeing in people recovering from illness or suffering from long-term conditions.

LANDSCAPE ARCHITECT

JOB DESCRIPTION

Landscape architects design, create, and manage open spaces in both man-made and natural environments. In this role, you work with other construction and engineering professionals to plan and manage projects as diverse as parks and recreational sites, pedestrian schemes, sports venues, and urban regeneration.

SALARY

Junior landscape architect ★★★★★
Senior landscape architect ★★★★★

INDUSTRY PROFILE

Growing demand for landscape architects due to environmental planning requirements • Salaries higher in private practice • Around 50 per cent of professionals are self-employed

AT A GLANCE

YOUR INTERESTS Design • Art • Environmental science • Architecture • Town planning • Information Technology (IT) • Geography

ENTRY QUALIFICATIONS A degree in a relevant subject and accredited status with a professional body are required to practise as a landscape architect.

LIFESTYLE Regular office hours are the norm, but the job is deadline driven, so evening and weekend work may sometimes be required.

LOCATION The work is office-based, although it features regular travel to survey projects, visit sites, and present plans to clients or the public.

THE REALITIES Improving urban and natural spaces for the benefit of the community and the environment is highly rewarding.

CAREER PATHS

A degree or postgraduate qualification in a relevant subject is usually required to find work as a landscape architect. Local authorities and private practices are the biggest employers, but jobs may also exist with environmental agencies, utility companies, supermarket chains, construction firms, and voluntary organizations. With experience, you can also work on a self-employed basis.

GRADUATE You will need a professionally accredited degree in a subject such as garden design, landscape architecture, planning, or environmental conservation.

POSTGRADUATE You can take a postgraduate-level conversion course in landscape architecture if you have a prior degree in a related subject, such as architecture, horticulture, or botany.

SKILLS GUIDE

 Effective communication skills for liaising with clients and construction staff.

 A flair for design and an awareness of the future need for creating aesthetic, sustainable spaces.

 The ability to understand client requirements and incorporate them into the site's design.

 Good IT skills to use Computer-aided Design (CAD) software to create designs and presentations.

 Commercial awareness, combined with an understanding of social and environmental issues.

▼ RELATED CAREERS

▶ **HORTICULTURAL WORKER** *see pp. 168–169*

▶ **ARCHITECT** *see pp. 194–195*

▶ **QUANTITY SURVEYOR** *see pp. 198–199*

▶ **TOWN PLANNER** *see pp. 200–201*

▶ **LANDSCAPER** Works to a landscape architect's designs and specifications to build features such as garden paving, patios, walls, and borders. Landscapers also use their knowledge of horticulture to plant and maintain vegetation.

▶ **LAND SURVEYOR** Carries out survey work to gather data for mapping an area of land in advance of building or engineering projects.

LANDSCAPE CONTRACTOR Works to realize a landscape architect's designs by hiring and overseeing construction staff and the machinery required to complete the job.

LANDSCAPE PLANNER Advises on land development proposals with the aim of protecting natural resources and historic or cultural sites in urban and rural settings.

LANDSCAPE MANAGER Helps to plan new landscapes and maintain existing ones, supervising and directing the work of landscape architects, monitoring progress, and advising on legal aspects of the planning process.

LANDSCAPE ARCHITECT To progress in this career, you will need to achieve professional status. You can then choose to specialize in a particular type of work – such as ecological design or highways landscaping – or become a partner or owner of a private practice.

LANDSCAPE SCIENTIST Carries out surveys of ecologically valuable habitats and advises on how to manage them in order to improve their long-term viability and enhance biodiversity.

ECOLOGIST

JOB DESCRIPTION

An ecologist studies the relationship between plants and animals, and their interaction with their physical environment. Ecologists may specialize in a particular habitat (such as a rainforest) or groups of species (such as lions). Their work could range from conducting research on global issues, to developing plans for local land management. A deep passion to protect the environment drives most ecologists.

SALARY

Newly qualified ecologist ★★★★★
Consultant ecologist ★★★★★

INDUSTRY PROFILE

Many potential employers, especially in government and environment agencies • Fierce competition for higher-level posts

CAREER PATHS

To work as an ecologist, you need a degree or postgraduate qualification in ecology or biological science. Opportunities exist with charities and Non-Governmental Organizations (NGOs) that campaign for the environment and wildlife, national and local government agencies, and environmental consultancies.

MARINE ECOLOGIST
Studies marine organisms and ecosystems to help preserve commercially important fish stocks and other marine life, protect biodiversity, and conserve habitats.

VOLUNTEER Volunteering for a conservation charity or taking countryside skills courses will improve your chances of employment, but a relevant degree is essential.

GRADUATE You should hold a relevant degree, and be experienced in carrying out field research and data analysis. Postgraduate degrees are becoming increasingly useful.

ECOLOGIST Early in your career, you will carry out field surveys, write reports, and provide advice to various organizations. With experience, you could move into management roles or work on environmental policy in a government department or with an NGO, before specializing in a number of different fields.

SKILLS GUIDE

 Good written and verbal skills to write and present reports and academic papers.

 A methodical approach to gathering data and using lab equipment for analysis of samples.

 Dedication and patience, as global projects may take many years to research and complete.

 Good team-management skills for advising and leading a team in a large project.

 Strong computer skills for the analysis, presentation, and accurate reporting of data.

RELATED CAREERS

▶ **COUNTRYSIDE CONSERVATION OFFICER**
Oversees environmental and countryside issues, including management of conservation activities. The role may carry responsibility for ensuring the public have access to the countryside and for making presentations for education or publicity.

▶ **OCEANOGRAPHER** Studies the seas and oceans. Also conducts research into the effects of climate change, and explores the impact of pollution on marine life.

▶ **ZOOLOGIST** Observes and studies animals and their behaviour in their natural habitats. This job usually requires a degree in zoology, animal ecology, animal behaviour, or conservation.

CONSERVATION ECOLOGIST
Plans and carries out programmes to preserve natural resources and encourage wildlife to flourish in a variety of environments.

BIODIVERSITY OFFICER
Works to protect endangered plant species and key habitats. Carries out fieldwork in order to make recommendations to conservation charities and government authorities.

AT A GLANCE

 YOUR INTERESTS Wildlife and environmental conservation • Botany • Biology • Chemistry • Geography • Mathematics • Statistics

 ENTRY QUALIFICATIONS A degree in a subject such as ecology, geography, or environmental science is essential. Postgraduate study is useful.

 LIFESTYLE Ecologists tend to be highly committed to wildlife and the environment. The job often requires long working hours.

 LOCATION Ecologists can work in an office, laboratory, or in the field. Travel to sites may mean being away from home for extended periods.

 THE REALITIES Long periods of field work and research can be physically exhausting. A driving licence is required for site-to-site travel.

ENGINEERING AND MANUFACTURING

If you enjoy learning how things work and improving them, there is a vast range of potential career options in this sector. Whether you are building new machines, conducting experiments, or analysing the science behind it all, you will need to be creative, methodical, and organized.

CIVIL ENGINEER
Page 176

By drawing up and following construction designs, civil engineers shape our environment. They oversee and deliver building projects on time and to budget.

DRILLING ENGINEER
Page 178

At the cutting edge of fossil fuel exploration and extraction on land and at sea, drilling engineers design and install the wells that open up oil and gas fields.

CHEMICAL ENGINEER
Page 180

Researching ways of using raw materials through new chemical processes, chemical engineers develop new substances and products for commercial profit.

MECHANICAL ENGINEER
Page 182

Anything with moving parts – from a watch to a train – has been designed by a mechanical engineer, making this the broadest of all the engineering disciplines.

MOTOR VEHICLE TECHNICIAN
Page 184

Using their practical skills and knowledge, motor vehicle technicians diagnose and fix problems, and replace worn parts to keep our vehicles on the road.

ELECTRICAL ENGINEER
Page 186

Designing, building, and maintaining a range of electrical systems and components, electrical engineers are the specialists whose job it is to keep the power on.

TELECOMS ENGINEER
Page 188

Working with telephones, mobile networks, radio, and the Internet, telecoms engineers ensure that telecommunications networks stay connected across the globe.

AEROSPACE ENGINEER
Page 190

Specializing in aircraft and space technology, aerospace engineers design, build, test, and maintain the vehicles that fly in – and beyond – our skies.

CIVIL ENGINEER

JOB DESCRIPTION

Civil engineers design and manage a wide range of engineering projects, both large and small, such as roads, bridges, and pipelines. A civil engineer's role is challenging and varied. It includes talking to clients, surveying sites, preparing designs (called blueprints), budgeting, assessing a project's environmental impact, and making sure a site meets health and safety standards.

SALARY

Newly qualified graduate ★★☆☆☆
Experienced civil engineer ★★★★★

INDUSTRY PROFILE

Worldwide sector • Steadily growing market • Many engineering jobs in the construction industry • Few opportunities for part-time work or self-employment

SKILLS GUIDE

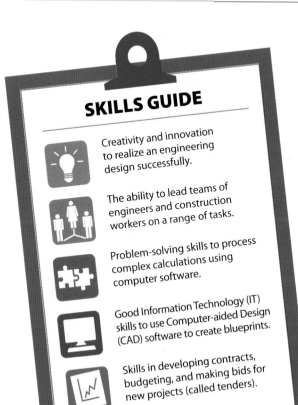

Creativity and innovation to realize an engineering design successfully.

The ability to lead teams of engineers and construction workers on a range of tasks.

Problem-solving skills to process complex calculations using computer software.

Good Information Technology (IT) skills to use Computer-aided Design (CAD) software to create blueprints.

Skills in developing contracts, budgeting, and making bids for new projects (called tenders).

AT A GLANCE

YOUR INTERESTS Engineering • Construction • Physics • Mathematics • Computer-aided Design (CAD) • Geology • Materials science

ENTRY QUALIFICATIONS Most entrants hold an engineering degree, but it is possible to combine work and study to qualify as an engineer.

LIFESTYLE Civil engineers usually work regular hours. However, most roles will require frequent travel to work sites.

LOCATION Depending on the nature of a project, civil engineers work in an office or at a building site. They may need to travel both locally or overseas.

THE REALITIES Projects may require staying away from home for periods of time. On-site environment is usually hazardous. Sites may be at great heights.

CAREER PATHS

A civil engineer can choose from a vast number of specialisms. These include transport, planning and designing roads and ports, working on dams and pipelines, dealing with waste and pollution, and many others.

> The giant rollercoasters in theme parks have all been designed by civil engineers.

GRADUATE A degree in civil engineering is the most common route into this career. Most companies will offer you a graduate training programme.

SCHOOL-LEAVER Although higher education is essential for a career in civil engineering, you can gain practical experience as an engineering technician while you study part-time to qualify for a degree course.

CIVIL ENGINEER After gaining experience, you can study for further qualifications and seek professional accreditation. This will allow you to progress to more senior posts and specialized roles.

CONTRACTING CIVIL ENGINEER Implements the designs of consulting engineers on site, overseeing the work of contractors, checking quality and progress, and buying in appropriate materials and equipment.

CONSULTING CIVIL ENGINEER Plans and advises on engineering projects, working closely with clients and architects. Produces detailed designs and oversees the entire project.

PROJECT MANAGER Is in charge of an engineering project and makes sure the solutions are delivered to the highest possible standards, on time and on budget.

▼ RELATED CAREERS

▶ **MECHANICAL ENGINEER** *see pp. 182–183*

▶ **STRUCTURAL ENGINEER** *see pp. 196–197*

▶ **QUANTITY SURVEYOR** *see pp. 198–199*

▶ **ENGINEERING GEOLOGIST** Primarily analyses the earth of a chosen site to ensure that a man-made structure will sit safely upon it.

▶ **MARINE ENGINEER** Designs and develops offshore structures, such as oil platforms, wind farms, and tidal barriers.

DRILLING ENGINEER

JOB DESCRIPTION

Drilling engineers are responsible for planning, coordinating, and managing oil and gas drilling operations. In this role, you oversee a new project, assessing a site's suitability for drilling, designing and testing the well, as well as monitoring its output and operation, and ensuring that it is closed off safely when the project is over. Employers include oil and gas companies, engineering firms, and specialist drilling contractors.

SALARY

Drilling engineer ★★☆☆☆
Senior drilling engineer ★★★★★

INDUSTRY PROFILE

Most jobs in multinational companies and specialist consultancies • Experienced drilling engineers very well paid • Number of jobs depends on current economic conditions

AT A GLANCE

 YOUR INTERESTS Geology • Physics • Engineering • Chemistry • Mathematics • Geography • Languages • Information Technology (IT)

 ENTRY QUALIFICATIONS A degree in a subject such as engineering, physics, or geology, or a related postgraduate qualification, is essential.

 LIFESTYLE Most drilling engineers work full-time. Long periods away from home and travel to drilling sites, which may be overseas, are common.

 LOCATION Drilling engineers may work offshore – on oil or gas platforms or support vessels – or in an office on land, often shuttling between the two.

 THE REALITIES Working on rigs may require helicopter travel. The work is physically challenging, and may involve harsh weather conditions.

▼ RELATED CAREERS

▶ **GEOSCIENTIST** *see pp. 148–149*

▶ **MECHANICAL ENGINEER** *see pp. 182–183*

▶ **ENERGY ENGINEER** Researches and develops methods of generating energy from different sources, including renewable forms, such as wind, wave, geothermal, and solar power.

▶ **MARINE ENGINEER** Designs, builds, and tests oil rigs, pipelines, remotely operated vehicles, ships, boats, and support vessels for the oil, gas, and marine-leisure industries.

▶ **MINING ENGINEER** Plans, designs, and monitors new and existing mining and quarrying sites. Mining engineers are also responsible for ensuring that sites are safe and working efficiently.

> The oil and gas sectors provide the raw materials for almost half the world's forms of energy.

CAREER PATHS

Drilling engineers typically gain on-the-job responsibility quickly, moving from managing a small well to larger wells with multi-million pound budgets in a relatively short space of time. Training programmes typically last for five years, and may include several changes of project and location.

GRADUATE You can apply for graduate training programmes with a degree in subjects such as geology, natural sciences, or any engineering discipline.

POSTGRADUATE You can improve your chances of entry into this career if you have a higher-level degree. You may also begin your career in a specialist area of drilling.

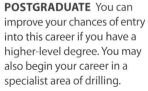

SKILLS GUIDE

 The ability to communicate with managers, engineers, and "roustabouts" (manual workers).

 Excellent team-working skills, and the willingness to live onboard rigs with colleagues for long periods.

 Good interpersonal skills in order to work, often very closely, with people from all over the world.

 Sharp analytical skills for effective decision-making about complex drilling operations.

 The ability to draw on subject knowledge and technical expertise to solve complex problems.

DRILLING ENGINEER Since some firms operate overseas, you may need to be fluent in a foreign language. With experience you can choose a particular specialism, or seek promotion to senior roles.

HORIZONTAL DIRECTIONAL DRILLING ENGINEER Specializes in techniques that enable wells to be drilled at an angle, in order to extract more oil and gas.

DEEP WATER DRILLING ENGINEER Specializes in drilling wells under the sea floor from floating or fixed platforms. These wells may be for the exploration of new gas or oil reserves, or for extraction.

OFFSHORE INSTALLATIONS MANAGER Manages drilling operations on a floating or fixed platform at sea or off the coast, ensuring that the project is run profitably and safely.

HIGH-PRESSURE HIGH-TEMPERATURE DRILLING ENGINEER Specializes in drilling oil and gas wells under high pressures and temperatures, which require complex extraction methods.

WELL TEST ENGINEER Conducts technical checks to ensure the optimum drilling and production of oil and gas. Also monitors operations, equipment, and staff to ensure health and safety standards are met.

CHEMICAL ENGINEER

JOB DESCRIPTION

Chemical engineers develop the technologies that turn raw materials into useful products, such as paints, glues, textiles, and plastics. Some work in laboratories, designing new – or improving existing – products, while others specialize in developing efficient manufacturing processes – the machinery and techniques used to produce the products while meeting quality and safety standards.

SALARY

Graduate industrial chemist ★★★★★
Senior engineer ★★★★★

INDUSTRY PROFILE

Huge global industry • Rising energy costs driving innovation • Manufacturing often based in countries with lower labour and resource costs

AT A GLANCE

YOUR INTERESTS Chemistry • Mathematics • Physics • Biology • Technology • Information Technology (IT) • Computing

ENTRY QUALIFICATIONS A degree in chemical, process, or biochemical engineering, as well as some practical experience, is essential.

LIFESTYLE Working hours are regular in research and development, but shift-work may be necessary in some processing and manufacturing fields.

LOCATION The work is usually based in an office, laboratory, or chemical plant. Chemical engineers may have to travel, sometimes overseas, to visit sites.

THE REALITIES This is a high-pressure job demanding swift problem-solving skills. Chemical engineers may be in charge of operating expensive facilities.

SKILLS GUIDE

Good interpersonal skills to interact with a range of people across the industry.

Problem-solving and analytical skills to manage complex projects and large budgets.

Mathematical skills and an ability to apply scientific principles to real-world problems.

Expertise in specialist computer software used to process data and control production lines.

The ability to predict and analyse the commercial results of scientific applications.

Creativity and innovation to define manufacturing processes that make industrial products.

▼ RELATED CAREERS

▶ **ENERGY ENGINEER** Researches and develops ways to generate energy from fossil fuels, such as coal and oil, as well as from renewable sources, such as wind, waves, and sunlight.

▶ **MINING ENGINEER** Surveys mining sites, and designs the structure of mines and the equipment for extracting resources from the ground.

▶ **NUCLEAR ENGINEER** Designs and maintains facilities in the nuclear energy industry. Nuclear engineers are also responsible for decommissioning nuclear facilities when they shut down.

▶ **PROCESS ENGINEER** Uses chemical and mechanical engineering knowledge to develop efficient manufacturing and production processes.

Graduates in chemical engineering are among the best paid of all college-leavers in their first jobs.

CAREER PATHS

After completing a degree and obtaining experience in the industry, an entrant usually needs to study further to gain professional accreditation. You can then choose to specialize in production, research and development, or the sales and marketing of your company's products, or you may decide to move into management.

GRADUATE You need a degree or postgraduate qualification in chemistry or a related subject. Larger employers in the field usually offer a graduate training scheme, through which it is possible to gain experience across the diverse areas of the business.

CHEMICAL ENGINEER Once qualified, you have the option of focusing on researching new products, improving industrial products already in use, or managing activity at a manufacturing plant. Experienced chemical engineers can become process engineers, research chemists, or environmental chemists.

PROCESS ENGINEER Designs, builds, and maintains the equipment used in the mass production of chemicals. Works in areas as diverse as pharmaceuticals and oil refineries, and oversees the running of a manufacturing plant.

RESEARCH CHEMIST Specializes in the development of new products and manufacturing techniques. Some of this work is at the cutting edge of science, such as advancing new medicines or treatments.

ENVIRONMENTAL CHEMIST Applies a knowledge of chemistry to study problems concerning pollution and waste management in order to find solutions that protect the environment.

MECHANICAL ENGINEER

JOB DESCRIPTION

As part of a production team, mechanical engineers design, build, test, and repair machinery that operate in many products, from dishwashers to automobiles to power stations. They use computer software to develop the mechanical devices, which they build into working prototypes.

SALARY

Junior mechanical engineer ★★★★★
Lead mechanical engineer ★★★★★

INDUSTRY PROFILE

Broadest engineering discipline, covering hi-tech areas to everyday technologies • Excellent job opportunities overseas

CAREER PATHS

Once qualified, mechanical engineers are expected to join a professional engineering body and continue learning throughout their career. They may choose to specialize in one area of engineering or work on large-scale projects. Opportunities in sales and marketing, or a role in an independent consultancy, offer a path into the business side of the profession.

BUSINESS MANAGER Manages people and commercial activities in the engineering sector. Usually has an interest in business, which leads to more corporate roles.

TECHNICIAN As a school-leaver, you may be able to find work as a trainee technician. This may involve installing and maintaining mechanical systems, but you will need to study part-time for a degree-level qualification if you wish to qualify as a mechanical engineer.

GRADUATE After completing an engineering degree you can join a graduate trainee scheme at a large company or take an entry-level position in a smaller firm.

MECHANICAL ENGINEER You will have many choices in this field, from working on the design of aircraft engines to developing wind turbines or improving the performance of cutting-edge medical technologies, such as prosthetic limbs or artificial hearts. Experienced mechanical engineers can move into a number of different roles.

SKILLS GUIDE

Excellent communication skills for collaborating with colleagues on a range of projects.

The creativity and innovation necessary to find working solutions to engineering problems.

The ability to handle pressure, while maintaining good working relationships.

Good computer skills to work with Computer-aided Design (CAD) programs.

A keen eye for detail and the ability to build and test working prototypes.

MATERIALS ENGINEER Develops and tests the properties of materials, such as their strength or resistance to corrosion, to see if they are fit for a specific purpose.

INDUSTRIAL PRODUCTION MANAGER Refines mechanical systems and deals with on-site problems that may arise at manufacturing facilities and production lines.

MINING ENGINEER Manages the safe operation of mechanized wells and mines for the efficient extraction of oil and minerals.

▼ RELATED CAREERS

▶ **AEROSPACE ENGINEER** *see pp. 190–191*

▶ **AUTOMOTIVE ENGINEER** Works in production plants, designing and manufacturing road vehicles. An automotive engineer may also build racing cars or other specialist vehicles.

▶ **BUILDING-SERVICES ENGINEER** Designs, installs, and maintains machinery in buildings, such as heating, lighting, and plumbing systems. Apprenticeships may be available to those with good secondary school qualifications.

▶ **MECHATRONIC ENGINEER** Develops products by combining mechanical, electronic, and computer components. These products include home appliances, cameras, and computer hard drives.

AT A GLANCE

YOUR INTERESTS Engineering • Science • Mathematics • Physical sciences • Design • Information Technology (IT)

ENTRY QUALIFICATIONS A degree in mechanical engineering is a minimum requirement; some employers require higher degrees.

LIFESTYLE Regular hours are the norm, though engineers in some sectors may need to travel or work overnight to meet project deadlines.

LOCATION Although the work is mainly office-based, engineers may need to make frequent visits to manufacturing and testing sites.

THE REALITIES Higher education in mechanical engineering is notoriously tough. Ongoing learning is essential to keep up to date with new technologies.

MOTOR VEHICLE TECHNICIAN

JOB DESCRIPTION

Motor vehicle technicians inspect faults and use computer-based tests to diagnose problems with a vehicle's mechanical or electrical systems, then repair, service, or replace any worn parts. This is a good profession for those who enjoy the challenge of dismantling, fixing, and maintaining mechanical systems.

SALARY

Novice technician ★★★★★
Senior technician ★★★★★

INDUSTRY PROFILE

Good opportunities for qualified technicians • Employers include car dealerships, garages, breakdown organizations, and freight and construction companies

AT A GLANCE

YOUR INTERESTS Motor vehicles • Mechanical systems • Engineering • Electronics • Physics • Mathematics • Information Technology (IT)

ENTRY QUALIFICATIONS Good school grades in science, mathematics, and English are usually required for trainee positions and vocational courses.

LIFESTYLE Most employees work full-time, but shift-work, overtime, and on-call hours – especially for breakdown services – are often required.

LOCATION The job is usually based in a workshop. Breakdown work requires travel as well as performing repairs outdoors and in all weather conditions.

THE REALITIES The job can be physically tiring, messy, and potentially dangerous due to the heavy, dirty, and hazardous nature of vehicle parts.

CAREER PATHS

Technicians often specialize in a make of vehicle or type of repair, such as front-end mechanics – the suspension, steering, and wheels. Options for career progression include self-employment or changing roles, such as garage repair work or managing the maintenance of a transport firm's vehicles.

TRAINEE As a school- or college-leaver, you can work as a trainee or apprentice motor vehicle technician, combining paid work with practical, on-the-job training.

COLLEGE GRADUATE You can gain a qualification before finding a job by taking a vocational course in motor vehicle technology. This will combine classroom instruction with workshop experience.

SKILLS GUIDE

 Strong communication skills to explain faults to clients who have limited technical knowledge.

 Strength for lifting and reaching inaccessible parts, and stamina to concentrate for long periods.

 Good problem-solving skills for investigating, diagnosing, and fixing mechanical faults.

 Manual dexterity to use a wide variety of tools and handle complex vehicle components.

 Precision and attention to detail to disassemble parts and reassemble them correctly.

▼ RELATED CAREERS

▶ **MECHANICAL ENGINEER** *see pp. 182–183*

▶ **AUTO DAMAGE APPRAISER** Inspects vehicles that have been damaged in accidents to estimate the cost of repair.

▶ **AUTO PARTS ADVISER/SALESPERSON** Orders and sells vehicle parts and accessories in addition to providing advice to customers on vehicle faults and other troubleshooting issues.

▶ **MOTOR VEHICLE BODY REPAIRER** Fixes, restores, and refinishes damaged vehicle parts. Repairers also inspect vehicles for damage, replace or repair affected body panels, and refinish paintwork.

Once qualified, the best way to find work is to approach employers directly – most jobs are not advertised.

FITTER Also known as a "fast fitter", this specialist role involves repairing, testing, and fitting vehicle parts, including tyres, brakes, exhausts, and batteries.

MOTOR VEHICLE TECHNICIAN
You perform preventative and repair work to make vehicles roadworthy. With experience, you could move into a senior workshop role or maintain a fleet of vehicles for a commercial firm.

MOBILE TECHNICIAN Assists drivers whose vehicles have broken down. Mobile technicians drive to the motorist's location, inspect the vehicle for faults, and make any necessary repairs or tow the vehicle to a repair centre or to the driver's home.

AIR-CONDITIONING/ REFRIGERATION TECHNICIAN Specializes in the repair and maintenance of air-conditioning systems, handling any refrigerants in a manner that meets statutory safety requirements.

ELECTRICAL ENGINEER

JOB DESCRIPTION

Electrical engineers are employed in a wide range of sectors to design, install, and maintain electrical systems and components. In this role, you might work on infrastructure projects (such as developing low-energy street lighting), power-generation networks, construction schemes, or consumer goods manufacturing. A key aspect of the job is to ensure that equipment meets relevant safety standards.

SALARY

Engineering technician ★★★★★
Experienced engineer ★★★★★

INDUSTRY PROFILE

Growing profession due to pace of technological innovation • Jobs in a wide range of sectors, from research and development to design services • Excellent career prospects

CAREER PATHS

Qualifying as an electrical engineer usually requires accreditation by a professional body, which can take several years of training. You can choose to specialize in one area, such as telecoms or research. Alternatively, you can become a self-employed consultant or seek a senior role within the management team of an engineering firm.

RELIABILITY TESTER Works for a microchip manufacturing company, testing the reliability of manufacturing processes and components for devices such as mobile phones.

TECHNICIAN You can find employment as an apprentice technician straight from school or college, and then train on the job to achieve the necessary qualifications to become an accredited electrical engineer.

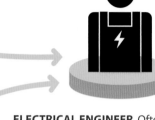

GRADUATE With a degree in electrical engineering or a related subject, you can apply for graduate trainee schemes, which are run by large electrical engineering firms.

ELECTRICAL ENGINEER Often working with specialists in other disciplines, you may carry out feasibility studies, coordinate the work of technicians, or conduct the testing and analysis of new systems. After gaining professional status, you can specialize or seek senior roles.

SKILLS GUIDE

Innovation and creativity for designing parts and equipment that fulfil the client's brief.

Strong leadership skills to ensure that colleagues work to relevant electrical safety standards.

Keen analytical skills to understand complex technical problems and devise cost-effective solutions.

High-level mathematical skills for recording, analysing, and interpreting product test data.

Proficiency in using computer software and hardware when installing and fixing equipment.

AT A GLANCE

YOUR INTERESTS Electrical circuitry • Engineering • Mathematics • Computing • Science • Physics • Technical drawing

ENTRY QUALIFICATIONS A degree or diploma in electrical engineering or a related subject is helpful. School-leavers can train as apprentices.

LIFESTYLE Most electrical engineers work regular office hours, but evening, weekend, or on-call work may be required in some sectors.

LOCATION The work is based in an office or workshop, but visits to service equipment, monitor installations, or oversee manufacturing are common.

THE REALITIES Continual learning is essential to keep pace with fast-changing technologies. Numerous career options are available.

TELECOMMUNICATIONS ENGINEER Specializes in the design and maintenance of electronic telecommunications technology, such as broadband, wireless networks, fibre optic cabling, and satellite systems.

CONSULTING ENGINEER Provides advice to clients on the design and build of electrical systems and components, from power distribution to fire safety systems and interior lighting.

RESEARCH ENGINEER Works at a university or research facility, carrying out research into emerging areas, such as nanoelectronics – electrical engineering on a molecular scale.

▼ RELATED CAREERS

▶ **SYSTEMS ANALYST** *see pp. 120–121*

▶ **NETWORK ENGINEER** *see pp. 124–125*

▶ **BROADCAST ENGINEER** Operates and maintains hardware and software used in television, radio, and other new-media broadcasts.

▶ **INFORMATION TECHNOLOGY (IT) CONSULTANT** Advises businesses on how to use IT systems to resolve operational issues.

▶ **ROBOTICS ENGINEER** Designs and builds robotic equipment for use in a variety of sectors, such as medical practice, drilling engineering, or motor vehicle manufacturing.

TELECOMS ENGINEER

JOB DESCRIPTION

A telecommunications – or telecoms – engineer works with a variety of technologies that enable the exchange of data and communications. These include mobile and fixed-line telephones, radio, cable or wireless broadband Internet, fibre optics, and satellite-based systems. As a telecoms engineer, you design, install, test, or repair these systems for clients that may range from large organizations to individual customers.

SALARY

Graduate trainee engineer ★★☆☆☆
Senior telecoms engineer ★★★★☆

INDUSTRY PROFILE

Growing sector due to increase of technologies • Employers include manufacturers of communications systems and devices, government departments, and telecoms providers

AT A GLANCE

YOUR INTERESTS Electronics • Information Technology (IT) • Electrical engineering • Software engineering • Mathematics • Physics

ENTRY QUALIFICATIONS A degree or higher qualification in electronic engineering, telecommunications, physics, or computing is essential.

LIFESTYLE Full-time office hours are the norm, but telecoms engineers may have to work overtime to meet deadlines. Self-employed contract work is common.

LOCATION Engineers mostly work in an office, but travel is required for site visits, meetings, or conferences. Working remotely from home is also possible.

THE REALITIES Meeting delivery deadlines can be stressful. However, working at the forefront of developing technologies is rewarding.

CAREER PATHS

Telecoms engineering is a broad field. Following a degree, most telecoms engineers join a graduate training programme and specialize in one area, such as computer networks or broadcast technology. You must continue learning throughout your career to keep pace with fast-changing technologies.

TECHNICIAN You can study at college for a vocational qualification that will enable you to work as a technician, testing and maintaining telecoms equipment. You can then study for a degree while employed.

GRADUATE With a degree-level qualification in a technical subject, you can enter a company's graduate training programme. You can increase your chances of entry with previous work experience, such as an industrial placement.

▼ RELATED CAREERS

▶ **SYSTEMS ANALYST** *see pp. 120–121*

▶ **ELECTRICAL ENGINEER** *see pp. 186–187*

▶ **TELECOMMUNICATIONS RESEARCHER**
Researches new forms of telecommunications technology – such as for telephones, television, or the Internet – for commercial firms or universities.

The global telecoms industry was valued at US$5 trillion in 2013, a rise of 6 per cent on 2012.

SKILLS GUIDE

 Good communication skills to explain complex design solutions to technicians and customers.

 Strong team-working skills to collaborate with other specialists on multidisciplinary projects.

 The ability to find creative, innovative, and cost-effective solutions to design challenges.

 Strong analytical skills for understanding a vast and evolving range of technologies.

 The ability to multitask and prioritize jobs to manage several projects at once.

BROADCAST ENGINEER
Operates and maintains hardware and software systems for broadcasting content via television, radio, and new-media channels, ensuring that the content is transmitted on time and to a high standard of quality.

SATELLITE ENGINEER Specializes in installing, configuring, and repairing satellite communications equipment used in areas including television services for home users or videoconferencing for businesses.

NETWORK ENGINEER Installs and maintains IT networks, such as fibre optic, wired, and wireless systems, used by businesses and Internet Service Providers (ISPs).

TELECOMS ENGINEER As a telecoms engineer, you must possess technical expertise to understand and design telecoms systems, and management skills to ensure that your projects are run efficiently. You can choose to work freelance or as a company employee.

SOFTWARE ENGINEER Writes, modifies, and tests the computer code that underpins most telecommunications technologies.

AEROSPACE ENGINEER

JOB DESCRIPTION

Aerospace engineers design, build, and maintain a range of aircraft and spacecraft, from passenger airliners and military jets to satellites and space vehicles. In this role, you might work on the parts that make up the aircraft's fuselage, wings, or undercarriage, or the instruments and electronic systems that enable the pilot and crew to operate the craft.

SALARY

Junior aerospace engineer ★★☆☆☆
Senior aerospace engineer ★★★★☆

INDUSTRY PROFILE

Global opportunities • Diverse industry shaped by technological advances • Jobs in aircraft manufacturing firms, airline operators, armed forces, and government research agencies

▼ RELATED CAREERS

▶ **MECHANICAL ENGINEER** *see pp. 182–183*

▶ **ELECTRICAL ENGINEER** *see pp. 186–187*

▶ **DESIGN ENGINEER** Works in a range of industries, developing ideas for the design of new products and researching ways to improve existing ones.

Defence is the biggest area within the aerospace sector, accounting for about 20 per cent of UK sales.

AT A GLANCE

YOUR INTERESTS Aviation, aircraft, and flight technology • Mathematics • Physics • Information Technology (IT) • Engineering • Chemistry

ENTRY QUALIFICATIONS A degree in aerospace engineering or similar, such as mechanical engineering or physics, is a minimum requirement.

LIFESTYLE Working hours are regular, but evening or weekend work may be necessary to meet project deadlines, or to deal with repairs and emergencies.

LOCATION Engineers may carry out design work in an office, but may also visit aircraft hangars, production sites, or aeronautical laboratories.

THE REALITIES The job bears great responsibility as the work has a direct impact on the functioning of aircraft and the safety of passengers and crew.

CAREER PATHS

Aerospace engineering offers good prospects for career development. Specializing in a particular area – such as astronautics – is common, and training courses to improve professional skills are possible throughout one's career.

TRAINEE You can find work as an aerospace technician or trainee apprentice without a degree, but further qualifications are required to become an engineer.

GRADUATE You need an aerospace-engineering or related degree to become an aerospace engineer. Many firms offer graduate trainee programmes.

AEROSPACE ENGINEER
In this sector, you may specialize in research and development, aircraft systems testing, or maintenance and production. You can advance into senior project management positions or specialize in a particular technical area, such as aerodynamics.

ROTORCRAFT ENGINEER
Designs and develops helicopter components such as engines, electrical systems, and blade technology.

ASTRONAUTICAL ENGINEER Specializes in the research, design, and development of vehicles for space exploration, including rockets and satellites.

AVIONICS AND SYSTEMS ENGINEER Designs electronic equipment used in civil and military aircraft, such as flight-control and weapon-combat systems.

AERODYNAMICIST Researches the effect of air flow on the speed and performance of vehicles in order to improve stability and fuel-efficiency, and reduce the environmental impact of aircraft.

MATERIALS AND STRUCTURES ENGINEER Designs and builds the body and framework of an aircraft, before testing it to ensure that the structure is strong and durable.

CONSTRUCTION

A vast sector with global opportunities, the construction industry requires a steady supply of skilled personnel to keep up with demand from domestic and commercial customers. If you enjoy being practical and hands-on, there is a range of career options available.

ARCHITECT
Page 194

Working at the forefront of building design, architects use their creative skills and technical knowledge to design structures of all kinds, from houses to concert arenas.

STRUCTURAL ENGINEER
Page 196

By modelling the way in which loads and forces affect structures, structural engineers use their expertise to ensure that buildings are designed and built within safe limits.

QUANTITY SURVEYOR
Page 198

Drawing on a knowledge of construction methods, costs, and materials, quantity surveyors ensure that building projects are completed efficiently and economically.

TOWN PLANNER
Page 200

Using a detailed knowledge of architecture and urban design to advise on planning policies, town planners help to shape and develop our towns and cities.

BUILDER
Page 202

From houses and offices to power stations and skyscrapers, builders use their knowledge of construction techniques to create structures from the ground up.

CONSTRUCTION MANAGER
Page 204

Construction managers plan schedules, supervise on-site workers, and monitor building progress to ensure that each job is completed on time and to budget.

CARPENTER
Page 206

Sculpting and joining a variety of wooden fittings or structural features – from kitchen cabinets to ceiling beams – carpenters work on a range of building projects.

ELECTRICIAN
Page 208

Ensuring that the power stays on in homes, offices, and commercial premises, electricians install and repair electrical equipment in line with safety regulations.

PLUMBER
Page 210

Providing the services that make buildings of all kinds safe and habitable, plumbers install and repair heating, water, and air-conditioning systems.

ARCHITECT

JOB DESCRIPTION

An architect plans and designs buildings for a range of clients, from companies developing huge retail or leisure facilities to individuals erecting their own homes. Architects may design new buildings, work on existing structures, or specialize in the restoration and conservation of historic sites. They are responsible for budgeting a project, making sure it runs on time, and for managing the workflow of the people involved.

SALARY

Newly qualified architect ★★☆☆☆
Senior architect ★★★★★

INDUSTRY PROFILE

Employment opportunities linked to the state of construction industry • Rising demand for architects due to growth in housing market • Fierce competition in the private sector

AT A GLANCE

YOUR INTERESTS Art • Design • Construction • Design technology • Materials science • Engineering • Physics • Mathematics

ENTRY QUALIFICATIONS An undergraduate degree in architecture is essential for gaining accredited status with a regulatory body.

LIFESTYLE Architects usually work regular hours, but project deadlines may demand them to work for longer hours.

LOCATION While the work is mainly office-based, architects also travel to construction sites to meet clients.

THE REALITIES Markets can be affected by changes in the economy. Pay can vary greatly between the public and private sectors.

CAREER PATHS

It takes a long time to qualify as an architect. You need to gain practical experience after completing a degree in architecture, after which you take a set of exams to earn professional accreditation. Once qualified, your progress depends on your reputation and field of activity. Large architectural practices offer opportunities for promotion, but many architects choose to set up their own business, or take jobs with property developers or local authorities.

DISTANCE LEARNING STUDENT You may be able to study by distance learning to gain professional accreditation as an architect. To become an architect, you need an accredited undergraduate degree.

GRADUATE An architecture degree can take up to five years, after which you will need to work and learn under professional supervision before registering as a qualified architect.

▼ RELATED CAREERS

▶ **LANDSCAPE ARCHITECT** *see pp. 170–171*

▶ **CIVIL ENGINEER** *see pp. 176–177*

▶ **STRUCTURAL ENGINEER** *see pp. 196–197*

▶ **QUANTITY SURVEYOR** *see pp. 198–199*

▶ **TOWN PLANNER** *see pp. 200–201*

▶ **INDUSTRIAL DESIGNER** Develops the appearance, usability, and function of a wide range of products using engineering and business expertise. Usually works alongside engineers and model-makers and draws up proposals for projects. May also be responsible for the costing of a designed item to make sure it is commercially viable.

SKILLS GUIDE

 Strong communication skills and the ability to liaise with clients and the construction team.

 A willingness to work in a team of construction personnel of varying skills and abilities.

 Artistic flair and creativity to generate unique and innovative design ideas.

 Efficient management skills for running design projects, both on a large and small scale.

 Good technical knowledge and a logical, analytical approach towards challenges.

 Attention to detail in order to produce drawings and designs to exact specifications.

RESIDENTIAL ARCHITECT Designs and builds homes and residential properties to be functional and visually appealing. Specialist knowledge of residential building regulations is also important.

 COMMERCIAL ARCHITECT Designs and builds retail, office buildings, and other large commercial structures, cooperating closely with engineers, and interior and landscape designers.

 **CIVIC ARCHITECT** Designs public buildings, usually working with a local authority, town council, or government agency.

 CONSERVATION ARCHITECT Specializes in the conservation of old buildings, ranging from ancient monuments to listed residential properties.

 **ARCHITECT** Once qualified, you will have already chosen a specific career path, from designing new homes to restoring old buildings.

STRUCTURAL ENGINEER

JOB DESCRIPTION

Structural engineers help to design buildings and infrastructure, such as bridges, railroads, dams, and tunnels. They analyse the forces that a structure may face, such as winds, pedestrian loads, and traffic, and work with architects and civil engineers to ensure that it is built to required standards of strength and safety.

SALARY

Trainee ★★★★★
Senior structural engineer ★★★★★

INDUSTRY PROFILE

Growing industry with opportunities across the globe • Employers range from governments to a variety of contractors and consultancies

AT A GLANCE

YOUR INTERESTS Engineering • Mathematics • Physics • Information Technology (IT) • Design • Geography • Drawing and model-making

ENTRY QUALIFICATIONS A degree in structural or civil engineering is needed. Postgraduate qualifications are required for more senior positions.

LIFESTYLE Regular office hours are the norm, although engineers may need to be on call to deal with emergencies, such as damaged or unstable buildings.

LOCATION Most engineers divide their time between an office and construction sites. They may occasionally need to travel overseas for work.

THE REALITIES Construction is one of the first sectors to be affected in an economic slump. Sites are often dusty and noisy, and can be dangerous.

▼ RELATED CAREERS

▶ **CIVIL ENGINEER** *see pp. 176–177*

▶ **ARCHITECT** *see pp. 194–195*

▶ **BUILDING CONTROL OFFICER** Ensures that building regulations and other laws are followed in the design and construction of houses, offices, and other buildings. Building control officers also make sure that property alterations, such as extensions and conversions, meet all the current regulations.

▶ **COMPUTER-AIDED DESIGN (CAD) TECHNICIAN** Uses computer design software to create plans for buildings and machinery. CAD technicians can work in a range of industries, including construction, manufacturing, and engineering.

Demand for structural engineers is increasing, partly due to growing numbers of aging buildings.

CAREER PATHS

Qualified structural engineers often specialize in working on one type of building or material – oil platforms or concrete structures, for example. With experience, many move into managing construction projects or become consultants.

TRAINEE You can study for an undergraduate engineering degree on the job while working as a trainee for an engineering company.

GRADUATE You will need an accredited degree in a subject such as civil or structural engineering to apply for jobs. Graduate training programmes are available.

SKILLS GUIDE

Good communication skills – both verbal and written – to deal with clients and prepare reports.

The ability to use mathematical analysis to determine whether a structure can withstand loads.

Strong problem-solving abilities to tailor designs to resolve issues that arise during the project.

Budgeting expertise and commercial awareness of business implications of design decisions.

Excellent organizational skills to schedule and fulfil all stages of the planning and design process.

STRUCTURAL ENGINEER After gaining experience in junior roles and passing your professional exams, you can practise as a qualified structural engineer. You can then choose a specialist area to work in.

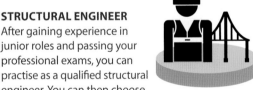

FORENSIC ENGINEER Investigates the reasons for failure or collapse of a structure in situations such as criminal damage, human error, or terrorist attack.

PROJECT MANAGER Liaises closely with all of the personnel on a construction project, ensuring that everything happens on time and to brief. A project manager may work independently or as leader of a team.

CONSERVATION AND RESTORATION ENGINEER Works on the conservation and restoration of historic buildings and structures, combining old and new construction methods.

HUMANITARIAN ENGINEER Contributes to disaster relief work in the reconstruction of infrastructure and buildings damaged by natural disasters.

SEISMIC ENGINEER Designs buildings in earthquake-prone countries to ensure that they can cope with seismic movements in the ground in order to minimize building damage and improve safety.

QUANTITY SURVEYOR

JOB DESCRIPTION

Quantity surveyors play a key role in every large construction project. With expertise in building techniques and materials, they calculate, monitor, and control the costs of a construction project to ensure value for money. They liaise with other experts, such as engineers, to ensure a project meets legal and quality standards.

SALARY

Junior quantity surveyor ★★★★★
Senior quantity surveyor ★★★★★

INDUSTRY PROFILE

Worldwide opportunities in areas of economic growth • Industry subject to economic downturns • Careers available in both public and private sectors

CAREER PATHS

Quantity surveyors can work on a variety of projects at any one time, such as the restoration of a historic monument or the construction of a giant skyscraper. When fully qualified, they can specialize in various fields, such as risk assessment, or helping to resolve legal disputes over building work.

INFRASTRUCTURE QUANTITY SURVEYOR
Specializes in building projects involving infrastructure, such as railways, ports, and airports, or energy and water networks.

SURVEYING TECHNICIAN
One possible route into the industry is by working as a surveying technician – measuring and surveying land – while studying for a degree part-time.

GRADUATE You should hold a degree in quantity surveying, but if you have graduated in another field, you may be able to take a conversion course to qualify as a surveyor.

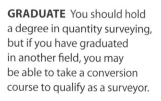

QUANTITY SURVEYOR Starting your career as a trainee surveyor, you will be expected to learn on the job to attain further qualifications and membership of a professional body. You will then be able to specialize in one of several sectors.

SKILLS GUIDE

 Good language skills for producing reports and communicating with many different suppliers.

 The ability to work as part of a team, and to motivate and negotiate with other people.

Excellent analytical skills and an organized, logical, and methodical approach to problem-solving.

 Strong numerical skills for calculating estimates and costs, and keeping track of budgets.

Extensive knowledge of commercial building methods, materials, and legislation.

 GROUP ACCOUNT DIRECTOR Supervises accounts and staff across a group of construction companies. This is a more senior and strategic construction role.

 **PROCESS ENGINEER** Helps to manage the processes and facilities in one of many possible energy industries, from oil and gas, to chemical and renewables.

The profession of quantity surveying emerged in the 1820s.

▼ RELATED CAREERS

▶ **CIVIL ENGINEER** *see pp. 176–177*

▶ **BUILDING CONTROL OFFICER** Visits sites to ensure that construction workers follow building regulations, such as fire and safety.

▶ **CLERK OF WORKS** Inspects project sites to ensure that construction professionals meet health, safety, and quality standards in the plans they draw up.

▶ **CONTRACTS MANAGER** Manages construction contracts, prepares documents for all project presentations, and estimates and oversees costs.

▶ **LAND SURVEYOR** Uses a range of techniques to survey land, take measurements, and gather data for companies planning to develop an area. Also known as a geomatic surveyor.

AT A GLANCE

 YOUR INTERESTS Construction • Structural engineering • Mathematics • Economics • Civil engineering • Physics • Geography

 ENTRY QUALIFICATIONS A degree in quantity surveying or a related subject, such as engineering, mathematics, or geography, is required.

 LIFESTYLE Quantity surveyors work regular hours. Overtime may be required to meet deadlines, as well as travel to various sites.

 LOCATION Travelling to meet clients and view sites may be required. Working away from home, even overseas, for several months is also common.

 THE REALITIES Time constraints can be stressful and long hours may be necessary to complete projects to strict deadlines.

TOWN PLANNER

JOB DESCRIPTION

Shaping the development of towns and cities is a balancing act between the economic and social needs of a community. Environmental concerns and the interests of certain areas, such as housing, business, and leisure, are all considered. As a town planner, you must examine and balance these issues, and make a judgement on planning applications proposed by individuals and companies.

SALARY

Assistant town planner ★★☆☆☆
Chief planning officer ★★★★★

INDUSTRY PROFILE

Jobs dependent on growing population, and their need for houses • Economic fluctuations affect the rise or fall of planning applications

CAREER PATHS

After graduation, town planners usually start their careers in local or regional government. With experience, they can progress to more senior planning roles within government agencies or choose to work with developers and construction firms in the private sector to help them negotiate complex planning regulations.

SENIOR PLANNING OFFICER Takes on complex planning projects, such as landscape conservation and large-scale urban developments. This involves supervising junior staff and keeping on top of larger budgets.

GRADUATE You can start with a town planning degree recognized by a professional planning body. Alternatively, you can study for a degree in geography, statistics, environmental science, or architecture, followed by postgraduate training in town planning.

TOWN PLANNER Once qualified as a town planner, you will generally start work as an assistant. After gaining experience, you have a choice between several career routes.

PLANNING CONSULTANT Works as a private consultant with property developers, government, charities, and other agencies on a range of major planning projects.

SKILLS GUIDE

 Good writing and presentation skills to communicate with a wide range of people.

 Time-management skills to meet deadlines on several projects running at once.

 Excellent problem-solving skills for analysing planning applications from clients.

 Knowledge of any new business developments, political initiatives, and environmental issues.

 Clear understanding of planning rules and regulations to be able to prepare detailed reports.

CHIEF PLANNING OFFICER
Manages a local or regional planning office and works with other branches of government to prepare the designs necessary to shape a town or region.

 Town planners have been around since the world's first towns and cities arose in Mesopotamia around 4500 BCE.

▼ RELATED CAREERS

▶ **ARCHITECT** *see pp. 194–195*

▶ **QUANTITY SURVEYOR** *see pp. 198–199*

▶ **HISTORIC BUILDINGS INSPECTOR** Ensures that a wide variety of historic buildings are preserved and maintained appropriately. Historic buildings inspectors are usually qualified to degree level in a relevant subject.

▶ **HOUSING MANAGER** Supports the development of new housing for local authorities and housing associations. Housing managers also work with people living in existing local authority-owned housing schemes to ensure that the buildings are maintained properly.

AT A GLANCE

 YOUR INTERESTS Urban design • Geography • Environmental studies • Mathematics • Landscape design • Information Technology (IT)

 ENTRY QUALIFICATIONS Urban planners typically require an undergraduate degree, a master's degree, and professional accreditation.

 LIFESTYLE Work hours are regular, but town planners may have to work overtime to meet clients, view sites, and attend public consultations.

 LOCATION Town planners work in an office some of the time, but travel is required to view potential sites and meet with developers and the public.

 THE REALITIES Dealing with tight schedules and budgets can be stressful. Town planning decisions may also be unpopular with local people.

BUILDER

JOB DESCRIPTION

Builders work on construction sites or existing structures, building anything from houses and office blocks to factories, roads, and bridges. As a builder, you must have a thorough understanding of building materials and health and safety requirements, and often work alongside other construction professionals – such as architects – to complete projects on schedule and to design plans.

SALARY

Junior builder ★☆☆☆☆
Experienced builder ★★★☆☆

INDUSTRY PROFILE

Job prospects improving with growth in housing market • Huge range of building projects, from motorway construction to house renovation • Building work available worldwide

CAREER PATHS

When first entering the construction industry, builders are likely to perform laborious tasks, such as moving materials and assisting other workers. Supervisory roles come as experience is gained. Most builders specialize in a particular area, such as welding or concrete, but it is possible to move into management and remain involved – at a supervisory level – in all stages of construction.

TRADESPERSON You can become a builder if you have experience as a building tradesperson, such as working as a bricklayer, roofer, plumber, plasterer, carpenter, or scaffolder.

SCHOOL-LEAVER You can enter the construction industry as a school-leaver with no qualifications by taking an apprenticeship with a building company.

COLLEGE-LEAVER You will improve your career prospects by studying for a trade qualification – such as bricklaying, carpentry, or plumbing – at college before finding work as a builder.

BUILDER As a builder, you can work on a self-employed basis or join a construction firm, where you could rise through the ranks to become a manager. With experience, you can specialize in roles such as a building technician.

SKILLS GUIDE

 Good numerical skills to interpret plans and designs and take accurate measurements on site.

 Strong team-working skills for collaborating with fellow construction staff.

 The flexibility to adapt to new projects and to travel to work at different building sites.

 Physical fitness and resilience to perform manual work in a range of weather conditions.

 Manual dexterity for using hand tools and construction machinery safely and efficiently.

BUILDING CONTRACTOR
Oversees a project for a building firm, hiring, managing, and coordinating the required construction workers and equipment to complete the job.

SITE SUPERVISOR
Manages the day-to-day activities of the bricklayers, electricians, carpenters, and other tradespersons on the building site.

STONE MASON
Specializes in restoring and creating stonework and decorative features. Masons work on new as well as historic buildings.

BUILDING TECHNICIAN
Estimates building costs, negotiates the purchase of materials, ensures quality standards are maintained, and supervises contractors on site.

AT A GLANCE

 YOUR INTERESTS Construction • Design technology • Technical drawing • Mathematics • English • Physical Education (PE)

 ENTRY QUALIFICATIONS There are no formal entry requirements. Most entrants learn their trade skills at college or as building apprentices.

 LIFESTYLE Most builders work regular hours. Evening and weekend work may be required to complete a project or to make the most of favourable conditions.

 LOCATION Builders usually work on construction sites or in buildings. Some travel is required; overnight stays are likely if sites are far from home.

 THE REALITIES The work is physically demanding and requires strength, agility, and resilience for working in poor weather or challenging conditions.

▼ RELATED CAREERS

▶ **CARPENTER** *see pp. 206–207*

▶ **ELECTRICIAN** *see pp. 208–209*

▶ **PLUMBER** *see pp. 210–211*

▶ **BUILDING SURVEYOR** Surveys properties, inspects damage, and makes recommendations for repair. Building surveyors also work on the design and development of new buildings and use their legal knowledge to advise clients on property legislations and building regulations.

▶ **SCAFFOLDER** Constructs scaffolding poles, platforms, and ladders to enable builders to access high-level exterior areas of a building. Scaffolders are also trained to use ropes and climbing equipment to reach inaccessible areas.

CONSTRUCTION MANAGER

JOB DESCRIPTION

Construction managers plan, coordinate, and oversee construction projects. They ensure that the work is completed according to the client's specifications, and take responsibility for budgets, schedules, health and safety standards, and hiring construction staff and subcontractors.

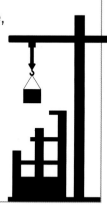

SALARY

Junior construction manager ★★☆☆☆
Senior construction manager ★★★★★

INDUSTRY PROFILE

Vast industry, with scope for working for employers of all sizes, in locations around the world • Sector vulnerable to economic fluctuations • High demand for construction managers

AT A GLANCE

YOUR INTERESTS Engineering • Design and construction • Project management • Mathematics • Physics • Economics

ENTRY QUALIFICATIONS A degree in civil engineering, building studies, or similar subject is usually required; work-based routes may be available.

LIFESTYLE Construction managers tend to work regular hours, but working in the evenings and on weekends may also be necessary to meet deadlines.

LOCATION The work is usually office-based, but construction managers make frequent site visits to oversee projects and check their quality and progress.

THE REALITIES It can take up to a decade to gain sufficient industry experience to be considered for construction management jobs.

CAREER PATHS

There is no defined route to becoming a construction manager, but in-depth industry experience is essential. Work opportunities are extensive, from large or small construction companies and specialist building-services contractors to utility firms, government departments, and housing associations.

ASSISTANT You can study for work-based qualifications in construction management while working as an assistant. If you have relevant prior experience, such as in surveying, this job can be attained without a degree.

GRADUATE You can enter the construction industry if you have a degree in a related subject, and gain the necessary experience to become a construction manager. Alternatively, you can apply for a graduate training scheme.

▼ RELATED CAREERS

▶ **LANDSCAPE ARCHITECT** *see pp. 170–171*

▶ **CIVIL ENGINEER** *see pp. 176–177*

▶ **CONSTRUCTION ARBITRATOR** Investigates and helps to resolve any disputes that arise during building projects. This is a role that requires extensive experience of the construction industry.

▶ **FACILITIES MANAGER** Ensures that business premises and the services required to use and maintain them – such as cleaning, parking, air conditioning, and security – meet the needs of the people who use the facilities.

SKILLS GUIDE

 Excellent communication skills for working effectively with people at all levels of the industry.

 Good organizational skills for coordinating teams to finish projects on time and to budget.

 Attention to detail to understand complex technical data, and focus to ensure objectives are met.

 Strong leadership and management skills for motivating and inspiring project personnel.

 The flexibility and focus to work on a number of different projects at the same time.

CONTRACTS MANAGER Identifies potential building contracts for their company to bid on, then manages the bidding process, and may monitor the execution of the subsequent contract.

BUILDING SURVEYOR Inspects property or land earmarked for construction. Provides the client with a report describing the state of the property and suggests options for repair and maintenance.

QUANTITY SURVEYOR Works on large construction projects, monitoring costs and liaising with experts, such as engineers, to ensure that legal and quality standards are met.

CONSTRUCTION MANAGER You will need solid experience in the construction industry to progress. Postgraduate study or professional accreditation may enhance your career prospects.

CONSULTANT Assists on projects and offers expertise and best-practice advice to complete them safely and efficiently. Consultants usually work for a consulting firm or a construction organization.

CARPENTER

JOB DESCRIPTION

A carpenter makes and installs the wooden elements of a building. These include its large structural pieces, such as the roof beams, floor supports, and wall partitions, as well as the internal fixtures, such as staircases, kitchen cabinets, doors, and skirting boards. Carpenters follow drawings and blueprints, and ensure that their work meets safety and quality standards.

SALARY

Trainee carpenter ★☆☆☆☆
Experienced carpenter ★★☆☆☆

INDUSTRY PROFILE

Self-employment is common • Market dictated by the economic state of the construction industry • Many experienced carpenters take on contracting roles in construction

CAREER PATHS

There are many opportunities for carpenters in the construction industry. While working, you can study for further vocational qualifications if you wish to specialize in areas such as cabinet-making or building conservation.

CABINET-MAKER Makes pieces of wooden furniture, such as chairs, tables, and cupboards. Some cabinet-makers also carry out restoration work on antique items and properties.

SCHOOL-LEAVER If you have an interest in carpentry, you can study for a certificate in carpentry or joinery in college to help you find employment. You can then study for higher diplomas if you wish to specialize.

APPRENTICE Some larger construction or kitchen-fitting companies may employ you as an apprentice straight from school, allowing you to learn on the job.

CARPENTER You may focus on one area of construction, such as making the frames of buildings, but most carpenters provide a wide range of services to their clients.

SKILLS GUIDE

The ability to work in a team, taking instructions from a site manager and guiding co-workers.

Creativity to make decorative elements of furniture, unique trims, and fittings.

Good numerical skills for taking accurate measurements and making calculations.

Manual dexterity for using a wide range of hand and power tools to cut, shape, and join materials.

Physical strength for lifting heavy items and holding them in place while fixing them into position.

BENCH JOINER Specializes in making wooden items in a workshop. These may include staircases, cupboards, doors, roof beams, and wardrobes.

KITCHEN FITTER Installs and fits kitchen cupboards, worktops, and trims. Fitters follow precise layouts drawn up by a designer to achieve the look requested by their customers.

SITE CARPENTER Makes the wooden sections of a property on a building site. Site carpenters also prepare scaffolds or forms (the moulds that hold poured concrete).

▼ RELATED CAREERS

▶ **PRODUCT DESIGNER** *see pp. 18–19*

▶ **BOAT BUILDER** Builds new boats or carries out repairs on existing vessels using a range of carpentry, engineering, and plumbing skills.

▶ **PAINTER AND DECORATOR** Applies paint, wallpaper, and other coatings to walls and surfaces of a building to improve its appearance.

▶ **ROOFER** Repairs and builds roofs on houses and commercial properties, using materials such as slates, tiles, and wood.

▶ **THEATRE SET DESIGNER** Creates the sets that are used for stage shows. Uses artistic skills and knowledge of lighting and costumes to create the right visual setting for the production.

AT A GLANCE

YOUR INTERESTS Woodwork • Engineering • Design technology • Construction • Mathematics • Science • Health and fitness

ENTRY QUALIFICATIONS College courses in carpentry or joinery are not essential, but will help you find work at the start of you career.

LIFESTYLE Working hours are regular, but early starts are common. Carpenters may need to work overtime on some projects.

LOCATION Some jobs require work on site in harsh weather. Carpenters may need to work away from home for long periods on jobs located far away.

THE REALITIES Carpentry can be physically demanding and hazardous, and the financial rewards are relatively modest.

ELECTRICIAN

JOB DESCRIPTION

Electricians install and repair electrical equipment, such as power circuits, lighting, switches, and other fittings. Most work on site, visiting homes, shops, offices, and factories. Others train in specialist areas, such as high-voltage systems used to transmit electricity over long distances, street lighting, or the electrical wiring that supplies power to heavy industries.

SALARY

Trainee electrician ★★★★★
Experienced specialist ★★★★★

INDUSTRY PROFILE

Wide variety of employment options • Self-employment is common • Salaries can vary considerably depending on specialism and experience

AT A GLANCE

YOUR INTERESTS Electronics • Mathematics • Physics • Engineering • Information Technology (IT) • Buildings and maintenance

ENTRY QUALIFICATIONS There are no set entry requirements, but employers offering apprenticeships look for a good basic education, and possibly a diploma.

LIFESTYLE Most electricians have regular hours, but may have to work evenings or weekends, or be on call for emergency repairs.

LOCATION Electricians work on site in a variety of settings, such as homes, factories, or shops, and therefore have to travel extensively.

THE REALITIES The job can involve working in cramped or dirty spaces. Keeping track of changing building regulations can be challenging.

▼ RELATED CAREERS

▶ **ELECTRICAL ENGINEER** *see pp. 186–187*

▶ **DOMESTIC APPLIANCE ENGINEER** Installs and repairs appliances, such as washing machines, electric cookers, and refrigerators in homes.

▶ **ENERGY ENGINEER** Develops new methods of extracting energy from existing methods, such as electricity, nuclear power plants, and wind turbines.

▶ **KITCHEN FITTER** Installs kitchen interiors, including worktops, cupboards, and trims, following designs and layouts accurately to achieve the look requested by the customer.

▶ **RAILWAY ENGINEER** Fits and maintains control panels, tracks, power lines, and other electrical equipment used on railways.

Most electricians qualify through an apprenticeship programme.

CAREER PATHS

The industry is tightly regulated, so it is essential to complete approved training and certification. Many electricians are self-employed or work on a contract basis for construction companies, but others are employed directly by manufacturers, engineering companies, or government bodies.

TRAINEE Apprenticeships are commonly available to school-leavers. These combine college study (such as a diploma course in electrotechnology) with on-the-job training for a complete overview of the electrician's role.

ELECTRICIAN Once qualified, you can take more vocational training courses to expand your range of skills or specialize in a specific area, to earn a better salary.

INSTALLATION ELECTRICIAN Fits lighting, sockets, network cables, and other electrical equipment in commercial and domestic properties.

MAINTENANCE ELECTRICIAN Repairs, tests, and certifies equipment used by businesses to ensure they meet safety standards.

HIGHWAYS ELECTRICIAN Specializes in installing and maintaining street lighting, traffic controls, and other electrical equipment used by the transport system.

ENGINEERING TECHNICIAN Works on industrial equipment, such as generators, production lines, and control systems. This requires further training.

SITE MANAGER Oversees the entire electrical installation at a business or residential construction site, or manages the electrical systems in a factory.

SKILLS GUIDE

 The ability to communicate effectively with customers, verbally and in writing.

 Analytical skills for diagnosing faults and finding cost-effective solutions to electrical problems.

 Good numeracy skills for calculating electrical loads and taking accurate measurements.

 Manual dexterity to perform complex wiring tasks, and handle power tools and other devices.

Physical fitness and the ability to work in confined spaces, in all weather conditions.

PLUMBER

JOB DESCRIPTION

Plumbers install and repair heating systems, boilers, water pipes, drainage systems, air-conditioning units, and domestic equipment such as washing machines. They work in homes, offices, or at industrial locations, and may be self-employed or an employee of a larger firm or business. The work involves using a wide range of equipment, from power tools to welding gear, often in wet and cramped conditions.

SALARY

Trainee plumber ★☆☆☆☆
Experienced plumber ★★★★☆

INDUSTRY PROFILE

Numerous employment opportunities, including growth in renewable energy systems • Self-employment common • Skilled plumbers in demand in many countries worldwide

▼ RELATED CAREERS

▶ **BUILDING-SERVICES ENGINEER** Designs and builds a wide range of systems within buildings, from lighting, heating, and power to internal features such as lifts and escalators. Works on large- and small-scale construction projects, and may have degree-level qualifications.

▶ **DOMESTIC APPLIANCE ENGINEER** Installs and repairs appliances, such as washing machines and refrigerators, in people's homes.

▶ **ENERGY ENGINEER** Develops new ways of producing energy, such as electricity, from a range of technologies, such as wind turbines.

▶ **KITCHEN-FITTER** Installs and fits kitchen worktops, cupboards, and decorative trims. Kitchen-fitters follow detailed plans to achieve the layout and look required by the customer.

▶ **REFRIGERATION AND VENTILATION ENGINEER** Designs, installs, and commissions air-conditioning systems in people's homes, offices, schools, and other premises.

AT A GLANCE

 YOUR INTERESTS Engineering • Mathematics • Physics • Design technology • Information Technology (IT) • English

 ENTRY QUALIFICATIONS There are no formal entry requirements. To work with oil and gas appliances, plumbers need to be certified and registered.

 LIFESTYLE Working hours are fairly regular although plumbers may need to work evenings or weekends, or remain on call in case of emergency repairs.

 LOCATION Travel between customers is essential – plumbers work in a variety of locations, such as customers' offices, homes, factories, and shops.

 THE REALITIES Being self-employed requires hard work and determination. Some work is carried out at unsociable hours, or in wet or cold conditions.

CAREER PATHS

Gaining qualifications and membership of a professional body are useful for working as a plumber, and are essential for gas installation. Domestic plumbing is the most common area of work, but there are several options for specialization.

SCHOOL-LEAVER
You can enter plumbing straight from school as an apprentice, training on the job and learning from experienced colleagues.

COLLEGE-LEAVER
You can study for college qualifications in plumbing and heating engineering before finding employment as a plumber.

PLUMBER As a plumber, you will stay up to date with safety standards and technological advances throughout your career. Once you have built a good reputation, you can set up and run your own business for domestic customers.

HEATING ENGINEER Specializes in the design, installation, and commissioning of a wide variety of heating systems, such as oil, gas, or electrical systems.

RENEWABLE ENERGY ENGINEER Designs, installs, and maintains eco-friendly domestic and industrial systems, such as solar panels or biomass heating systems, which use organic fuels rather than gas, oil, or electricity.

GAS SERVICE TECHNICIAN Installs, repairs, and services gas appliances and systems such as cookers, water-heating boilers, and gas fires.

INDUSTRIAL PLUMBER Works on major plumbing projects at factories, hospitals, and offices to ensure heating, water, and drainage systems are running efficiently.

PLUMBING ESTIMATOR Assesses the scope of new plumbing projects and estimates the cost of labour and fittings. This is usually a senior role within a large plumbing firm.

TRANSPORT

With international travel and trade on the increase, the transport industry is a growing sector across the world. Opportunities are increasingly available in the fields of air, road, rail, and maritime transport, in both planning roles and as a crew member, driver, pilot, or captain.

AIRLINE PILOT

JOB DESCRIPTION

Piloting an aircraft is an exciting job that offers the chance to see the world. It is also a role that carries heavy responsibilities, as pilots are in charge of an expensive aircraft and must ensure the safety and comfort of the passengers. They also work to strict schedules and standards. Before they qualify, pilots must undergo a period of intense training in order to fly a commerical aircraft.

SALARY

Newly qualified pilot ★★☆☆☆
Experienced captain ★★★★☆

INDUSTRY PROFILE

Industry run by a few large companies • Male-dominated profession • Demand slowing due to reduction in low-cost airlines • Little scope for part-time work

AT A GLANCE

YOUR INTERESTS Aviation • Mathematics • Physics • Engineering • Travel and tourism • Information Technology (IT) • Meteorology

ENTRY QUALIFICATIONS A pilot's licence is essential. Pilots may train at university, private flying school, or through the armed forces.

LIFESTYLE Unusual working hours go with the job, and pilots usually work in shifts. They will often spend long periods away from home.

LOCATION Pilots on long-haul flights typically spend a rest day at their destination before flying home. Short-haul pilots usually return to base each day.

THE REALITIES Private training for a pilot's licence is costly and there is a lot of competition for good jobs. Pilots spend most of their time in the cockpit.

CAREER PATHS

Gaining a pilot's licence is the first step towards a career as a pilot. With sufficient experience and flying hours, you can work towards becoming a first officer and then a captain. Pilots can work for passenger airlines, charter airlines, freight carriers, or private jet operators.

PRIVATE PILOT You can train for a pilot's licence with a private flying school. It may take up to 18 months to clock up the required flying hours.

ARMED FORCES PILOT If you serve for a given period of time as a pilot in the armed forces, you may be able to take a conversion course to qualify as a commercial pilot.

GRADUATE A degree in aviation studies or a similar subject will help your chances of finding a role with an airline company.

▼ RELATED CAREERS

▶ **AEROSPACE ENGINEER** *see pp. 190–191*

▶ **AIR-TRAFFIC CONTROLLER** *see pp. 216–217*

▶ **AIRLINE CABIN CREW** *see pp. 308–309*

▶ **HELICOPTER PILOT** Usually flies as the sole pilot, servicing oil platforms, conducting police work, flying on search-and-rescue missions, or carrying out survey work. Training for this role is costly and intensive. Fewer companies operate helicopters than airplanes, so job opportunities are more scarce.

 Pilots train on flight simulators once every nine months to renew their flying licence.

SKILLS GUIDE

 An ability to understand and remember technical and procedural information.

 Excellent skills in spoken and written English – the international language of the aviation industry.

 An ability to remain focused under pressure and think quickly to resolve problems.

 Manual dexterity, sharp eyesight, a good level of physical fitness, and excellent coordination.

 Confidence and good communication skills to interact with the crew in a calm manner.

LONG-HAUL PILOT Flies larger aircraft on longer routes, after having gained sufficient experience on short-haul routes.

CORPORATE JET PILOT Flies smaller planes, often to smaller airports for private customers.

 CARGO PILOT Flies cargo planes, often overnight when airports carry fewer passengers. Shifts are usually fairly predictable, allowing for greater stability in home life.

 AIRLINE MANAGER Works as a manager for an airline or for an airport. The job does not involve much time spent in the cockpit.

 **FIRST OFFICER** Shares duties with the captain in commanding the plane. After five to ten years' experience, you can progress to senior first officer, then captain.

 **CAPTAIN** Following rigorous training and selection, you can become captain, taking overall control of piloting the aircraft.

 INSTRUCTOR Trains new pilots on simulators, and works on airline company guidelines.

AIR-TRAFFIC CONTROLLER

JOB DESCRIPTION

Air-traffic controllers are responsible for managing aircraft traffic, ensuring that flights are completed safely and that airport runways and parking stands are used efficiently. In this role, you must be calm under pressure while tracking aircraft in flight and directing them at take-off, landing, and also on the ground.

SALARY

Trainee controller ★★★★★
Senior controller ★★★★★

INDUSTRY PROFILE

Highly competitive industry • Aviation sector growing as global air traffic increases • Concerns for job security due to privatization of airlines and airport authorities

CAREER PATHS

Most controllers train with their country's aviation authority to gain the licence required to work. Training can take several years to complete, and involves specializing in one area of air-traffic control. Progression comes in the form of increased seniority and responsibility – changing to a different specialism is rare, due to the high cost of retraining.

AREA CONTROLLER
Tracks and monitors aircraft as they fly across one of a number of defined areas of air space. The job is usually based at a large regional control centre.

SCHOOL- OR COLLEGE-LEAVER
You can apply to join a trainee programme run by a national aviation authority. A rigorous application process tests your skills, aptitude, and general health. You must also pass a background check to get security clearance.

ASSISTANT In some regions, you can apply directly to airport operators to work as an air-traffic control assistant, training on the job to qualify as a controller.

AIR-TRAFFIC CONTROLLER As an air-traffic controller, you will be trained to specialize in one of three distinct roles: area controller, approach and departure controller, or tower/aerodrome controller. With experience, you can take on management responsibility.

SKILLS GUIDE

 Good speaking and listening skills for communicating with pilots and other personnel.

 Excellent organizational skills to coordinate the arrival and departure of simultaneous flights.

 Good numerical skills to ensure accurate calculation of the speed of aircraft and distance travelled.

 The ability to solve complex and urgent problems with rapid, safe, and innovative solutions.

 Concentration, accuracy, and attention to detail for ensuring that aircraft safety is maintained.

APPROACH AND DEPARTURE CONTROLLER Maintains contact with aircraft pilots as flights arrive or depart from an airport, arranging the sequence of landing and take-off, and keeping pilots updated on weather conditions and other vital information.

TOWER/AERODROME CONTROLLER Works in an airport control tower to guide pilots in to land. Tower controllers also direct planes on the ground to ensure they reach the correct parking stand. They also coordinate the movement of service vehicles, such as baggage carts.

▼ RELATED CAREERS

▶ **AIRLINE PILOT** *see pp. 214–215*

▶ **AIRLINE CABIN CREW** *see pp. 308–309*

▶ **AIRCRAFT MAINTENANCE ENGINEER** Performs routine maintenance checks on aircraft to inspect them for defects, carry out repairs, and keep them in excellent flying condition. Aircraft maintenance engineers also undertake functional checks on internal aircraft systems, such as engines and instrument panels.

In the USA alone, air-traffic controllers coordinate the movements of up to 50,000 planes a day.

AT A GLANCE

 YOUR INTERESTS Aviation • English • Mathematics • Physics • Engineering • Information Technology (IT) • Electronics • Transport

 ENTRY QUALIFICATIONS A good general education, including English and mathematics, is needed to train. A degree or college diploma is useful.

 LIFESTYLE Working hours are regular, but controllers work in shifts to cover nights, weekends, and holidays in order to track flights over a 24-hour period.

 LOCATION Controllers usually work on computers and radar tracking equipment in an office, or within an airport control tower or centre.

 THE REALITIES Responsibility for the safety of aircraft and passengers requires intense concentration, and can be stressful and exhausting.

TRANSPORT PLANNER

JOB DESCRIPTION

Transport planners study and advise on the growth and management of road, rail, and aviation transport networks, and the impact they have both locally as well as nationally. They also examine transport patterns, such as walking or cycling, and recommend improvements to transport systems to meet government targets.

SALARY

Graduate trainee ★★★★★
Consultancy director ★★★★★

INDUSTRY PROFILE

Wide range of employers • Growth in areas such as sustainable transport and environmental conservation • Increasing demand for experienced transport planners

▼ RELATED CAREERS

▶ **CIVIL ENGINEER** *see pp. 176–177*

▶ **TOWN PLANNER** *see pp. 200–201*

▶ **LOGISTICS MANAGER** *see pp. 226–227*

▶ **CAR FLEET MANAGER** Manages a fleet of vehicles belonging to a company. Duties include overseeing servicing and maintenance, replacing vehicles when they reach a certain mileage, and ensuring vehicles are stored securely when not in use.

In the USA in 2012, 65 per cent of transport planners were employed by local governments.

AT A GLANCE

 YOUR INTERESTS Town planning • Geography • Engineering • Mathematics • Economics • Environmental science • Information Technology (IT)

 ENTRY QUALIFICATIONS Most entrants have a degree in a relevant subject. Non-graduates can train and study for a degree on the job.

 LIFESTYLE Regular office hours are the norm, but evening and weekend work may be necessary to meet deadlines or to attend public consultations.

 LOCATION The work is mainly office-based, but travel to visit projects, survey sites, and to meet clients is a common feature of the job.

 THE REALITIES Advising on a project and seeing it through to completion may take a long time. A shortage of staff with experience means salaries are rising.

CAREER PATHS

Transport planners are employed by public-sector bodies, private-sector consultancies, rail and bus providers, and logistics companies. Most study for professional accreditation or a postgraduate qualification in transport planning in order to improve their career prospects.

ASSISTANT With a good school education or college qualification, you may find employment as a planning assistant, and then study for a degree on the job.

GRADUATE You can apply for a job in transport planning with a degree in any discipline, but employers prefer subjects such as town planning, civil engineering, and geography.

SKILLS GUIDE

Good written and verbal skills for delivering reports and making recommendations.

The ability to work well with different personnel, from company directors to construction workers.

Strong analytical skills for studying complex data and devising new transport strategies.

Excellent numerical skills to gather, analyse, and interpret data and provide statistics.

Expertise in transport-modelling programs and presentation software for writing reports.

Keen commercial and political awareness in order to gather support for transport proposals.

TRANSPORT PLANNER
Your work as a planner is extremely varied, ranging from improving road safety to reducing traffic pollution in an urban area. You can advance your career by moving between the public and private sectors.

TRAFFIC ENGINEER
Conducts research into traffic flow and safety, and designs new roads or reconfigures existing ones to achieve the most efficient movement of vehicles and pedestrians.

TRANSPORT MODELLER
Uses computerized software to create transport models that simulate different scenarios, then analyses them in order to identify what action to take.

SUSTAINABLE TRANSPORT PLANNER
Specializes in policy and planning for sustainable forms of transport, such as low-emission vehicles and road networks that promote public transport.

TRANSPORT PLANNING CONSULTANT Provides advice to a wide range of clients, such as local and national authorities, hospitals, and construction firms. Consultants also develop plans, conduct assessments, and write transport proposal reports.

SHIP'S CAPTAIN

JOB DESCRIPTION

A ship's captain takes overall command of a vessel, its cargo or passengers, and crew. In this role, you oversee the navigation and handling of the ship, manage the crew, and ensure the safe and timely passage of cargo or passengers. Each class of vessel – from cruise ships and ferries to tankers and cargo ships – requires specialist skills, and every captain has a legal duty to keep an accurate log of voyages.

SALARY

Newly qualified officer ★★★★★
Experienced captain ★★★★★

INDUSTRY PROFILE

Industry currently growing • Wide range of opportunities across various sectors • Reduced demand for travel and goods during economic downturn can affect job prospects

AT A GLANCE

YOUR INTERESTS Seas and oceans • Ships and sailing • Geography • Mathematics • Engineering • Physics • Information Technology (IT)

ENTRY QUALIFICATIONS A good general education is required to train as a ship's officer. A degree in maritime science or similar subject is desirable.

LIFESTYLE Captains work in shifts and may also be on call. Leave periods vary in length, but are often one-for-one – the same length as your previous voyage.

LOCATION The captain is stationed on the ship's bridge, but also has an office onboard for paperwork. Captains spend long periods of time away from home.

THE REALITIES Responsibility for crew and passenger safety, and valuable cargo, makes this a high-pressure job. Overtime and reimbursed living costs boost pay.

CAREER PATHS

To become the captain of a ship, it is necessary to qualify as an officer in the merchant navy. As you gain experience and qualifications as a deck (navigation) or technical officer, you progress through the ranks, taking ever more responsibility for the work of other officers and crew until you can apply for the post of captain.

TRAINEE With good school grades in English, science, mathematics, and IT, you can apply to train as an officer. Training allows you to study while gaining onboard experience in junior positions.

GRADUATE You can apply for accelerated officer-training posts, or a range of junior officer positions, with a specialist industry-accredited degree.

▼ RELATED CAREERS

▶ **NAVY SAILOR** *see pp. 234–235*

▶ **COASTGUARD** *see pp. 238–239*

▶ **FISHING VESSEL SKIPPER** Manages the running of a commercial fishing vessel. Roles include piloting, navigation, using fish-locating sonar, and bringing in, storing, and arranging the sale of the catch. Fishing vessel skippers need a minimum of 18 months' sea-faring experience to qualify for the job.

▶ **MARINA MANAGER** Coordinates staff and services in a leisure marina, from allocating moorings to ensuring that maintenance and refuelling facilities are available. The job may also include contacting potential customers, marketing, and maintaining financial records.

SKILLS GUIDE

Excellent communication skills for making clear radio transmissions, often in international waters.

The ability to form an effective team from crew members who may be of different nationalities.

Strong leadership skills and the ability to motivate, instruct, and inspire confidence in your crew.

Effective problem-solving skills for dealing with issues or emergencies in a calm, controlled manner.

Excellent numerical skills in order to perform accurate navigational calculations.

CRUISE LINER CAPTAIN
Commands all onboard staff, from engineers to entertainers, oversees operational functions, such as planning routes and docking at port, and socializes with passengers at the captain's table.

CONTAINER SHIP CAPTAIN
Has responsibility for loading and unloading containers safely, and for navigating and course-setting this class of exceptionally large vessel.

SUPPORT VESSEL CAPTAIN
Commands a range of specialist vessels, such as survey ships, anchor-handling ships for oil rigs, and transport vessels for positioning new offshore wind farms.

SHIP'S CAPTAIN To become the captain of a ship, you will spend several years working in different officer roles. After reaching the rank of captain, you can choose to command a vessel at sea or work onshore for a maritime agency or port authority.

TANKER SHIP CAPTAIN Oversees the transport of liquids, such as oil, or gases, and bulk cargos, such as grain, ore, and coal. Tanker captains have specialist training in transporting hazardous materials safely.

TRAIN DRIVER

JOB DESCRIPTION

This skilled profession involves driving passenger or goods trains on local or national rail networks, stopping at stations or depots to collect and deliver passengers or cargo. The role requires acute concentration over long periods of time, and the ability to react quickly and calmly to unexpected situations. Drivers often specialize in a particular type of train, such as high-speed trains.

SALARY

Trainee train driver ★☆☆☆☆
Experienced train driver ★★★★☆

INDUSTRY PROFILE

Large industry • Passenger transport is the largest employer, followed by freight services • Competitive field, with many more applicants than jobs

AT A GLANCE

YOUR INTERESTS Trains and railway equipment • Travel and transport • Vehicle mechanics • Mathematics • Physics • Engineering • Geography

ENTRY QUALIFICATIONS A good school education is usually sufficient, but some rail companies may ask for higher-level qualifications.

LIFESTYLE Train drivers work in shifts that could begin or end at any time of the day or night, during the working week, and at weekends and holidays.

LOCATION When working on long-distance routes, overnight stays may be required. Most drivers must live within an hour's travel from their home depot.

THE REALITIES As they have to work alone for long periods, train drivers must be self-motivated. Experienced staff are well-paid and receive free rail travel.

▼ RELATED CAREERS

▶ **TRUCK DRIVER** *see pp. 224–225*

▶ **BUS DRIVER** Drives a bus on a particular route, picking up and setting down passengers at marked bus stops. Bus drivers ensure the safety of passengers, sell tickets, and check bus passes.

▶ **COACH DRIVER** Drives a coach – either hired by a private group, or a public service that makes scheduled stops – to destinations such as airports, tourist attractions, or major cities. Coach drivers load and unload luggage, take fares, and check passenger lists.

▶ **RAIL ENGINEERING TECHNICIAN** Builds, maintains, and repairs train engines, carriages, and wagons. Servicing a train's mechanical and electrical systems is an important part of the job.

▶ **TRAM DRIVER** Operates electrically powered trams on a fixed rail route in a town or city, taking on and dropping off passengers at stations.

CAREER PATHS

Prospective train drivers must first pass a series of aptitude tests and medical examinations. Once they have qualified, they undergo further training specific to the route and class of train on which they will be operating.

RAIL TECHNICIAN While most firms require drivers to be 21, you can join a rail technician apprenticeship as a school-leaver. This can lead to a trainee driver job.

TRAINEE You can apply for a place as a trainee driver with a national or regional rail company, then undergo practical and theoretical training to qualify as a driver.

SKILLS GUIDE

Attention to detail in order to interpret line-side signals and follow rules and procedures.

Good communication skills for answering customer enquiries when not in the driver's cab.

Strong problem-solving skills to resolve issues, such as service delays or a lack of trains or staff.

Physical and mental resilience to concentrate for long periods of time while driving at high speed.

A willingness to work flexibly when colleagues are absent or services are disrupted.

TRAIN DRIVER As well as controlling the train, you must check the engine and the train's systems before setting off, follow line-side signals, and make announcements to passengers. With experience, you can move into training, safety, or management roles.

TOUR TRAIN DRIVER Operates trains on themed or heritage railways, including vintage or steam-powered engines, which require specialist skills to drive.

DRIVER TRAINER Instructs new recruits to become drivers, training them in railway regulations, signals, the principles of train movement and handling, and route awareness.

DRIVER INSPECTOR Assesses the abilities of other train drivers to ensure they are working efficiently and safely by accompanying them on train journeys and simulations to ensure that safety standards are met.

LIGHT-RAIL TRAIN DRIVER Operates passenger trains or trams on urban underground and light-rail services. This specialist role involves rapid passenger transfers and frequent stops.

TRAIN OPERATIONS MANAGER Works in a management position for a train operating company, overseeing areas such as driver rotas, schedule changes, and the maintenance and deployment of trains.

TRUCK DRIVER

JOB DESCRIPTION

Truck drivers transport goods via local, national, or international road networks. In this role, you may be responsible for planning a delivery schedule and devising a route, keeping an accurate record of journeys, checking and maintaining your vehicle, and loading and unloading items. With additional licences, you can drive specialist trucks, such as tankers and hazardous-substance vehicles.

SALARY

Novice truck driver ★★★★★
Experienced truck driver ★★★★★

INDUSTRY PROFILE

Employers range from small haulage companies to multinational logistics firms • High demand for truck drivers • Drivers of trucks carrying hazardous loads command highest pay levels

AT A GLANCE

YOUR INTERESTS Driving • Transport • Travel and distribution • Motor vehicle engineering • Vehicle mechanics • Health and safety

ENTRY QUALIFICATIONS While there are no formal educational requirements, a full driving licence is required to start training as a truck driver.

LIFESTYLE Driving hours are regulated, with rest breaks required for safety. Most drivers work 42 hours a week, driving by day or night as required.

LOCATION Truck drivers spend the majority of their driving time inside the truck's cab. Long periods away from home are common.

THE REALITIES Driving long-distance is physically exhausting, and overtime pay can be limited. The job offers the chance to travel at home and abroad.

CAREER PATHS

A full car driving licence is required before taking the specialist theory and practical examinations required to gain a truck driver's licence. After qualifying, it is common for drivers to move between employers in different sectors.

SCHOOL- OR COLLEGE-LEAVER You can qualify as a truck driver from the age of 18. Studying mechanics or transport at school or college will improve your prospects.

CAREER CHANGER You can take the various truck driver's tests while working in another job, then switch careers once you have the necessary qualifications.

▼ RELATED CAREERS

▶ **TRAIN DRIVER** *see pp. 222–223*

▶ **CAR FLEET MANAGER** Manages a fleet of company cars for a business, overseeing servicing and maintenance of the vehicles and their safe and secure storage when not in use, and replacing them after they have reached a set mileage.

▶ **DISPATCH DRIVER** Transports and delivers items that require urgent, secure, or confidential delivery by motorcycle, car, van, or bicycle.

▶ **FORKLIFT TRUCK DRIVER** Uses a forklift truck to move heavy goods around warehouses, factories, and industrial premises, or to load and unload goods onto trucks, container units, or into industrial storage.

SKILLS GUIDE

 Good writing skills for maintaining accurate records of journeys, cargo, and maintenance.

 Flexibility to deal with route changes, bad weather, traffic conditions, and breakdowns.

 Good organizational skills for planning routes and delivery schedules efficiently.

 Manual dexterity for loading, securing, and handling unusual goods safely.

 Physical and mental resilience to concentrate for long periods while driving, often on the same routes.

 Attention to detail for following route directions and delivery instructions correctly.

HAZARDOUS LOAD DRIVER
Transports potentially dangerous chemicals, fuels, and hazardous waste. Hazardous load drivers need specialist training and must also hold an appropriate licence.

TRANSPORT MANAGER
Manages the work of drivers by planning routes and schedules, liaising with customers, and organizing contracts with staff and clients.

CONSTRUCTION/ MINING PLANT OPERATOR
Specializes in driving industrial vehicles – such as dumper trucks, diggers, and earth-movers – in various sectors, from mining and construction to waste management.

TRUCK DRIVER
As a truck driver, you will need to retake a driving test every five years in order to keep your licence. You can drive different types of truck, such as hazardous-load tankers, by obtaining specialist licences.

In the USA, 80 per cent of all transported goods are moved by truck.

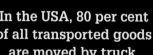
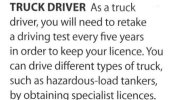

LOGISTICS MANAGER

JOB DESCRIPTION

Logistics managers coordinate the transport and storage of products and raw materials, liaising with suppliers, manufacturers, and retailers to ensure customers receive the goods they order. The rise of e-commerce – the sale of goods via electronic systems, such as the Internet – has increased demand for stock control and delivery services, making logistics managers crucial to today's economy.

SALARY

Logistics manager ★★★★★
Senior logistics manager ★★★★★

INDUSTRY PROFILE

Increasing demand for logistics managers due to rapid expansion of the sector • Advances in computerized stock ordering and management have revolutionized the field of logistics

CAREER PATHS

Careers in logistics have been transformed by new technologies, such as online ordering and real-time tracking of goods. Entry-level roles may involve managing distribution, warehousing, Information Technology (IT) systems, or individual contracts with customers. These lead to senior positions in management and in planning distribution networks.

BUSINESS DEVELOPMENT MANAGER Works on the commercial development of a logistics company, negotiating new contracts, seeking new business opportunities, and increasing orders from existing customers.

SCHOOL- OR COLLEGE-LEAVER
You can gain work experience by applying for apprenticeship schemes, which are offered by many employers. You can supplement this with a combination of short courses and private study.

GRADUATE You can apply for graduate training schemes with a degree in any discipline. However, subjects such as logistics, business, transport, or geography can boost your chances of gaining a place.

LOGISTICS MANAGER To ensure your company's business is run efficiently, you must use IT systems to monitor stock levels, fuel costs, and estimated supply times continually. With experience, you can work in a range of industries, such as mining and oil.

SKILLS GUIDE

Excellent communication skills to keep suppliers and customers fully informed.

Effective team-working skills for coordinating the work of every member of the supply chain.

Strong leadership abilities to motivate a range of people – from lorry drivers to managers.

Sharp analytical skills and a logical approach for effective scheduling and stock control.

The ability to use IT systems efficiently for tracking goods, supply levels, and costs.

LOGISTICS CONSULTANT Provides specialized services, often on a freelance basis, helping firms to plan and set up efficient supply chains and advises on global transport networks.

QUALITY MANAGER Focuses on minimizing shipment errors, delays, and goods damaged in transit. Quality managers also review the supply chain to identify areas that can be improved.

In the UK, one in 12 people work in an area of logistics, from air and sea to road, rail, or warehousing.

▼ RELATED CAREERS

▶ **TRANSPORT PLANNER** *see pp. 218–219*

▶ **CRANE OPERATOR** Uses a crane to load containers and items of cargo on and off ships, trucks, and trains, to be transported locally or around the globe.

▶ **HUMANITARIAN AID WORKER** Manages the collection, transport, and delivery of food, clothing, medicines, and other vital supplies to people following natural disasters or during conflicts.

▶ **PURCHASING MANAGER** Buys in any product or service required for a business to help it carry out its core activities.

AT A GLANCE

YOUR INTERESTS Mathematics • IT • Planning • Business studies and efficiency • Management • Geography • Languages

ENTRY QUALIFICATIONS A degree is required to join most company training schemes, but junior personnel can work their way up with on-the-job training.

LIFESTYLE Large logistics firms operate around the clock, so logistics managers may be required to work full-time hours in shifts.

LOCATION Mostly office-based, but logistics managers may also need to visit warehouses and suppliers during the working week.

THE REALITIES Travel, often to international destinations, is common. Long hours are often required, but the rewards can be generous.

SECURITY AND EMERGENCY SERVICES

If you want to take an active role in helping people and society, a career in the security and emergency services may be for you. Some jobs in this sector involve international travel, but all of them require an active approach and a willingness to engage with people.

SOLDIER
Page 230

Deployed in war zones to fight at the front line, gather intelligence, or perform support roles, soldiers risk their lives to serve their country and defend its citizens.

ARMED FORCES PILOT
Page 232

Providing airborne firepower, transport, and rescue capabilities, armed forces pilots are often the first line of attack and defence in today's high-tech conflicts.

NAVY SAILOR
Page 234

Working at sea on aircraft carriers, patrol boats, and a range of other naval vessels, sailors aim to protect citizens and commercial ships in the oceans.

ROYAL MARINES COMMANDO
Page 236

Rapid-response soldiers trained to operate on land and at sea, Royal Marines commandos are members of the crack units parachuted into high-risk areas of conflict.

COASTGUARD
Page 238

Taking to the oceans whatever the weather conditions, coastguards go to the aid of people, ships, boats, and other craft that get into difficulty at sea or on the shore.

POLICE OFFICER
Page 240

Serving the public with honesty, integrity, and diligence, police officers work to deter criminal activity, solve crimes, and help to improve society at large.

PRISON OFFICER
Page 242

Supervising the activities of inmates in jail, prison officers maintain order and ensure that the prisoners are secure and supported while serving their sentences.

PROBATION OFFICER
Page 244

Probation officers work with prisoners released on licence from jail or on community sentences to ensure that they complete their sentences and reintegrate after release.

INTELLIGENCE OFFICER
Page 246

Specialists in investigating matters of national security, intelligence officers use a variety of means – from covert surveillance to data monitoring – to protect citizens.

FIREFIGHTER
Page 248

Protecting the public and property from fires, natural disasters, and accidents, firefighters risk their own safety to assist people in hazardous situations.

PARAMEDIC
Page 250

Responding quickly to emergency call-outs, paramedics use their medical training to provide emergency care to people with different types of injuries and illnesses.

SOLDIER

JOB DESCRIPTION

Soldiers work to protect their country from external – and sometimes internal – threats. In times of war, they perform a range of activities, from fighting on the front line to helping civilians caught in conflict zones. Soldiers can specialize in combat roles or support functions – such as engineering, medicine, intelligence, and logistics – and might also perform aid work and peace-keeping missions.

SALARY

Starting salary ★★★★★
Chief of staff ★★★★★

INDUSTRY PROFILE

Job opportunities in different divisions each year • Pay levels are low for new recruits • In recent years, funding cuts have caused redundancies and fewer vacancies

AT A GLANCE

YOUR INTERESTS Armed forces • National defence • Physical Education (PE) • Sports • Engineering • Information Technology (IT) • Science

ENTRY QUALIFICATIONS There are no academic requirements to become a rank-and-file soldier, but more senior roles require a degree-level qualification.

LIFESTYLE There are no set working hours. Long periods away from home during exercises and combat missions are a major feature of the job.

LOCATION Soldiers can be based anywhere in the world. Even when stationed at a home base, they must be prepared to travel at very short notice.

THE REALITIES This job involves high levels of risk, particularly for front-line infantry. The work is highly physically demanding.

▼ RELATED CAREERS

▶ **NAVY SAILOR** see pp. 234–235

▶ **POLICE OFFICER** see pp. 240–241

▶ **BODYGUARD** Provides personal protection to high-profile figures and celebrities, either as part of a 24-hour protection team or at high-risk events, such as when making public appearances.

▶ **STORE DETECTIVE** Monitors and protects merchandise on sale in shops and stores. Store detectives are authorized to stop and search individuals suspected of theft.

The number of soldiers in the British Army is being cut to 82,000 by 2018 – a fall of 20 per cent.

CAREER PATHS

Army soldiers are under contract to serve in the armed forces for a specified number of years. While in service, they can train in different areas to enhance their prospects for promotion, and gain transferable skills that are recognized by civilian employers once they have left the army.

SCHOOL- OR COLLEGE-LEAVER You do not need any specific qualifications to enlist in the army, as long as you pass physical, medical, and aptitude assessments.

GRADUATE You will need a degree to train as an officer or join one of the army's technical units, in a subject of your choice (for the former) or relevant to the specialism (for the latter).

SKILLS GUIDE

The ability to communicate well with colleagues, senior officers, and civilians at home and abroad.

Team-working skills for building good relationships with troops and officers, and following orders.

The flexibility to adjust to an ever-changing work environment, location, and requirements.

Physical fitness and psychological strength to serve courageously in life-threatening situations.

Determination, self-discipline, and respect for authority to fulfil the duties of a soldier.

SOLDIER Whether you are an officer or rank-and-file soldier, you will be trained in a particular combat or supporting role. Promotion to more senior positions is possible with experience and demonstration of ability.

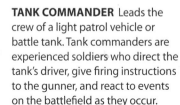

TANK COMMANDER Leads the crew of a light patrol vehicle or battle tank. Tank commanders are experienced soldiers who direct the tank's driver, give firing instructions to the gunner, and react to events on the battlefield as they occur.

MEDICAL OFFICER Provides medical care to military personnel. Medical officers hold a medicine, pharmacy, or physiotherapy qualification, and take cadet or accelerated officer training to prepare for army life.

INTELLIGENCE OFFICER Seeks out and analyses information about the enemy to help inform battle strategy and assist troops serving on the battle front.

LOGISTICS SPECIALIST Manages transport vehicles and supply chains to ensure that munitions and supplies – such as fuel, food, and medical items – reach their destination. Troops in this area take basic soldier training, then receive specialist training in logistics.

PARATROOPER Trained to parachute behind enemy lines, paratroopers perform rapid assaults to secure specific targets and achieve defined strategic aims.

ARMED FORCES PILOT

JOB DESCRIPTION

Pilots in the armed forces fly fast jets, multiengine aircraft, or helicopters on a range of combat and support missions. They may fly during conflicts, in military exercises, or on humanitarian aid missions. These pilots fly some of the most advanced aircraft in the world, operate weaponry, conduct search-and-rescue missions, and perform assault roles on airborne or ground targets.

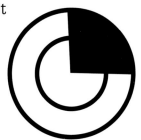

SALARY

Trainee pilot ★★★☆☆
Chief of staff ★★★★★

INDUSTRY PROFILE

Highly competitive entry • Recruitment to some nations' air forces has reduced due to recent budget cuts • Male-dominated field, but women can pilot some types of military aircraft

▼ RELATED CAREERS

▶ **AIRLINE PILOT** *see pp. 214–215*

▶ **HELICOPTER PILOT** Usually flies as the sole pilot, servicing oil platforms, conducting police work, flying on search-and-rescue missions, or carrying out survey work. Training for this role is costly and intensive. Fewer companies operate helicopters than planes, so opportunities are more scarce.

▶ **PILOT TRAINER** Works for commercial flying schools or as a trainer in the armed services, teaching new pilots how to fly a range of aircraft. Pilot trainers are very experienced pilots.

The first female fighter pilots in the US air force entered training in 1993.

AT A GLANCE

YOUR INTERESTS Aviation • Armed forces • Mathematics • Physics • Engineering • Information Technology (IT) • Leadership • Physical Education (PE)

ENTRY QUALIFICATIONS A degree is usually required to enter pilot training, although it is possible to train as a school-leaver in some countries.

LIFESTYLE The job is highly varied, with a range of intellectual and physical demands. Working hours are long when on operations.

LOCATION Physical locations can vary enormously. Although pilots may have a base, they can be stationed anywhere in the world during training and combat.

THE REALITIES The work is physically, intellectually, and emotionally demanding, with a high level of risk and responsibility for the lives of others.

CAREER PATHS

After basic training, pilots are selected to fly a particular type of aircraft. If they pass a competitive selection process, further promotion through the ranks is possible. Pilots can advance to senior roles that might include commanding an air base, making tactical decisions, or liaising with government officials. After leaving the armed forces, pilots can retrain as commercial pilots or instructors.

GRADUATE You will require a degree in a technical discipline – some universities offer courses sponsored by the military. In some countries, you can apply to join after leaving school, especially if you have experience of flying as a private pilot or air cadet.

TRAINEE You need to fulfil citizenship and age criteria, and pass rigorous physical and mental tests to be selected for training. You will begin as an officer at a military training school or academy, before starting the initial phase of flight training.

SKILLS GUIDE

 Excellent communication skills for working effectively with senior staff and ground and flight crew.

 The ability to work well as part of a team, often in dangerous and stressful situations.

 The flexibility to adapt to the requirements of different missions, and to learn new technology.

 An analytical approach and the ability to take critical decisions in high-pressure situations.

 High levels of fitness for dealing with the physical demands of flying and operational duties.

 Attention to detail and precise thinking to fly advanced aircraft and correctly carry out orders.

ARMED FORCES PILOT After between 13 and 26 weeks of initial flight training, you can specialize in either fast jets, multiengine aircraft, or helicopters. After your military career is over, you could use your expertise to become a flight instructor or civilian airline pilot.

AIRLINE PILOT Flies commercial passenger, cargo, or private aircraft. Military pilots can take a conversion course to qualify as a commercial aircraft pilot, and so continue their flying careers after leaving the armed forces.

FAST JET PILOT Flies combat aircraft on ground-assault or air-intercept missions. Training fast jet pilots is very expensive and only the very best candidates are selected.

MULTIENGINE AIRCRAFT PILOT Flies larger planes used for transporting personnel and materials, conducting search-and-rescue missions, refuelling, or surveillance.

HELICOPTER PILOT Specializes in flying helicopters on military transport, support, or search-and-rescue duties, or in ground-assault missions.

NAVY SAILOR

JOB DESCRIPTION

Navy sailors defend their country and its allies against seaborne threats, working in a variety of roles onboard military vessels – from patrol boats to aircraft carriers and submarines. Typical roles include protecting commercial shipping from piracy, patrolling the oceans and locating mines, providing naval support and firepower during military operations, or delivering aid following natural disasters.

SALARY

Newly qualified sailor ★★★★★
Chief of Naval Staff ★★★★★

INDUSTRY PROFILE

Many different roles available in a range of settings and locations • Most navies require a constant supply of new recruits, although cuts in funding have reduced vacancies

AT A GLANCE

YOUR INTERESTS Boats and sailing • Maritime security • Physical Education (PE) • Sports • Engineering • Geography • Information Technology (IT) • Science

ENTRY QUALIFICATIONS There are no set entry requirements for enlisted sailors, but officers must hold a degree to be considered for training.

LIFESTYLE Long periods at sea far from home are a constant feature of the job. The hours can be irregular during training and combat missions.

LOCATION Stationed at a naval base at home or abroad, sailors might be posted anywhere in the world during exercises or for combat.

THE REALITIES The work is physically demanding and carries high personal risk, particularly during combat. Courage and determination are essential.

CAREER PATHS

Enlisted sailors and officers can be promoted to senior positions by passing competitive selection procedures. All navies provide on-the-job training – right up to degree level – which can lead to qualifications in specialist fields, from flying to weapons maintenance, logistics, and engineering. Once your period of service is over, these qualifications can be used in a civilian career.

SCHOOL-LEAVER You can join the navy as an enlisted sailor with a good general school education. You will need to pass a variety of aptitude, medical, and fitness tests to be selected.

GRADUATE You will need a degree to train as a naval officer in a specialized area, such as logistics, medicine, engineering, or flying.

SKILLS GUIDE

 Good team-working skills to work effectively as part of a large crew and follow orders correctly.

 The flexibility to adapt to new technology and a rapidly changing working environment.

 Good organizational skills, self-discipline, and the ability to work in an orderly manner.

 Determination and courage to perform duties regardless of threats to personal safety.

 High levels of strength, fitness, and agility to work in all conditions for extended periods of time.

▼ RELATED CAREERS

▶ **SHIP'S CAPTAIN** *see pp. 220–221*

▶ **SOLDIER** *see pp. 230–231*

▶ **ROYAL MARINES COMMANDO** *see pp. 236–237*

▶ **COASTGUARD** *see pp. 238–239*

▶ **MERCHANT NAVY OFFICER** Works onboard commercial cruise ships, container boats, passenger ferries, oil tankers, and support vessels, including tug boats. Merchant navy officers can be deck officers, responsible for the navigation, deck operations, maintenance, and overall running of the ship; or they can be engineering officers, responsible for maintaining the electrical and mechanical machinery onboard the ship.

WARFARE OFFICER Specializes in naval combat using the latest weapons technology and leads a team of sailors.

ENGINEERING OFFICER Leads a team of technicians to maintain and repair a ship's systems, such as the engines, hydraulics, and hull.

LOGISTICS OFFICER Ensures that a ship is stocked with equipment and supplies that are suitable for its mission, and plans how the vessel will be resupplied on shore and at sea.

SPECIAL OPERATIONS OFFICER Uses special weapons and tactics to carry out functions such as covert reconnaissance, combat, demolition, and counter-terrorism.

SAILOR As an enlisted sailor, you can apply for officer training once you have gained experience and demonstrated key skills. Officers can gain promotion to senior roles, up to admiral level.

MEDICAL OFFICER Provides medical care – from vaccinations to emergency surgery – to sailors on training, during combat, or on relief missions.

SUBMARINER Works as part of a submarine crew far beneath the sea, specializing in areas such as navigation, nuclear engineering, and weapons technology.

ROYAL MARINES COMMANDO

JOB DESCRIPTION

Royal Marines commandos are highly trained soldiers who are expert in performing unconventional and high-risk missions, such as raids or rescues behind enemy lines. They are ready to be deployed at short notice – by land, sea, and air – to military or humanitarian crises anywhere in the world.

SALARY

Royal Marines commando ★★★★★
Royal Marines officer ★★★★★

INDUSTRY PROFILE

Royal Marines commando units contain around 4,800 fighting servicemen • Recruitment occurs annually, and is highly competitive

AT A GLANCE

YOUR INTERESTS Defence and security • Physical Education (PE) • Sports • Engineering • Geography • Information Technology (IT) • Science

ENTRY QUALIFICATIONS There are no academic requirements, but applicants must be British citizens, male, aged 16 to 32, and have good physical fitness.

LIFESTYLE Royal Marines commandos remain on call at all times. The hours may be long and irregular, with long periods away from home.

LOCATION Based at barracks in the UK, commandos may be deployed anywhere in the world, from mountains and jungles to deserts and marine environments.

THE REALITIES Operations can occur in extreme conditions, from -40˚C (-40˚F) to desert heat, are often challenging, and carry high risk of death.

▼ RELATED CAREERS

▶ **MARINE ENGINEER** Designs, oversees the installation of, and maintains systems and equipment on a variety of ships and offshore installations. On boats and submarines, marine engineers are responsible for all the onboard electrical and mechanical systems.

▶ **OUTDOOR ACTIVITIES INSTRUCTOR** Leads groups of people in a range of outdoor activities, such as climbing, camping, canoeing, archery, windsurfing, sailing, mountain biking, survival skills, and problem-solving challenges.

▶ **SPECIAL AIR SERVICE (SAS) RESERVE** Working for the military on a part-time basis, SAS reserves carry out a range of operations in different parts of the world to support the activities of the British Army's SAS Regiment.

Commandos must march 48 km (30 miles) in full battle kit in under eight hours as one of the final tests of basic training.

CAREER PATHS

After passing a pre-selection process that involves academic testing and three days of physical training, and completing a gruelling 32-week basic training course, recruits join a commando unit as a general duties marine.

ROYAL MARINES SEA CADET If you are aged between 13 and 18, you can prepare for joining the Royal Marines by becoming a sea cadet.

GENERAL DUTIES MARINE You must pass pre-selection and basic training to become a general duties marine, and will then join an operational commando unit.

ROYAL MARINES COMMANDO After two years as a general duties marine, you earn your green beret and can serve in a specialist operational unit. Commandos with higher qualifications, more experience, or a degree, can apply to become an officer or move into other specialized areas.

SPECIAL BOATS SERVICE (SBS) OFFICER Carries out special operations and counter-terrorism missions. SBS officers are trained experts in swimming, diving, parachuting, and navigation, as well as in survival skills and reconnaissance.

ASSAULT ENGINEER Builds bridges, field defences, obstacles, and other structures for commando operations. Assault engineers are also trained in demolition and using explosives.

COMBAT INTELLIGENCE MARINE Gathers and analyses enemy information and produces intelligence reports and briefs that are used to plan operations.

SIGNALS SPECIALIST Provides communications between land, sea, and air forces using satellite links and hand-held radios.

PILOT OFFICER Flies helicopters to deliver troops and supplies to the front line, and also carries out reconnaissance missions.

COASTGUARD

JOB DESCRIPTION

Coastguards undertake search-and-rescue missions in coastal areas, providing emergency support to ships and people in difficulty at sea. They also monitor shipping movements, recommend safety procedures to the public, and are responsible for checking and maintaining safety equipment, as well as reporting any pollution incidents and illegal shipping activities in a specific area.

SALARY

Coastguard watch assistant ★★★★★
Coastguard watch officer ★★★★★

INDUSTRY PROFILE

National governments and charities are main employers of coastguards • Opportunities for voluntary, on-call working • Most employers are based in coastal areas

CAREER PATHS

Coastal rescue services are provided by on-call volunteer coastguard rescue officers – who usually have other jobs, and are paid for the hours they work – and salaried coastguard watch officers. Prior seafaring experience is essential, and the job involves intensive training in navigation, radio use, health and safety, and legal procedures.

VOLUNTEER You can gain experience by becoming a voluntary coastguard rescue officer. You will be trained to help with coastal rescue missions, and must live near the base of coastguard operations.

SCHOOL- OR COLLEGE-LEAVER You can work as a coastguard watch assistant in an operations centre, gaining experience of taking emergency calls, providing information to the public, updating logs, and other administrative tasks.

▼ RELATED CAREERS

▶ **SHIP'S CAPTAIN** see pp. 220–221

▶ **NAVY SAILOR** see pp. 234–235

▶ **CUSTOMS OFFICER** Monitors and prevents illegal trade across international borders.

▶ **FISHING VESSEL SKIPPER** Takes overall responsibility for a commercial fishing boat, planning routes, ensuring that the crew are safe, and arranging sale of the catch once in port.

COASTGUARD As a newly qualified coastguard, you start your career as a watch officer. After thorough training, you coordinate operations from the shore and take part in emergency cliff rescues, coastal searches, and boat-assistance missions.

SKILLS GUIDE

 Excellent communication skills for giving clear instructions over radio and in person during rescues.

 The ability to work effectively as part of a team in dangerous and high-pressure conditions.

 Good leadership skills for directing rescues, which may involve multiple air- and sea-rescue teams.

 The ability to solve complex, high-risk problems in dangerous conditions while protecting lives.

 Excellent numeracy skills for keeping accurate logs and using navigational equipment.

AT A GLANCE

 YOUR INTERESTS Sailing and navigation • Public safety • Sciences • Mathematics • Geography • Meteorology • Physical Education (PE)

 ENTRY QUALIFICATIONS A good school education is required, together with a high level of fitness, and good eyesight and hearing.

 LIFESTYLE Coastguards provide round-the-clock emergency cover, so evening, weekend, and on-call work is possible at all times.

 LOCATION The work is based either at an operations centre, or in a coastguard station. All coastguard facilities are based in coastal areas.

 THE REALITIES This job is physically demanding, and involves responsibility for the lives of others. Working in rough seas is often dangerous.

COASTGUARD WATCH MANAGER
Supervises a team of coastguard watch assistants, officers, and voluntary staff in the daily operations of a coastguard unit.

HEAD OF MARITIME OPERATIONS
Oversees the coastguard agency's services, such as search and rescue, ship surveying and inspection, maritime law enforcement, and counter-pollution activities.

HEAD OF COASTAL OPERATIONS
Commands and manages all coastal operations and staff. Evaluates risk, develops policies, and implements safe working procedures for staff.

CHIEF COASTGUARD
Responsible for the national search-and-rescue services' planning and policy development, the chief coastguard is the most senior person within the coastguard agency.

POLICE OFFICER

JOB DESCRIPTION

Police officers are responsible for maintaining law and order on a local and national level. In this role, you may conduct patrols to reassure the public and deter criminal activity, work with community groups to promote lawful behaviour, respond to calls from the public for assistance, catch and prosecute offenders, and investigate crimes by gathering evidence and questioning suspects and witnesses.

SALARY

Trainee police officer ★★☆☆☆
Senior police officer ★★★★☆

INDUSTRY PROFILE

A varied, diverse, and expanding profession • Strong competition for entry-level jobs • Opportunities for promotion and career development are good

▼ RELATED CAREERS

▶ **PROBATION OFFICER** *see pp. 244–245*

▶ **BODYGUARD** Accompanies individuals or groups of people and takes any necessary action to protect them from harmful or violent situations. Bodyguards are usually hired by important public figures, such as government officials.

▶ **CUSTOMS OFFICER** Monitors, investigates, and prevents illegal trade across international borders. Activities include intelligence gathering, cooperating with international agencies, and inspecting suspicious cargo at ports and airports.

▶ **STORE DETECTIVE** Uses closed-circuit television and in-store observation of shoppers and staff to prevent shoplifting or damage to property in retail stores and shopping malls.

Policing is a high-risk job – 58,000 officers are assaulted in the USA every year.

AT A GLANCE

YOUR INTERESTS Law enforcement • Psychology • Sociology • Physical Education (PE) • English • Mathematics • Information Technology (IT)

ENTRY QUALIFICATIONS Entry requirements vary, but potential officers must pass stringent aptitude and fitness tests as well as background checks.

LIFESTYLE Official working hours are regular, but shift-work to cover evenings, weekends, and holidays may be required. Overtime is available.

LOCATION The work is in a wide range of settings, from investigating crime scenes to desk work at a police station or testifying in a court of law.

THE REALITIES Police officers encounter high-risk situations and work long and unsociable hours. Serving a community can be highly rewarding.

CAREER PATHS

Although competition for entry-level jobs is high, police work offers good prospects for career progression. After successfully completing a two-year initial training period, officers achieve the rank of constable, and can then specialize in a range of different roles. Promotion through senior roles is based on performance. Officers are also encouraged to take ongoing training throughout their career.

SCHOOL- OR COLLEGE-LEAVER
You need a good general education to apply for trainee positions. The exact entry requirements vary between regional police forces, but experience of community work, volunteering alongside police officers in your local area, or working as a police community support officer will improve your career prospects.

SKILLS GUIDE

The ability to communicate clearly and confidently in potentially dangerous situations.

Good team-working skills for collaborating on cases with colleagues and specialist officers.

The capacity to behave with tact, diplomacy, and respect when dealing with the public.

Solid problem-solving skills to respond quickly, effectively, and appropriately to crisis situations.

Physical strength to pursue and apprehend criminals, and mental stamina to stay calm at all times.

POLICE OFFICER
After a two-year probationary period involving extensive training in investigative methods, policing skills, and legislation, you can progress by choosing from a range of specialisms.

SPECIALIST OFFICER
Prevents crime or apprehends criminals using specialist training or techniques. Specialist officers can work in areas such as child protection, vice, fraud, or narcotics (drugs), or undergo training in the use of firearms and special tactics, such as anti-terrorism.

RIVER POLICE
Performs river or coastal patrols on specialist police vessels, investigating illegal activity and arresting criminals. River police are given training in areas including advanced boat handling or diving.

DETECTIVE
Investigates serious crimes, including murder, assault, theft, sexual offences, and fraud. A detective's duties include gathering information, collecting evidence, and interviewing suspects.

TRAFFIC/TRANSPORT OFFICER
Specializes in road safety, dealing with traffic offences, attending road accidents, and performing checks on vehicles to ensure they are insured and taxed.

PRISON OFFICER

JOB DESCRIPTION

Prison officers supervise the activities of convicted offenders in a prison. The role involves monitoring inmates at all times, enforcing regulations, and maintaining order, which often means searching prisoners and their cells. Officers also watch out for those at risk of harm, and supervise the movement of prisoners in the vicinity. With experience, they may train new recruits or oversee a part of the institution.

SALARY

Entry-level officer ★★★★★
Senior officer ★★★★★

INDUSTRY PROFILE

Increasing job opportunities due to rising prison populations • Work mainly in the public sector but private prisons operate in some countries alongside government facilities

CAREER PATHS

Prisons are usually run by national or state authorities. To become a prison officer, you will need to be a citizen of the country in which you work. Once trained, and with experience, you can apply for more senior roles within the service, or use your skills in other related areas, such as counselling and rehabilitation.

SPECIALIST OFFICER Trains in various areas, such as drug and alcohol counselling, suicide prevention, health care, or physical education, with the aim of helping prisoners overcome their problems and adjust to life after prison.

TRAINEE To be accepted as a trainee, you will need to be at least 18 years of age and pass a number of physical and mental assessments. Basic training usually lasts for several weeks.

▼ RELATED CAREERS

▶ **POLICE OFFICER** *see pp. 240–241*

▶ **PROBATION OFFICER** *see pp. 244–245*

▶ **PSYCHOLOGIST** *see pp. 254–255*

PRISON OFFICER As well as running the prison community, you help rehabilitate prisoners and work towards providing them with new skills that will be useful in the future. Experienced prison officers can progress to become either specialist officers or senior officers.

AT A GLANCE

 YOUR INTERESTS Law and the legal system • Psychology • Sociology • Languages • Physical education • Counselling and helping people

 ENTRY QUALIFICATIONS There are no formal requirements, but you will need a reasonable school education and be able to pass a series of aptitude tests.

 LIFESTYLE Prison officers are usually expected to work shifts, including nights, weekends, and holidays.

 LOCATION Prison officers are based permanently in the prison, supervising inmates indoors and during outdoor activities in prison yards.

 THE REALITIES The work conditions can be stressful. Prison officers may have to deal with inmates who are prone to aggression, and try to resolve their disputes.

SKILLS GUIDE

 Good communication and mediation skills to help defuse potentially volatile situations.

 Strong team-working skills to work alongside other personnel to control and safeguard inmates.

 The ability to stay calm and remain patient despite stressful and challenging circumstances.

 Strength and endurance for dealing quickly and efficiently with displays of aggression from inmates.

 Keen powers of observation to detect any unusual activities and behaviours in prison.

 **SENIOR OFFICER** Supervises a small team of other officers or takes responsibility for one wing (area) of the prison. As well as making sure prison officers carry out their duties, senior officers must undertake administrative work in the prison office. This role is a promotion, following several years' experience and some further training.

 **PRISON GOVERNOR** Manages a prison and takes responsibility for controlling budgets and other resources, supervising junior officers, and liaising with social workers and other agencies involved in the rehabilitation and welfare of inmates.

One-fifth of UK inmates are employed in prison workshops, such as manufacture and textiles.

PROBATION OFFICER

JOB DESCRIPTION

Probation officers work with criminal offenders before, during, and after they are sentenced by the courts. In this job, you ensure that offenders carry out their sentences, and help them return to the community, monitoring them carefully and working towards their rehabilitation. You may work with courts, prison and police services, and social and community organizations on initiatives to prevent reoffending.

SALARY

Probation services officer ★★★★★
Probation officer ★★★★★

INDUSTRY PROFILE

Political factors determine the resources available to probation services • Intense scrutiny of the profession by media and government

CAREER PATHS

Probation officers work for a regional or national probation service, or for a private company that specializes in the rehabilitation of offenders. Routes into the career vary greatly country by country, but a relevant degree and vocational qualifications are expected. Once qualified, you can choose to move into managing the work of other officers, or specialize in one area of offender rehabilitation.

REHABILITATION OFFICER Helps people addicted to drugs, alcohol, or other substances, or those with behavioural issues, to lead active, independent lives.

TRAINEE You can join a regional probation service once you have completed vocational qualifications. Experience of working with prisoners or providing support to victims of crime is helpful. You will then study for a degree in community justice to qualify fully as a probation officer.

GRADUATE If you hold a degree in criminology, police studies, community justice, or criminal justice, you can combine working for a probation service with studying for a diploma in community justice, which will qualify you to work as a probation officer.

PROBATION OFFICER You supervise offenders on parole or assess the risks they may pose to the community, and write reports for the courts and prison authorities. You may specialize in areas including high-risk offenders, people with addiction problems, or hostel management.

SKILLS GUIDE

 The ability to work with people from all walks of life, and to understand their individual needs.

 Good team-working skills for collaborating with the agencies involved in offender care.

 The ability to listen, negotiate, and remain calm when dealing with challenging behaviour.

 An organized approach and the ability to prioritize work for handling several cases at once.

 The ability to make objective and analytical assessments of behaviour and circumstances.

HOSTEL MANAGER
Oversees the running of a hostel that provides accommodation for offenders who have recently left prison, or who are undergoing treatment for addiction.

PROFESSIONAL DEVELOPMENT OFFICER
Advises and guides ex-offenders through the options available to them regarding education, training, and work, and helps them integrate into society following a prison term.

▼ RELATED CAREERS

▶ **POLICE OFFICER** *see pp. 240–241*

▶ **PRISON OFFICER** *see pp. 242–243*

▶ **COUNSELLOR** *see pp. 256–257*

▶ **SOCIAL WORKER** *see pp. 258–259*

▶ **FORENSIC PSYCHOLOGIST** Works with offenders in prisons and in the community to devise and deliver treatment programmes that will counter antisocial behaviour. Also carries out research to profile and understand criminal behaviour, and may give expert testimony in court and advise parole boards and police forces.

AT A GLANCE

 YOUR INTERESTS Sociology and social work • Law • Psychology • Politics • Counselling • English • Mathematics • Information Technology (IT)

 ENTRY QUALIFICATIONS Entry requirements vary, but a degree and vocational training in probation work are usually needed.

 LIFESTYLE Office hours are regular, but probation officers may need to work late or at weekends to deal with heavy caseloads.

 LOCATION The work of probation officers is mainly office-based, but they may need to travel frequently to courts, police stations, and prisons.

 THE REALITIES Making positive changes to people's lives is satisfying, but dealing with offenders and victims of crime can be distressing.

INTELLIGENCE OFFICER

JOB DESCRIPTION

Intelligence officers protect their country from security threats and serious and organized crime, such as terrorism or human trafficking. They may use data-analysis skills to interpret intelligence from "sources" – people with access to sensitive information – about organizations or individuals who pose a risk to national security.

SALARY

Post-school trainees ★★★★★
Senior officers ★★★★★

INDUSTRY PROFILE

Growing job sector due to heightened global security concerns • Cyber crime is a major area of growth • Option for working freelance

CAREER PATHS

To become a government intelligence officer, applicants must hold appropriate citizenship and pass a series of physical, psychological, and background checks. Your career path will depend on the skills for which you were recruited, but there is scope for specializing in particular areas – such as military intelligence – and progressing to senior roles in an agency.

GRADUATE You can enter the intelligence service after undertaking undergraduate study in any subject, but must achieve a degree classification of 2.2 or above.

▼ RELATED CAREERS

▶ **CYBER-SECURITY ANALYST** *see pp.132–133*

▶ **FORENSIC SCIENTIST** *see pp.146–147*

▶ **CRIMINAL INTELLIGENCE ANALYST** Examines crime data to investigate patterns in criminal activity, target individual offenders or gangs, and plan future crime-reduction initiatives.

▶ **CRYPTOLOGIST** Deciphers codes, puzzles, or cryptograms (puzzles that consist of a short piece of encrypted text), or creates them in order to protect private information.

INTELLIGENCE OFFICER After a period of on-the-job training, you can serve in your first post for 18 months to three years. You can specialize in certain areas, or take a job rotation to another department or agency.

AT A GLANCE

YOUR INTERESTS Psychology • Current affairs • Languages • Mathematics • Science • Information Technology (IT) • History • Economics

ENTRY QUALIFICATIONS Intelligence officers usually have a degree, or higher, qualification in a subject related to their specialism, such as forensics.

LIFESTYLE Intelligence officers work regular office hours, but overtime may be required during investigations.

LOCATION Most intelligence officers are mainly office-based, but may need to travel to the scene of a crime or to a location that is under surveillance.

THE REALITIES Intelligence work can be intensive and must be kept secret. During selection, candidates are subject to intrusive vetting procedures.

SKILLS GUIDE

Excellent written and verbal skills for writing and presenting intelligence reports.

The ability to work with fellow colleagues and specialists from other agencies.

Excellent observational, analytical, and research skills, and an aptitude for creative problem-solving.

Proficiency in computer software for identifying significant data, and analysing and recording it.

An organized approach to tasks – which might be over the long term – and the ability to prioritize.

HUMAN OPERATIONS OFFICER

Gathers intelligence by making contact with sources, ranging from covert conversations with unsuspecting targets to the interrogation of suspects. Also plans and executes cover missions and briefs government officials.

IMAGERY INTELLIGENCE OFFICER

Collects vital information via satellite and aerial photography. The information received will form the basis of many military operations.

SIGNALS INTELLIGENCE OFFICER

Specializes in gathering intelligence by analysing intercepted communications, both personal (such as telephone calls) and electronic (such as encrypted emails).

The United States' intelligence agency, the CIA, monitor 5 million tweets every day.

FIREFIGHTER

JOB DESCRIPTION

Firefighters are emergency personnel who rescue and protect people, animals, and property in a range of accidents or emergencies, from fires, traffic incidents, and floods, to bomb threats and environmental hazards. They educate the public on fire prevention and safety, and respond to emergency call-outs in order to extinguish fires, bring trapped people or animals to safety, and administer first aid before medical services arrive.

SALARY

Newly qualified firefighter ★★☆☆☆
Station manager ★★★★☆

INDUSTRY PROFILE

Competitive industry in which applicants often outnumber vacancies • Challenging profession with a tough selection process • Good opportunities for promotion and career development

AT A GLANCE

YOUR INTERESTS Health and safety • Community welfare and service • Physical Education (PE) • English • Mathematics • Science

ENTRY QUALIFICATIONS A reasonable standard of school education is required. Firefighters must pass a series of physical and psychological tests.

LIFESTYLE Firefighters work on call or in shifts to provide 24-hour cover. They typically work two day shifts and two night shifts a week, totalling 42 hours.

LOCATION Firefighters are based at a fire station that houses firefighting equipment, and travel to locations to respond to emergencies as they occur.

THE REALITIES The job can be stressful and physically demanding. Firefighters are exposed to dangerous situations, such as unstable, smoke-filled buildings.

▼ RELATED CAREERS

▶ **SOLDIER** *see pp. 230–231*

▶ **POLICE OFFICER** *see pp. 240–241*

▶ **PARAMEDIC** *see pp. 250–251*

▶ **DOG HANDLER** Works with trained dogs to detect and prevent crime, protect property, or find missing people. Dog handlers may work for the police force, the fire and rescue services, the armed forces, the security industry, or customs and border control.

In 2013 in the UK, 60 per cent of emergency calls to the fire service were false alarms.

CAREER PATHS

Trainees usually start their careers working as firefighters at a local fire brigade, each of which recruits on a local basis. Other employers include airports and the military services. Progressing to senior roles depends on gaining qualifications in areas such as advanced firefighting techniques, emergency medical technology, and disaster management (coordinating the response to disasters).

TRAINEE Your personal and physical attributes are more important than academic results, but a good general education is useful. To gain experience before applying, you can volunteer in support roles or be placed as an observer with a local fire brigade.

FIREFIGHTER Once you have gained front-line experience, you will have good prospects for advancing to senior and management roles. You can also specialize in a particular area, such as hazardous materials, fire investigation, or fire inspection.

SKILLS GUIDE

 Physical strength and endurance to carry heavy equipment and injured or stranded victims.

 Good verbal and written skills to communicate clearly and write accurate incident reports.

 Strong team-working skills for collaborating effectively and quickly with emergency staff.

 Good interpersonal skills for responding sensitively and reassuring people in distress.

 Excellent problem-solving skills for effective decision-making in life-or-death emergencies.

FIRE PREVENTION OFFICER Visits homes and business premises to check that they are free from fire hazards and meet fire-and-safety regulations, such as having working fire alarms and extinguishers.

FIRE INVESTIGATOR Examines evidence at the scene of an incident to determine the causes of a fire, explosion, or other accident. Fire investigators are usually experienced former firefighters.

AIRPORT FIREFIGHTER Responds to aviation emergencies using specialist equipment, including suppressant foam for fighting aviation-fuel fires.

STATION MANAGER Manages the crew on shift – or watch – at a fire station, and ensures that crew are fully trained and firefighting equipment and vehicles are in a good working condition. With experience, station managers can become regional managers, looking after fire stations in a certain region.

PARAMEDIC

JOB DESCRIPTION

Paramedics are health care experts who usually work as part of an ambulance crew. When called to the scene of an accident or emergency, paramedics assess the patient's condition and provides essential, sometimes life-saving care. They are trained to deal with minor injuries, such as cuts and fractures, as well as critical health conditions, such as heart attacks or strokes.

SALARY

Newly qualified paramedic ★★ ★ ★ ★
Senior paramedic ★★★ ★ ★

INDUSTRY PROFILE

Number of jobs set to grow • Most employment with ambulance and health service providers • Some opportunities in the armed forces

CAREER PATHS

To work as a paramedic, you will need to obtain a degree- or diploma-level qualification and professional certification. Once qualified, there are opportunities for further training in clinical practice or in rapid-response units.

EMERGENCY CARE PARAMEDIC
Works alongside other medical staff in hospitals, prisons, or other institutions, providing emergency treatments on site. Further training is required to gain additional clinical skills.

STUDENT PARAMEDIC
Depending on your location, you may be able to join the ambulance service as a trainee after secondary school. You may need to study on the job for a degree or diploma.

GRADUATE You can study for a degree or diploma in paramedic science or paramedic emergency care. These courses often include clinical placements with health care providers and are the most popular routes into the profession.

PARAMEDIC With experience, you can specialize in heading up an emergency response team, which involves making quick decisions about surgical procedures and using advanced life-support techniques.

SKILLS GUIDE

 Team-working skills for cooperating with other health personnel in emergency situations.

 Strong leadership and organizational skills to direct team members during medical crises.

 Compassion and empathy when giving emotional support to patients and their families.

 Quick-thinking and decision-making skills for responding effectively to emergency situations.

 The confidence to carry out emergency procedures quickly in often tough conditions.

 High levels of physical fitness to use patient-lifting devices and other equipment safely.

AT A GLANCE

 YOUR INTERESTS Health and medicine • Biology • Chemistry • Physics • Mathematics • English • Helping and caring for others

 ENTRY QUALIFICATIONS A degree- or diploma-level qualification is essential, as are excellent driving skills.

 LIFESTYLE Working hours are regular but usually involve shifts, covering nights, weekends, and holidays.

 LOCATION Based at a hospital or an ambulance station, paramedics travel to emergencies and spend a lot of time on the road.

 THE REALITIES The work is physically tough and can be emotionally draining. Accident sites are often harrowing, so one needs to keep calm and focused.

 CRITICAL CARE PARAMEDIC Provides advanced care for patients being transported between medical facilities: this may include managing airways, administering drugs, and monitoring signs of life.

 **RAPID RESPONSE PARAMEDIC** Works as part of a specialist rapid response team, providing emergency care via a motorcycle, car, or air ambulance (helicopter) unit.

▼ RELATED CAREERS

▶ **FIREFIGHTER** *see pp. 248–249*

▶ **DOCTOR** *see pp. 276–277*

▶ **NURSE** *see pp. 278–279*

▶ **MIDWIFE** *see pp. 280–281*

▶ **AMBULANCE CARE ASSISTANT** Moves disabled, elderly, or vulnerable people to and from health clinics, and for routine hospital admissions.

SOCIAL CARE AND TEACHING

Careers in this sector focus on improving the lives of individuals, families, groups, and the wider society by caring for, training, developing, and supporting people. If you enjoy working with others, and have good interpersonal skills, this may be the field for you.

PSYCHOLOGIST
Page 254

Applying scientific methods to analyse human behaviour, emotions, and thought processes, psychologists also deliver therapies to treat psychological conditions.

COUNSELLOR
Page 256

Using a range of behavioural and talking therapies, counsellors help their clients to explore, understand, and overcome their personal issues and problems.

SOCIAL WORKER
Page 258

Working closely with hospitals, schools, and prisons, social workers aim to improve people's lives by providing help, support, and advice during difficult times.

YOUTH WORKER
Page 260

Helping young people to reach their potential, youth workers provide a range of activities for children and teenagers, and offer them advice and support.

CARE HOME MANAGER
Page 262

Working in a residential care home, care home managers ensure that elderly or unwell residents are looked after in a supportive and stimulating environment.

NURSERY WORKER
Page 264

Encouraging the young children in their care to learn through play, nursery workers organize activities, read stories, and play games to help them develop key skills.

PRIMARY SCHOOL TEACHER
Page 266

In order to give children the best start to their education and encourage their social development, primary school teachers work to make learning fun and engaging.

SECONDARY SCHOOL TEACHER
Page 268

With excellent communication skills, understanding, and a good sense of humour, secondary school teachers use their subject knowledge to educate and inspire students.

HIGHER EDUCATION LECTURER
Page 270

Working in a university or college, lecturers combine teaching degree-level or postgraduate students with academic research in their chosen area of expertise.

LIBRARIAN
Page 272

With a passion for knowledge, librarians catalogue, store, and retrieve information in public, college, and university libraries, and increasingly, in collections held online.

PSYCHOLOGIST

JOB DESCRIPTION

Psychologists apply scientific methods to analyse and explain human behaviour. They use this understanding to help people overcome mental health problems, or to shape the way we organize many areas of society – for example, the way we are taught, and how people are treated and rehabilitated in hospitals and prisons. Specialist branches of psychology require postgraduate training.

SALARY

Trainee psychologist ★★★★★
Consultant psychologist ★★★★★

INDUSTRY PROFILE

Large sector • Growing demand for psychologists as new areas of expertise develop • Most jobs in educational services and health care • Self-employment is common

AT A GLANCE

YOUR INTERESTS Psychology • English • Biology • Mathematics (especially statistics) • Helping and caring for people

ENTRY QUALIFICATIONS Graduate-level and postgraduate qualifications are essential; psychologists must be registered to be able to practise.

LIFESTYLE Depending on their specialism, psychologists usually work normal office hours. If employed in a hospital, they might work shifts.

LOCATION Psychologists usually see clients in an office or clinic, but they may also be expected to make visits to homes or institutions.

THE REALITIES The job can be emotionally stressful. In some branches of the profession, a psychologist can be on call for long periods of time.

CAREER PATHS

A minimum of a degree is needed to enter this profession. With relevant work experience, you can then study for a postgraduate qualification that will enable you to specialize in a certain area, from clinical to occupational psychology.

ASSISTANT You can gain valuable experience before your degree studies by working as a psychology assistant or for a mental health charity.

GRADUATE To qualify as a psychologist, you need a degree, as well as an accreditation by a professional body. If you have a degree in another discipline, you can take a conversion course.

SKILLS GUIDE

 Excellent verbal and written communication, and the ability to listen carefully to clients.

 The ability to work with other health care professionals to ensure the welfare of patients.

 An interest in science and a strong commitment to carry on learning new skills.

 The ability to relate to people and remain calm with clients who may be distressed.

 Good problem-solving and decision-making skills, and the discipline to follow set guidelines.

▼ RELATED CAREERS

▶ **COUNSELLOR** see pp. 256–257

▶ **SOCIAL WORKER** see pp. 258–259

▶ **SPEECH AND LANGUAGE THERAPIST** see pp. 290–291

▶ **CAREERS ADVISER** Works with adults or children to help them make choices about their future careers. Provides information and guidance about learning and work opportunities that are available.

The study of the human mind and behaviour dates back to ancient Greece.

OCCUPATIONAL PSYCHOLOGIST
Analyses the working environment of an organization and suggests ways to improve staff welfare and productivity in the workplace.

EDUCATIONAL PSYCHOLOGIST Liaises with families and schools to address behavioural and learning difficulties in children and young people.

FORENSIC PSYCHOLOGIST
Works with prison and probation services to develop effective programmes that aim to prevent people from reoffending.

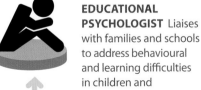
COUNSELLING PSYCHOLOGIST
Helps people to manage difficult life events and circumstances, such as dealing with grief, anxiety, or depression.

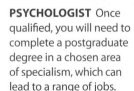

PSYCHOLOGIST Once qualified, you will need to complete a postgraduate degree in a chosen area of specialism, which can lead to a range of jobs.

CLINICAL PSYCHOLOGIST
Deals with the assessment and treatment of mental and physical health problems in clients.

SPORTS PSYCHOLOGIST
Helps athletes and sports teams to overcome psychological barriers to their performance and training on the field of play.

COUNSELLOR

JOB DESCRIPTION

People may seek a counsellor's help when they face difficult life events or if they have trouble coping with everyday tasks. Using talking therapies to build trust, counsellors create a safe place for their clients to help them make choices that lead to positive changes in their lives. A counsellor needs to have a high regard for confidentiality and professional ethics, and may use different counselling styles according to the client's needs.

SALARY

Newly qualified counsellor ★★☆☆☆
Experienced counsellor ★★★☆☆

INDUSTRY PROFILE

Employment opportunities in a variety of settings • Growing demand for counselling in workplaces • Some freelance opportunities available • Strong competition for jobs

CAREER PATHS

Counsellors require maturity and experience, and many take up the job as a new career later in life for this reason. A degree in social work or psychology is useful, but you can also become a counsellor by studying for a vocational qualification part-time. There are many forms of counselling and a variety of career paths.

SCHOOL/COLLEGE COUNSELLOR Works with young people to help them cope with difficult home circumstances, stressful experiences at school, or difficulties in learning and behaviour.

TRAINEE COUNSELLOR You can move into the profession by taking courses accredited by a professional counselling body. A previous degree is not necessary to study the courses, but the training usually lasts three to four years.

GRADUATE You can study counselling at degree level, or take a postgraduate qualification if you already hold a degree in another subject.

MENTAL HEALTH COUNSELLOR Once qualified, most counsellors choose to specialize in a number of areas. You may need a postgraduate degree for some of these paths.

SKILLS GUIDE

 Excellent verbal, written, and listening skills for effective communication with clients.

 The ability to work with people in health care and refer clients to further sources of help.

 An interest in working with diverse organizations and with different kinds of people.

 High levels of empathy, patience, and a non-judgemental attitude towards people in general.

 Good organizational skills for managing a large number of clients in a given period.

 The ability to help clients resolve their issues and find ways to improve their lives.

AT A GLANCE

 YOUR INTERESTS Psychology • Sociology • Biology • Health care • Helping and supporting people

 ENTRY QUALIFICATIONS An appropriate degree and extensive therapy training is essential, as is accreditation by a professional body.

 LIFESTYLE Short-term freelance contracts are quite common. The majority of the work is one-on-one, but it may involve group therapy.

 LOCATION Most counsellors are based in an office, but may need to visit clients in the community as part of their work.

 THE REALITIES Counsellors may hear about distressing situations, so the job can be emotionally stressful. Pay rates vary according to experience.

 FAMILY AND MARRIAGE COUNSELLOR Helps couples to improve their relationships with each other and their families, or to resolve specific problems by encouraging communication and reflection.

 REHABILITATION COUNSELLOR Supports people with disabilities, social disadvantages, or health problems to help them engage more fully with their family, work colleagues, and society in general.

 **ADDICTION COUNSELLOR** Supports people with drug, alcohol, or gambling problems to help them deal with the issues underlying their addiction.

▼ RELATED CAREERS

▶ **PROBATION OFFICER** see pp. 244–245

▶ **PSYCHOLOGIST** see pp. 254–255

▶ **SOCIAL WORKER** see pp. 258–259

▶ **DEBT ADVISER** Works with charities and publicly funded bodies to provide unbiased and confidential advice about debt and money problems. Debt advisers also help people to budget and take a sensible approach to spending.

▶ **LIFE COACH** Helps people to achieve goals in their lives by working out their aims and discussing ways to achieve desired outcomes. Life coaches need to be good listeners, empathic, and be able to work with many personality types.

SOCIAL WORKER

JOB DESCRIPTION

For those committed to creating positive changes in people's lives, social work can be a rewarding career. Social workers provide help, support, and advice to vulnerable people in the community. They work closely with agencies, such as schools, hospitals, and probation services, to recommend ways in which struggling members of society can improve their lives.

SALARY

Newly qualified social worker ★★★★★
Social work manager ★★★★★

INDUSTRY PROFILE

Large number of employment opportunities • Growing demand for social workers due to an ageing population • Majority of work in the public sector

AT A GLANCE

YOUR INTERESTS Sociology • Health and social care • Psychology • Childcare • Helping and caring for people

ENTRY QUALIFICATIONS A degree in social work or a related field is essential. Some jobs require a master's degree and accreditation by a professional body.

LIFESTYLE Full-time workers have regular office hours, but they may occasionally need to work in the evening. Part-time jobs are available.

LOCATION Although social workers work mostly from an office, they regularly visit clients at home or in schools and other community settings.

THE REALITIES Working with troubled clients, and making difficult decisions that will affect a young person's future, can be emotionally challenging.

▼ RELATED CAREERS

▶ **PSYCHOLOGIST** *see pp. 254–255*

▶ **COUNSELLOR** *see pp. 256–257*

▶ **OCCUPATIONAL THERAPIST** *see pp. 292–293*

▶ **FAMILY SUPPORT WORKER** Offers practical and emotional support to people who are experiencing problems in their personal lives, such as families going through divorce, people with disabilities, and children whose parents are in prison.

▶ **SUBSTANCE MISUSE WORKER** Supports people to overcome their dependence on alcohol and over-the-counter or illegal drugs, providing practical advice and referrals to other specialist organizations to plan recovery and treatment programmes.

▶ **YOUTH WORKER** Works with young people to help promote personal, social, and educational development in their lives. Methods of support include befriending, counselling, mentoring, and arranging activities for youngsters.

CAREER PATHS

Social workers choose to specialize in one of many areas, such as homelessness or education, or move into management and training. Because of their experience of social issues, they may be consulted on social policy by members of the local government.

ASSISTANT SOCIAL WORKER As a school-leaver, you may be able to find work as a social work assistant in a local authority or charity.

GRADUATE To become a fully registered practitioner, you will need a degree in social work. If you hold a degree in another subject, postgraduate courses are also available.

SOCIAL WORKER Once qualified and registered, you will be assigned a caseload while continuing your development. Later on, you may choose to specialize in one particular area.

SKILLS GUIDE

 The ability to listen to, understand, and talk to clients in order to provide them with practical solutions.

 Good team-working skills, and the ability to work with organizations such as the police and schools.

 Empathy to understand a client's challenges in life and develop a good relationship with them.

 Excellent organizational skills to maintain accurate records for multiple cases and clients.

 The ability to solve problems efficiently to help people lead better and more fulfilling lives.

Tact and perseverance with clients who are reluctant to accept help.

EDUCATION WELFARE OFFICER Supports families to ensure that children are attending school and getting the best from their education.

MENTAL HEALTH SOCIAL WORKER Works alongside health professionals and charities to help people with mental health problems adjust to a normal life at home in their local community.

HEALTH CARE SOCIAL WORKER Supports patients adjusting to long periods of time in hospital. Also assists those who have been discharged after a long-term illness or who are coping with a disability.

CHILDREN'S SERVICES SOCIAL WORKER Specializes in supporting children and families who are at risk or in trouble with the law.

YOUTH WORKER

JOB DESCRIPTION

Youth workers support and empower young people – often from disadvantaged or at-risk backgrounds – to improve their personal and social development. They may act as a mentor or counsellor, organize activities, or run a drop-in centre. Youth workers may specialize in working with young people in a particular local area or with specific needs, and may be employed by a charity, faith-based group, or government body.

SALARY

Newly qualified youth worker ★★★★★
Youth service manager ★★★★★

INDUSTRY PROFILE

Increasing employment opportunities • Most youth workers employed in the public sector, but jobs also exist in charitable and voluntary sectors

AT A GLANCE

 YOUR INTERESTS Social work • Sociology • Psychology • Physical Education (PE) • Languages • Team sports • Performing arts • Music

 ENTRY QUALIFICATIONS A good secondary education and a degree or postgraduate qualification in social work or community services are useful.

 LIFESTYLE Working hours vary, with evening and weekend duties often required. Part-time and self-employed work is available.

 LOCATION Most of the work is office-based, but many youth workers visit clients in their homes, at school, in the community, or in prison.

 THE REALITIES Working with disadvantaged young people requires resilience, and may occasionally involve conflict or threats to personal safety.

CAREER PATHS

Most youth workers are graduates, with many courses including both academic study and practical work to allow students to gain hands-on experience while studying. You can specialize in a number of areas and will be able to apply for more managerial and senior roles after around five years of experience in the job.

ASSISTANT YOUTH WORKER
You can work as an assistant as a school-leaver by volunteering for a local authority or charity. You can then study for a degree.

GRADUATE You will need  an undergraduate degree in a relevant subject – or a postgraduate conversion course – and professional accreditation to apply for a job as a youth worker.

▼ RELATED CAREERS

▶ **ADVICE WORKER** Provides impartial and confidential advice to individuals suffering from a variety of social, financial, legal, and employment problems. Advice workers can also mediate on behalf of a client, by writing letters or attending tribunals, for example.

▶ **FAMILY SUPPORT WORKER** Works with families with problems to provide practical and emotional support, such as caring for children whose parents are divorcing or apart due to a prison sentence.

▶ **HOUSING OFFICER/MANAGER** Works for social housing associations and rehabilitative housing projects, providing on-site advice and support to residents and specific vulnerable groups, such as the homeless, minority groups, ex-offenders, or disabled people.

SKILLS GUIDE

 Excellent interpersonal skills and emotional maturity for relating to young people and their problems.

 The ability to work closely with other professionals, such as police, teachers, and probation officers.

Creative skills for organizing activities that build young people's self-esteem and personal skills.

 Good written and verbal skills for producing reports for funding, regulatory, or community groups.

 Strong self-management skills for handling a number of different cases at the same time.

SUBSTANCE MISUSE WORKER Supports individuals seeking to overcome a dependency on illegal, prescription, or over-the-counter drugs and alcohol. Also provides referrals to other professionals, such as social workers, to plan a recovery and treatment programme.

 STUDENT COUNSELLOR Provides support and structured therapy to help young people overcome emotional and social problems that may affect their studies. Counsellors usually work in a student-services department at a college, school, or university.

 YOUTH/COMMUNITY CENTRE LEADER Organizes sports, arts, drama, and other activities at a local youth club, community centre, or faith centre. Leaders also develop and run projects that help young people deal with issues such as bullying or drug abuse.

YOUTH WORKER You may work with teenagers and young adults in areas that suffer from high unemployment and limited opportunities. With experience, you can move into management roles.

CARE HOME MANAGER

JOB DESCRIPTION

A care home manager oversees the day-to-day running of a residential care home and ensures that its residents receive a high standard of care. In this role, you manage the home's staff, ensure that it runs as a successful business, and plan activities, coordinate medical care, and provide support for residents.

SALARY

Newly qualified manager ★★★★★
Experienced manager ★★★★★

INDUSTRY PROFILE

Qualified managers in demand • Growing sector in many countries due to ageing population and increasing need for care • Jobs in public, private, charitable, and voluntary sectors

▼ RELATED CAREERS

▶ **NURSE** *see pp. 278–279*

▶ **ACCOMMODATION WARDEN** Manages the day-to-day running of accommodation provided by sheltered housing, youth hostels, and student residences. May also oversee the care and upkeep of the building, as well as providing assistance to the people who live there.

▶ **CARE ASSISTANT** Supports health care professionals in hospitals, care homes, sheltered housing, and other care environments. Depending on the setting, a care assistant may prepare equipment and provide hands-on support, or administer routine personal care directly to patients.

In 2012, more than 8.3 million elderly people received long-term care services in the USA.

AT A GLANCE

YOUR INTERESTS Health care • Sociology • Psychology • Mathematics • Biology • Physics • Chemistry • Business studies

ENTRY QUALIFICATIONS An accredited degree in a relevant subject, professional registration, and at least two years' managerial experience are required.

LIFESTYLE Work is normally done in shifts to provide continual care. Managers may need to be on call to deal with emergencies at the home.

LOCATION The work may be based at a care home, sheltered accommodation, nursing home, or hospice. Some travel may be required for meetings or outings.

THE REALITIES This is an emotionally and physically demanding job, especially if living on site. Regular inspections by regulatory bodies can be stressful.

CAREER PATHS

Prospects for advancement in the residential care industry are good. As well as specializing in a particular client group, experienced managers may move into freelance consultancy or regional management, or become care home inspectors.

ASSISTANT You can gain experience by working on either a paid or voluntary basis after leaving school, and then study for qualifications in social care.

QUALIFIED CARER You need a degree-level qualification in social work, nursing, or a similar subject, as well as professional registration and management experience, to apply for managerial jobs.

SKILLS GUIDE

Empathy, patience, and sensitivity for working with patients who have a range of medical needs.

Physical and mental stamina in order to manage demanding and distressing situations.

Effective leadership skills to manage and motivate a team of care workers and domestic staff.

Strong organizational skills for supervising and coordinating the varied activities of a care home.

Good business-management skills for recruitment, budgeting, marketing, and fundraising duties.

CARE HOME MANAGER In this role, you care for residents of a home, meeting their physical, emotional, and medical needs. You can choose to specialize in a particular type of care home, or move into senior management roles.

CHILDREN'S HOME MANAGER Delivers care to children who have been placed under the protection of a local authority. A qualification in the social care of children is required to work in this field.

ELDERLY CARE HOME MANAGER Specializes in the management of residential care for elderly people, who may have mental and physical health problems and complex medical needs.

DOMICILIARY CARE MANAGER Works for a registered care agency, managing a team of health care professionals who administer care in a patient's own home.

HOSPICE CARE MANAGER Coordinates care, counselling, and support for patients in a hospice, an institution for seriously or terminally ill patients. A nursing qualification is required for this specialist role.

NURSERY WORKER

JOB DESCRIPTION

Nursery workers care for, educate, and supervise babies and young children at play, helping them to develop and learn. In this role, you are responsible for safeguarding the children and will encourage them to develop their numeracy, language, and social skills through games, activities, and excursions. Much of the work is with children under the age of five, but some nurseries offer after-school and holiday care for older children.

SALARY

Nursery nurse ★★★★★
Nursery manager ★★★★★

INDUSTRY PROFILE

Growing sector in most parts of the world due to rapidly expanding population • Wide variety of employment options, including part-time and self-employed work

CAREER PATHS

Nursery workers are employed in many settings – from public- and private-sector day nurseries to playgroups and children's centres – so job prospects in this sector are good. Specialist areas, such as caring for children with disabilities or learning difficulties, require additional qualifications.

HOSPITAL NURSERY NURSE Works with hospitalized children up to the age of five, caring for the needs of newborn babies or using play as a means of helping older children to cope with illness or hospital treatments.

NURSERY ASSISTANT You can volunteer or work as a supervised nursery assistant after leaving school, combining on-the-job experience with studying for a diploma or certificate in childcare.

TRAINEE You can undertake a traineeship or apprenticeship that mixes practical training in a nursery setting with studying for an approved certificate or diploma at college.

NURSERY WORKER Most employers encourage you to continue your professional development, with courses in areas such as child welfare and preparing young children for school. With experience, you can specialize in different types of childcare.

SKILLS GUIDE

Perseverance and patience for motivating young children to engage in play activities.

Excellent communication skills for interacting with children, parents, other carers, and nursery staff.

Creativity and imagination for planning activities to stimulate the children to learn and play.

Attentiveness, empathy, and intuition to understand children's social and emotional needs.

Keen observational skills to assess children and keep written reports on their development.

Good organizational skills for following health and safety rules and ensuring each child stays safe.

PLAY WORKER Runs holiday play schemes for companies or works in after-school clubs, organizing activities such as sports, drama, and outings for children of all ages.

NANNY/CHILDMINDER Looks after young children in a domestic setting. Nannies work in the home of a client family; childminders work from their own homes, caring for one or more children while their parents are at work.

NURSERY MANAGER Oversees the day-to-day running and business operation of a nursery. Managers recruit staff and plan all the childcare and educational activities at the centre.

▼ RELATED CAREERS

▶ **CARE ASSISTANT** Supports health care professionals in hospitals, care homes, sheltered housing, and other care environments. Duties include setting up equipment and providing support to co-workers, or working directly with patients to provide routine personal care.

▶ **CHILDREN'S NURSE** Provides care and treatment for children under the age of 18, working with doctors, social workers, and health care assistants to assess the physical condition and needs of patients.

▶ **EARLY YEARS TEACHER** Teaches young children between the ages of three and five, covering subjects in the school curriculum. Jobs can be found in state or private schools.

AT A GLANCE

YOUR INTERESTS Education • Caring for children • Psychology • Sociology • Arts and crafts • Storytelling • English • Physical Education (PE)

ENTRY QUALIFICATIONS A certificate or diploma in childcare is required. A degree in early years learning may hasten promotion in the industry.

LIFESTYLE Nursery workers usually work 40 hours a week. Many nurseries are open from 8am to 6pm, or longer, to fit in with parents' work routines.

LOCATION In addition to day nurseries, playgroups, and children's centres, nursery workers can work in nursery schools or in households as nannies.

THE REALITIES Working with children requires patience and stamina. Starting salaries are usually low, and working hours may be longer than average.

PRIMARY SCHOOL TEACHER

JOB DESCRIPTION

Teaching at primary level is ideal for those who enjoy working with young children and are interested in education. Primary school teachers need creativity and enthusiasm to design lessons to help children learn new skills and develop their interests. It can be rewarding to help shape a child's educational, emotional, and social growth.

SALARY

Newly qualified teacher ★★★★★
Head teacher ★★★★★

INDUSTRY PROFILE

Primary schools may be governed by the state or privately run • Many jobs available worldwide • Pay levels generally low to begin with but increase with experience

AT A GLANCE

YOUR INTERESTS Working with children • English • Mathematics • Science • Arts and crafts • Information Technology (IT) • Problem-solving

ENTRY QUALIFICATIONS Employers usually look for a degree in a specific subject or in education, along with a further qualification in teaching.

LIFESTYLE Hours are long and teachers work year-round, using time outside teaching hours to plan lessons, attend parents' evenings, and do further training.

LOCATION While most work is classroom-based, there are also teaching opportunities in hospitals and schools run by the armed forces.

THE REALITIES Class sizes may be very large in urban and inner-city areas. Teachers may need to handle children with varying abilities.

CAREER PATHS

Primary school teachers work with children between five and 11 years of age. Once qualified, and with several years of experience, teachers can choose to coordinate school-wide efforts in key areas, such as numeracy, literacy, or special needs, or take up senior positions, such as a deputy headship or headship.

ASSISTANT If you do not have formal qualifications, you can support qualified teachers as a teaching assistant while studying for a foundation degree.

GRADUATE To become a primary school teacher, you must have a good general education, especially in English, mathematics, and science. Most teachers hold a degree and a postgraduate teaching qualification. You may have opportunities to study and train on the job.

▼ RELATED CAREERS

▶ **SOCIAL WORKER** see pp. 258–259

▶ **SECONDARY SCHOOL TEACHER** see pp. 268–269

▶ **NURSERY SCHOOL MANAGER** Handles the day-to-day running of a preschool playgroup or nursery school, planning and supervising activities, and interacting with parents and other staff.

> Teachers on average work 10 hours and 40 minutes a day. Less than half of that time is spent teaching children.

SKILLS GUIDE

 Good communication skills for giving instructions and relaying information clearly and simply.

 Creativity and innovation when designing activities to inspire and educate young children.

 Flexibility and adaptability to respond to different needs and situations.

 Good team-working and people skills for daily interaction with colleagues and parents.

 The ability to solve a wide range of problems, both academic and social.

 A good sense of humour and patience with young children in day-to-day classroom situations.

HEAD TEACHER Runs the school, from leading and managing teachers to deploying the school's resources effectively.

PRIMARY SCHOOL TEACHER In this role, you take charge of the class assigned to you, often specializing in a specific subject. As you gain experience, you will have a number of future career options.

 SPECIAL EDUCATIONAL NEEDS TEACHER Works with children who have a range of special educational needs. Extra training is required for this job.

 SECONDARY SCHOOL TEACHER Teaches one or two subjects to pupils aged between 11 and 18. Qualified primary school teachers will need to prove their specialist subject knowledge and undertake further courses and training.

 PRIVATE TUTOR Works with private students to improve their performance in a particular subject or to prepare them for an examination.

SECONDARY SCHOOL TEACHER

JOB DESCRIPTION

Secondary school teachers prepare and teach young people, and help shape their interests and develop their future career options. They teach students usually between the ages of 11 and 18, and often specialize in one or two subjects from the curriculum. Many also mentor and provide learning support to pupils.

$$\Sigma = mc^2$$

SALARY

Newly qualified teacher ★★☆☆☆
Head teacher ★★★★★

INDUSTRY PROFILE

Greater demand for private tutors •
Higher salary for teachers with advanced skills or who are in leadership roles •
Part-time work is available

CAREER PATHS

Secondary school teachers use curriculum-based teaching to prepare pupils of different abilities for school-leaving examinations. They also liaise with parents, school governors, and other experts. With training and experience, they can move into a variety of senior roles at a school or branch into education policy and management or curriculum development.

HEAD OF DEPARTMENT
Assumes management responsibilities for the department in their subject area, such as mathematics or English. This role generally requires several years of teaching.

TRAINEE In some countries, you can train and study on the job. Graduates in one subject can usually take a conversion course to teach another subject.

GRADUATE You will need a good standard of general education followed by a degree in a subject in the school curriculum and a postgraduate professional teaching qualification.

SECONDARY SCHOOL TEACHER As a qualified teacher, you can teach pupils aged between 11 and 18, in one or two subjects. Experienced secondary school teachers may become head of department, work as a private tutor, or work for a government or local authority.

SKILLS GUIDE

Excellent communication skills, and the ability to convey information during lessons and assemblies.

Creativity for planning stimulating lessons, and to inspire and motivate students.

The ability to manage large groups of people and deal with unruly behaviour.

Highly developed organizational and time-management skills to prepare and deliver lessons.

Flexibility in teaching style and the ability to adapt to the individual needs of students.

HEAD TEACHER Oversees the leadership and management of a school. Head teachers manage staff and make strategic decisions about the needs of the school and budget constraints.

EDUCATION MANAGER Acts in an advisory capacity for local authorities and government bodies, making decisions on education policy and strategy.

PRIVATE TUTOR Offers private tutoring to pupils who need extra support beyond school lessons or to prepare them for examinations. This part-time role offers flexible hours.

AT A GLANCE

YOUR INTERESTS Working with children • Teaching • Problem-solving • Strong interest in at least one subject taught at school

ENTRY QUALIFICATIONS Most secondary school teachers have a relevant degree and, usually, a postgraduate teaching qualification.

LIFESTYLE The work runs through the academic year. A lot of time is used outside school hours to plan lessons, mark homework, and meet parents.

LOCATION Most jobs are in secondary schools, but you could also work in a local education authority or move into private tuition.

THE REALITIES The role may involve long hours, children with unruly behaviour, and evening work, but helping children can be very rewarding.

▼ RELATED CAREERS

▶ **PRIMARY SCHOOL TEACHER** *see pp. 266–267*

▶ **HIGHER EDUCATION LECTURER** *see pp. 270–271*

▶ **ADULT EDUCATION TEACHER** Works with people aged 19 and over to provide tutoring, training, and assessment in the workplace and in classrooms.

▶ **CAREERS ADVISER** Helps children and adults to make choices about their careers. This job includes giving information and advice about learning opportunities and employment.

▶ **EDUCATION OFFICER** Escorts parties of school children around a museum or art gallery, and provides information on exhibits. This position may require a relevant degree and teaching qualification.

HIGHER EDUCATION LECTURER

JOB DESCRIPTION

If you are knowledgeable in a particular subject at a postgraduate level and have a passion for teaching, you could be a successful lecturer. Higher education lecturers teach courses that lead to undergraduate or postgraduate degrees. They may combine delivering lectures with carrying out research in their area of specialism.

SALARY

Lecturer ★★★☆☆
Professor ★★★★★

INDUSTRY PROFILE

Sector predicted to expand globally in line with developing economies • Growth in opportunities in online education • Employment mostly on short-term contract basis

AT A GLANCE

YOUR INTERESTS Teaching • Writing scholarly articles • Planning and problem-solving • Reading and research within a chosen field • English

ENTRY QUALIFICATIONS A PhD is usually required, although a master's degree may suffice for more junior posts at some colleges.

LIFESTYLE Longer hours are needed if doing research, as well as giving lectures and tutorials. There may be part-time opportunities.

LOCATION Lecturers work in universities, colleges, or research institutes. Field work in an area of research may take them abroad or allow for a year-long sabbatical.

THE REALITIES Administrative tasks take up the bulk of the working day outside teaching hours. Competition for senior academic posts is intense.

▼ RELATED CAREERS

▶ **DISTANCE-LEARNING LECTURER** Supports and teaches distance-learning students remotely (very occasionally conducting seminars at university study centres and summer schools). Provides feedback on assignments, helps students understand material, and prepares them for examinations and end-of-module assessments.

▶ **INDEPENDENT RESEARCHER** Holds a research post or fellowship at a national or international research council, charity, or commercial organization. This position usually follows many years' experience in academic research.

▶ **ONLINE TUTOR** Delivers materials, tutorials, and feedback through online learning platforms. Online tutors can usually work part-time and from home. Entry qualifications vary.

According to surveys, the best lecturers have public speaking skills, in-depth subject knowledge, and the desire to motivate students.

CAREER PATHS

Lecturers in higher education must be experts in their field, but need not have any formal teaching qualifications; some colleges prefer candidates who hold a postgraduate teaching certificate. Progress is related to your academic profile – which is formed in part by the quality of your published research – and your networking skills.

GRADUATE You need a degree and (usually) a postgraduate qualification. Experience of teaching seminars or marking papers during your higher studies will also help you to become a lecturer.

INDUSTRY PROFESSIONAL A good academic background plus experience in industry will help you to find lecturing posts in subject areas such as finance or business studies.

SKILLS GUIDE

 In-depth specialist knowledge and proficiency in a chosen area of expertise.

 Excellent communication skills for delivering lectures to students and colleagues.

 Well-developed leadership and management skills to direct a research team.

 Good organizational skills to juggle teaching responsibilities, administrative tasks, and research.

 High level of perseverance and dedication to complete research projects to a publishable standard.

HIGHER EDUCATION LECTURER Lecturers generally start their careers with a series of temporary contracts. Once your academic profile rises, you should be able to find a permanent position.

LECTURER/ASSISTANT PROFESSOR Delivers lectures, tutorials, and seminars while carrying out original research and publishing papers to raise their profile.

READER OR COURSE LECTURER Teaches classes and carries out scholarly work for publication in academic journals. Also responsible for administrative tasks related to the department.

PROFESSOR Leads the research culture of their faculty and focuses primarily on their scholarly activities.

VICE CHANCELLOR Directs an institution's teaching and research, funding, and administration. The vice chancellor is the head of the university or college, with the position equivalent to being the director of a company.

LIBRARIAN

JOB DESCRIPTION

Librarians organize and manage collections of books, journals, magazines, and electronic documents. Some of these collections are available to the public, while others are owned by universities, museums, or professional bodies, such as hospitals or law firms. Librarians select and buy books and other documents, catalogue them so they can be located, and help the public to find information.

SALARY

Library assistant ★★★★★
Senior librarian ★★★★★

INDUSTRY PROFILE

Rising employment opportunities in industry • Growing use of electronic resources has led to budget cuts in some public library services

CAREER PATHS

A degree and a higher qualification in information management is usually required to become a librarian. Libraries range from small, local collections for children, to vast archives of medical, technical, or historical documents. Your career path will depend on your academic background and the area in which you choose to specialize.

LIBRARY ASSISTANT

You can gain experience by working as an assistant. Your duties will include arranging books on shelves, and dealing with enquiries from users. You will need to study for a degree to progress.

DEGREE
A degree in librarianship gives you the ideal start in this career, but you can enter this profession with a degree in any subject and then study towards a postgraduate qualification in information management.

PUBLIC LIBRARIAN

Helps users with research into printed and online information, and organizes collections that serve the needs of the local community and often act as a hub for local events and cultural activities.

LIBRARIAN
Experienced librarians develop a deep knowledge of the collections they manage and are skilled researchers. You can work in local or regional libraries, but at the highest levels, you may manage large university libraries or national collections.

SKILLS GUIDE

 Interpersonal skills to interpret the needs of users and direct them to the desired resources.

 Excellent organizational ability for maintaining extensive catalogues and managing staff.

 Patience to deal with requests from library users and to track down elusive resources.

 The ability to think analytically to develop new or revised systems, procedures, and work flows.

 Good computer skills for helping with online research and keeping abreast of new technologies.

 Strong team-working skills for interacting with staff, volunteers, and community agencies.

 ACADEMIC LIBRARIAN Works in higher education and research institutes, providing specialist library support to students, researchers, and lecturers.

 MUSIC LIBRARIAN Manages a collection of musical scores, books, and recordings. Music libraries are held at universities, national archives, and by record companies.

 MEDICAL LIBRARIAN Works for a hospital or health care provider, maintaining collections of medical documents on clinical trials, treatments, and procedures.

▼ RELATED CAREERS

▶ **ARCHIVIST** Stores and maintains materials that record the culture, history, and achievements of individuals or groups of people. These may include letters, photographs, maps, books, and objects. Archivists may work for community groups, military regiments, companies, or national bodies.

▶ **BOOKSELLER** Buys books from publishers or wholesale suppliers and sells them to customers. Helps customers track down hard-to-find books.

▶ **INFORMATION SCIENTIST** Collects, stores, catalogues, and distributes printed and digital information within an organization. Most information scientists work in scientific, research, or technical companies to ensure that staff are kept up to date with new regulations and developments.

AT A GLANCE

 YOUR INTERESTS English • Literature • Reading • Research • Public information • Sciences • History • Information Technology (IT)

 ENTRY QUALIFICATIONS A degree is essential; postgraduate qualifications in information systems or library science may be required.

 LIFESTYLE Some libraries stay open late and over weekends, or host readings, so librarians may need to work beyond regular office hours.

 LOCATION Most of the working day is spent within the library building at a school, university, hospital, or academic institution.

 THE REALITIES Library users can be difficult, but helping people to find elusive information that they need is rewarding.

HEALTH AND MEDICINE

The health care sector is a large industry with a variety of roles based in hospitals or in the community. If you have an interest in promoting health and wellbeing and an aptitude for science and technology, health and medicine could be for you.

DOCTOR
Page 276

The medical profession is built upon the expertise and skill of doctors, who diagnose illness and injuries, and prescribe treatments to protect our health.

NURSE
Page 278

Supporting doctors and other skilled medical personnel, nurses provide hands-on care and treatment to patients in a range of settings, from hospitals to health centres.

MIDWIFE
Page 280

Caring for expectant mothers and unborn children during pregnancy and throughout labour, midwives play the vital role of delivering new life into the world.

DENTIST
Page 282

From promoting good dental hygiene to performing reconstructive oral surgery, dentists apply a range of treatments to teeth and gums to promote dental health.

PHARMACIST
Page 284

Ensuring that the appropriate medications are given to patients, pharmacists sell prescription and over-the-counter drugs to customers and advise on their safe use.

RADIOGRAPHER
Page 286

Using X-ray equipment, radiographers create detailed internal images of the body for diagnostic purposes, or deliver radioactive treatment for tumours or tissue defects.

PHYSIOTHERAPIST
Page 288

Experts in massage techniques, exercise programmes, and complementary therapies, physiotherapists work to encourage physical rehabilitation after injury or illness.

SPEECH AND LANGUAGE THERAPIST
Page 290

Speech difficulties can be caused by trauma or may have been present from birth. Speech and language therapists work with their patients to overcome or manage these problems.

OCCUPATIONAL THERAPIST
Page 292

Based in hospitals or clinics, occupational therapists offer advice and practical help with everyday tasks to people in need due to illness, injury, ageing, or disability.

OPTOMETRIST
Page 294

Working on the front line of eye health, optometrists use specialist equipment to test patients' eyesight, prescribing glasses or contact lenses where required.

DOCTOR

JOB DESCRIPTION

Doctors examine patients to diagnose illnesses, injury, and medical conditions, and prescribe an appropriate course of treatment or refer them to specialists for further care. They also might advise patients on how to lead a healthy lifestyle, and may work in a wide variety of settings, such as hospitals, community health centres, the armed forces, or in medical research.

SALARY

Junior doctor ★★★☆☆
Consultant ★★★★★

INDUSTRY PROFILE

Many and varied global opportunities • Medical training is lengthy, but job prospects are good due to the need for health care • Can specialize in a certain type of care and work flexibly

AT A GLANCE

YOUR INTERESTS Medicine • Caring for people • Physics • Chemistry • Biology • Mathematics • Psychology • Anatomy and physiology • Ethics

ENTRY QUALIFICATIONS A recognized medical degree is essential, followed by a foundation programme, and training in a chosen area.

LIFESTYLE Doctors work long hours and in shifts, especially during the earlier years of their career. Medical practitioners are never fully off duty.

LOCATION Doctors may work in hospitals, General Practice surgeries, or in the community. Some choose to work in the armed forces.

THE REALITIES The medical profession is competitive and training is long and demanding. Responsibility for patients brings intense scrutiny.

CAREER PATHS

Medical career paths differ from country to country. In some countries, applicants can enter medical school directly after secondary education; in others, a first degree (often termed a "pre-med") is required. You will then undergo general training, before receiving specialist training in your chosen area. Most doctors aspire to become consultants, the most senior practitioners in the profession.

GRADUATE You will need to complete a medical-school degree – entry to which is fiercely competitive – typically lasting between four and five years.

JUNIOR DOCTOR As a junior doctor, you work and study on a foundation programme (or "residency"), which lasts for two years.

SKILLS GUIDE

 Empathy to understand people's problems, a caring approach, and the ability to put people at ease.

 Excellent communication skills for explaining diagnoses and treatments with clarity to patients.

 Analytical skills for assessing illness and injury, and diagnosing the best course of treatment.

 Precision and dexterity to carry out both complex surgery and common medical procedures.

 Good technical and computer skills to keep records and operate sophisticated medical hardware.

▼ RELATED CAREERS

▶ **PSYCHOLOGIST** *see pp. 254–255*

▶ **NURSE** *see pp. 278–279*

▶ **DIETICIAN** Works with patients who have eating disorders, are underweight or overweight, or have food allergies, devising appropriate treatment programmes for them. Dieticians may also be employed by the food industry to give advice about ingredients, and to analyse food products.

▶ **PHYSICIAN ASSOCIATE** Helps doctors to diagnose and treat patients, recording medical histories, reporting test results, and compiling plans to manage a patient's treatment. In order to train, candidates need a science-related degree, or experience as a qualified health professional.

GENERAL PRACTITIONER (GP) Based in a surgery within a community, GPs are usually the first point of contact for patients experiencing health problems.

PHYSICIAN Also called a medical specialist, works in a hospital or clinic in general medicine – the diagnosis and treatment of complex medical problems, usually in adults.

SURGEON Works with a team of medical specialists to treat injuries, diseases, and defects by operating on patients. There are numerous specialist areas within surgery.

PSYCHIATRIST Works with patients suffering from mental illnesses, diagnosing problems and devising treatment programmes that may include medication and counselling.

NON-CLINICAL SPECIALIST Specializes in an area of medicine that has little contact with patients, such as radiology, pathology, or epidemiology (the study of how disease spreads).

DOCTOR Once qualified, you undergo four to five years of specialist training in one of more than 60 different areas, such as paediatrics, radiology, anaesthetics, surgery, General Practice, or psychiatry.

CLINICAL SPECIALIST Practises one area of medicine, such as obstetrics and gynaecology; Ear, Nose, and Throat (ENT) conditions; or emergency medicine.

NURSE

JOB DESCRIPTION

Nurses provide care and assistance for people who are ill, injured, or suffering from health problems. They administer treatments and therapies, plan patient care, and provide advice and practical support. There are opportunities to specialize and work at different locations, including hospitals, health centres, schools, and hospices, as well as in private practices.

SALARY

Newly qualified nurse ★★★★★
Nurse consultant ★★★★★

INDUSTRY PROFILE

Great demand for nurses across the world • Numbers set to rise along with the ageing population and advances in medical science • Pay levels very structured

▼ RELATED CAREERS

▶ **DOCTOR** *see pp. 276–277*

▶ **MIDWIFE** *see pp. 280–281*

▶ **HEALTH PROMOTION ADVISER** Inspires and motivates people to adopt a more healthy lifestyle.

▶ **HEALTH VISITOR** Visits patients' homes to provide care after surgery or childbirth. Is also on hand to discuss any other health issues.

▶ **SCHOOL NURSE** Visits children in schools to provide vaccinations and health checks, and to teach them about diet and exercise.

There are more nurses in the health care profession than in any other role.

AT A GLANCE

 YOUR INTERESTS Biology • Health and social care • Caring for people • Science • Psychology • Sociology • Medicine and pharmaceuticals

 ENTRY QUALIFICATIONS A nursing degree and membership of an association are needed to practise. Some colleges allow candidates to study nursing part-time.

 LIFESTYLE Nurses usually work a regular number of hours. However, this includes work in the evenings, night shifts, and weekends.

 LOCATION Nurses work out of surgeries, hospitals, day care centres, or hospices. They may also see patients for home visits or talk to children in schools.

 THE REALITIES Nursing can be physically and emotionally demanding. Financial rewards improve with further qualifications and increased responsibility.

CAREER PATHS

Depending on where one studies, nurses may need to choose an area of specialism during their degree, although they can usually change direction later. Experienced nurses are valued in hospital management and public health roles.

SKILLS GUIDE

 Good communication skills to help with dealing with people from different backgrounds.

 The ability to work successfully as part of a team in the busy health care profession.

 Natural compassion and empathy to provide support to suffering patients.

 A sense of humour to motivate patients suffering from challenging conditions.

 Physical strength to lift patients and move equipment; stamina to endure long hours of stress.

ASSISTANT Working as an assistant can provide useful experience before you apply for a nursing degree programme.

GRADUATE You need to hold a nursing degree to register as a nurse. This undergraduate course can take up to four years to complete.

NURSE Most nurses train in general adult nursing, where there are the largest number of training places and job vacancies. You can specialize during or after training.

 **CHILDREN'S NURSE** Works with children of all ages to provide health care in children's homes and hospitals.

PRACTICE NURSE Takes samples, removes or replaces dressings, and performs other general health checks. Doctors rely heavily on the help of practice nurses to support them.

DISTRICT NURSE Works with patients recovering at home, people with terminal illnesses, or the elderly. Many nurses provide care in their community settings rather than in hospitals.

MENTAL HEALTH NURSE Helps patients in their recovery from mental health conditions. Administers appropriate medication and works with patients to help them lead fuller, more independent lives.

LEARNING DISABILITY NURSE Assists people with learning disabilities to improve the quality of their lives. Assesses people's needs and creates tailored care plans for them.

MIDWIFE

JOB DESCRIPTION

A midwife supports and protects the health of a mother-to-be and her baby during pregnancy, helps to deliver the baby during childbirth, and may give care in the weeks that follow. They also provide counselling, advice, and medical assistance to help women and their families deal with the emotional and practical issues associated with pregnancy, labour, and the immediate care of the newborn baby.

SALARY

Newly qualified midwife ★★☆☆☆
Consultant midwife ★★★★★

INDUSTRY PROFILE

Many vacancies across the world • Demand for midwives growing as birth rates rise • Regulated profession with positions available in hospitals and in the community

AT A GLANCE

YOUR INTERESTS Women's health and welfare • Health and social care • Biology • Science • Mathematics • Social sciences • English

ENTRY QUALIFICATIONS A degree in midwifery is required and midwives must be entered onto a professional register in order to practise.

LIFESTYLE Due to the unpredictable nature of childbirth, midwives work in shifts. Community midwives may also be on call to provide emergency cover.

LOCATION Midwives work in hospital wards, community health centres, or birthing units. Community midwives visit patients in their homes.

THE REALITIES Pregnancy and labour can involve medical complications and emergencies, which can be traumatic. Shift-work can be tiring.

▼ RELATED CAREERS

▶ **COUNSELLOR** *see pp. 256–257*

▶ **CHILDREN'S NURSE** Provides health care to children of all ages in hospitals, children's homes, and schools. Children's nurses have to work closely with parents.

▶ **HEALTH VISITOR** Visits patients in their homes to provide care following surgery, after childbirth, or for a range of other health issues.

▶ **NEONATAL NURSE** Provides nursing care for newborn babies who are premature or sick. Neonatal nurses work in specialist units in hospitals.

▶ **SONOGRAPHER** Uses ultrasound to examine unborn babies, checking their development and screening them for medical conditions.

In the UK, more than 90 per cent of births take place in a hospital setting.

CAREER PATHS

Midwifery is a degree-level career that offers opportunities for working in a range of settings around the world. Midwives may be based in hospitals, maternity clinics, midwife units, and birth centres, or even make home visits.

NURSE You can take a nursing degree, then specialize in midwifery by undertaking on-the-job training after you have qualified as a nurse.

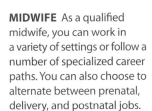

GRADUATE A good level of education and work experience will help you when applying for a midwifery degree, which is the usual route of entry into the job.

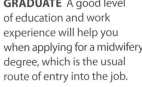

SKILLS GUIDE

Good communication skills for interacting with patients from different backgrounds.

The ability to work with other health care professionals, such as doctors and health visitors.

Compassion and empathy for delivering care with sensitivity to expectant parents.

Persistence, a good sense of humour, and the ability to motivate patients and staff.

Physical strength to lift patients and move equipment. Stamina to endure long hours and stress.

MIDWIFE As a qualified midwife, you can work in a variety of settings or follow a number of specialized career paths. You can also choose to alternate between prenatal, delivery, and postnatal jobs.

HOSPITAL MIDWIFE Works in the prenatal, labour, and postnatal wards of hospitals to provide care to expectant and new mothers.

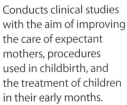

COMMUNITY MIDWIFE Runs clinics for expectant mothers, refers cases to medical staff if required, and cares for women in labour, especially those having home births.

CLINICAL RESEARCHER Conducts clinical studies with the aim of improving the care of expectant mothers, procedures used in childbirth, and the treatment of children in their early months.

CONSULTANT MIDWIFE Provides specialized care in complicated deliveries, such as Caesarian sections, as well as helping to train new midwives. May also participate in research programmes to assess and improve midwifery methods.

MIDWIFERY TEAM MANAGER Manages a team of midwives in a hospital maternity unit, combining hands-on duties with overseeing the work of other midwives.

DENTIST

JOB DESCRIPTION

Dentists diagnose and treat damage, disease, and decay to the teeth and gums, and provide cosmetic treatments to improve their appearance. They also educate and advise patients on effective cleaning techniques, mouth hygiene, and diet to maintain oral and dental health. Dentists might work in a hospital to carry out reconstructive surgery for patients with facial injuries, or perform routine dental care in a clinic.

SALARY

Newly qualified dentist ★★★☆☆
Senior dental practitioner ★★★★★

INDUSTRY PROFILE

Good job prospects and opportunities for career advancement • High salaries • Continued growth in demand for dental services • Strong competition for training places

AT A GLANCE

YOUR INTERESTS Medicine • Biology • Chemistry • Physics • Mathematics • English • Information Technology (IT) • Public health

ENTRY QUALIFICATIONS A degree in dentistry is required. Work experience, such as shadowing a dentist, will help when applying for courses.

LIFESTYLE Work hours vary by practice, and may include evening or weekend duties, and periods on call over holidays.

LOCATION Most dentists work in a consulting room within a private dental practice, a hospital, or a clinic. Travel for work purposes is rare.

THE REALITIES Dentists might have to work with patients who are unhygienic or who have oral diseases. Some patients might become stressed during treatment.

CAREER PATHS

A minimum of four years of study is required to become a dentist, after which students can choose between different branches of dentistry. Most dentists work on a self-employed basis as general practice dentists, owning or being a partner in a clinic. Switching between general practice and hospital dentistry is less common.

SCHOOL- OR COLLEGE-LEAVER
If your grades from school or college do not meet the minimum level required for entry into a degree course, you may be able to take a year-long foundation course before entering dental school.

GRADUATE You will need to study at dental school for a degree in dentistry in order to practise as a dentist. Undergraduate courses last five years, although science graduates may take a shorter four-year course.

▼ RELATED CAREERS

▶ **DOCTOR** *see pp. 276–277*

▶ **OPTOMETRIST** *see pp. 294–295*

▶ **DENTAL HYGIENIST** Advises patients on how to look after their teeth and gums to help prevent tooth decay and gum disease. Dental hygienists use dental instruments to clean and polish patients' teeth and to remove dental plaque.

▶ **DENTAL TECHNICIAN** Designs and constructs a range of dental devices to repair decaying teeth, replace lost teeth, and to improve the general appearance of teeth. Although technicians work closely with dentists, they have limited contact with patients.

SKILLS GUIDE

 Excellent communication skills to interact with patients and explain treatments to them.

 Strong leadership abilities for recruiting, training, and managing a dental practice team.

 Good interpersonal skills to understand patients' problems and to put them at ease.

 Excellent manual dexterity for carrying out intricate dental work using medical instruments.

 Attention to detail and precision to ensure that treatments are administered accurately.

ORTHODONTIST Corrects the abnormal alignment of the teeth and jaws by fitting dental appliances, such as tooth braces and space retainers.

MAXILLOFACIAL SURGEON Offers reconstructive surgery to patients who have defects or injuries – such as cleft palates, accident injury, or tumours – to the mouth, teeth, jaws, and face.

HOSPITAL DENTIST Treats patients in a hospital setting, carrying out complex dental and surgical procedures. Hospital dentists may specialize in restorative surgery, or in paediatric dentistry – treating children – for example.

COMMUNITY DENTIST Works at specialist centres, mobile clinics, or care homes to offer dental care to children, people with special needs or physical disabilities, and the elderly.

DENTIST To qualify as a dentist, you must undergo further on-the-job training after finishing dental school. You can specialize in areas including root canal work, or undertake postgraduate training in hospital dentistry.

PUBLIC HEALTH DENTIST Assesses the dental needs of a region, rather than of an individual patient. Also gives advice on preventing dental disease, and ensures that dental services meet public needs.

PHARMACIST

JOB DESCRIPTION

Pharmacists are responsible for the safe supply of medicines to hospital patients and the general public. They prepare medicines for use, checking the dosage, ensuring compatibility with other drugs a patient may be taking, and labelling the medicines clearly. Pharmacists also give advice to customers on prescription drugs, over-the-counter products, and the treatment of minor ailments.

SALARY

Trainee pharmacist ★★★★★
Senior pharmacist ★★★★★

INDUSTRY PROFILE

Good employment opportunities • Expanding sector due to development of new medical products and increasing life expectancy, leading to rising demand for pharmaceuticals

CAREER PATHS

After a relatively lengthy training and qualification period, pharmacists can choose from a wide range of career options. Moving between the different branches of pharmacy – such as clinical, hospital, or retail work – is common, while experience can bring opportunities in management, sales, consultancy, research, or training.

CLINICAL PHARMACIST
Works in a hospital, clinic, or doctor's surgery with other medical specialists, ensuring that patients receive the correct medication and that regulations on prescriptions are followed.

PHARMACY TECHNICIAN You can apply for a job as a pharmacy assistant or technician after a period of foundation-level study, but will need a degree to become a pharmacist.

GRADUATE To obtain a licence as a registered pharmacist, you need to take a four-year degree in pharmacy followed by a one-year training period with a pharmacist in a shop or hospital.

PHARMACIST As a pharmacist, you can study for postgraduate qualifications or take professional training to enhance your skills. You could choose to specialize in a particular area, such as complementary medicine, or move into research.

SKILLS GUIDE

 Good communication skills to listen to patients' needs and give instructions on taking medicines.

 Strong mathematical skills for using scientific formulae and making complex calculations.

 Excellent interpersonal skills and the ability to deal sympathetically and clearly with customers.

 Good analytical skills and scientific understanding for diagnosing a patient's medication needs.

 An eye for detail and a systematic approach to ensure medications are dispensed accurately.

 **COMMUNITY PHARMACIST** Provides health care advice and dispenses or sells medications in a retail pharmacy. Community pharmacists may also deliver medication to house-bound patients and visit care homes.

 INDUSTRIAL PHARMACIST Conducts research into the properties of new drugs, testing and developing products in order to bring them to market. Industrial pharmacists also perform checks to ensure that existing drugs meet safety and quality standards.

 **NUCLEAR PHARMACIST** Specializes in preparing and dispensing radioactive drugs, which are used in hospitals and clinics to treat cancer, and to diagnose disorders.

▼ RELATED CAREERS

▶ **PHARMACOLOGIST** *see pp. 140–141*

▶ **BIOCHEMIST** Studies chemical reactions in living organisms, proteins, cells, and DNA to understand the effects of drugs, foods, allergies, and disease.

▶ **BIOMEDICAL RESEARCH SCIENTIST** Performs clinical trials and laboratory tests to research new methods for treating diseases, ailments, and health conditions.

▶ **HOMEOPATH** Treats physical, psychological, and emotional conditions by using natural substances to stimulate the body's natural healing processes.

▶ **TOXICOLOGIST** Conducts experiments to research the impact of toxic and radioactive materials on people, animals, and the environment.

AT A GLANCE

 YOUR INTERESTS Medicine • Health care • Chemistry • Biology • Physics • Mathematics • Anatomy • English • Social welfare

 ENTRY QUALIFICATIONS A degree in pharmacy is required, followed by study for professional qualifications needed by regulatory bodies.

 LIFESTYLE Work can either be full-time or part-time. Some weekend work may be required for pharmacists who work in hospitals or on the high street.

 LOCATION The work is community-based, in a pharmacy or retail store, or in a hospital or clinic, either on the ward or in a dispensary.

 THE REALITIES Mistakes in dispensing medication can endanger patients' health. Preparing and dispensing medicines can be repetitive in nature.

RADIOGRAPHER

JOB DESCRIPTION

A vital part of a hospital team, radiographers use X-rays and sound waves to specialize in either diagnosing disorders and injuries, such as broken bones, or to treat illnesses, such as some types of cancer. They combine an academic knowledge of anatomy and human biology with the technical skills needed to operate sophisticated equipment. Their caring and compassionate approach puts patients at ease.

SALARY

Newly qualified radiographer ★★☆☆☆
Consultant radiographer ★★★☆☆

INDUSTRY PROFILE

Growing profession within the health care industry • Opportunities in government-run and private settings • Rapidly changing techniques require regular training

AT A GLANCE

YOUR INTERESTS Biology and human anatomy • Physics • Information Technology (IT) • Medicine • Helping people • Problem-solving

ENTRY QUALIFICATIONS A degree or postgraduate qualification is important, although in-service study can also be undertaken as an assistant to qualify.

LIFESTYLE Diagnostic radiographers work in shifts, while those working in the therapeutic branches of radiography have more regular hours.

LOCATION Radiographers mainly work in a hospital or clinic, within a specialized radiography unit or in an operating theatre.

THE REALITIES Shift-work does not suit everyone, and financial rewards are modest. The hospital environment can be physically and emotionally stressful.

CAREER PATHS

The radiography profession is split into two distinct strands. Diagnostic radiographers use imaging technologies, such as X-rays, Computed Tomography (CT), and ultrasound to diagnose illness and injury. Therapeutic radiographers use targeted doses of radiation to treat patients with conditions such as cancer.

ASSISTANT Helping radiographers in day-to-day work as an assistant, you may be able to undertake in-service study to qualify as a radiographer.

GRADUATE When opting for a degree in radiography, you will need to choose between diagnostic and therapeutic radiography.

▼ RELATED CAREERS

▶ **DOCTOR** *see pp. 276–277*

▶ **CLINICAL SCIENTIST** Specializes in the research, development, and testing of medical equipment and advances in diagnostic techniques.

▶ **MEDICAL PHYSICIST** Develops new methods and technologies to investigate and treat illness, and also assists medical staff with the use and maintenance of complex medical equipment.

▶ **RADIOLOGIST** Interprets the results of radiographic tests before planning and carrying out treatments, including taking cell samples (biopsies) from the patient. Radiologists are qualified hospital doctors who have specialized in the diagnosis and treatment of illness.

SKILLS GUIDE

 Clear and effective communication skills for dealing with patients of all ages and from all backgrounds.

 Care and consideration for others for dealing sympathetically with patients who are ill and weak.

 Good team-working skills for coordinating patient treatments with other health care staff.

 A natural flair for working with complex technology and sophisticated scanning equipment.

 An eye for detail when interpreting scans to maintain high standards of patient care.

DIAGNOSTIC RADIOGRAPHER
In this role, you use high-tech scanning equipment to diagnose illness and injury.

SPECIALIST RADIOGRAPHER
Uses advanced types of diagnosis radiography, such as ultrasound or Magnetic Resonance Imaging (MRI), and becomes involved in research into new imaging techniques.

THERAPEUTIC RADIOGRAPHER
This type of radiography involves you planning and delivering doses of radiation to treat patients suffering from cancer.

CONSULTANT RADIOGRAPHER
Works in a range of settings, including hospitals, to develop and promote new and exciting research.

PHYSIOTHERAPIST

JOB DESCRIPTION

Physiotherapists play a vital part in treating people with physical difficulties resulting from injury, disability, illness, or ageing. A physiotherapist uses various treatments, including massage, hydrotherapy, and exercise to help patients recover or manage their condition. They usually work in hospitals alongside other health care experts, such as nurses, occupational therapists, and social workers.

SALARY

Physiotherapy assistant ★★☆☆☆
Consultant physiotherapist ★★★★☆

INDUSTRY PROFILE

Strong competition for jobs • Most opportunities in government sector health services • Growing demand for sports physiotherapists and private practitioners

AT A GLANCE

YOUR INTERESTS Physical therapy • Massage • Exercise • Health and social care • Sports • Biology • Anatomy • Health science • Psychology

ENTRY QUALIFICATIONS An undergraduate or postgraduate degree is necessary, along with a commitment to ongoing training throughout career.

LIFESTYLE Physiotherapists typically have a normal working week, although some clinics open in the evening and on weekends.

LOCATION Most therapists work in hospitals, nursing homes, doctor's surgeries, in the community, and sometimes in schools.

THE REALITIES Treating patients over several weeks or months can be physically and mentally demanding, but rewarding when patients show improvements.

CAREER PATHS

Physiotherapists have several career options. They could work in doctor's surgeries or choose one of the specialisms within the profession. Clinical experience in physiotherapy may open up a career in hospital or health service management, or in teaching. Many physiotherapists also move into private practice once they have gained extensive experience.

ASSISTANT As a school- or college-leaver, you can start by assisting a qualified physiotherapist and study part-time for a degree.

GRADUATE Before starting to practise physiotherapy, you will need an undergraduate or postgraduate degree in physiotherapy, followed by registration with the Chartered Society of Physiotherapy.

▼ RELATED CAREERS

▶ **OCCUPATIONAL THERAPIST** *see pp. 292–293*

▶ **PERSONAL TRAINER** *see pp. 300–301*

▶ **MASSAGE THERAPIST** Uses massage to ease the aches and pains of patients and clients, treat specific muscular problems, such as spasms and sprains, or enhance their general wellbeing. Massage therapists also use their skills to provide rehabilitation or relief to people with long-term illnesses or sports injuries.

▶ **SPORTS SCIENTIST** Applies a science-based knowledge of sports and human biology to work with athletes, doctors, and other health care professionals. Helps athletes to improve their performance and take better care of their bodies. Also conducts research in health and sports.

SKILLS GUIDE

 Effective communication skills to interact with a wide range of patients and health care workers.

 The ability to work in teams alongside a range of other health care professionals.

 Empathy and sensitivity in understanding patients' problems to provide the right treatment.

 Problem-solving skills to diagnose and treat conditions, which may require technical equipment.

 Physical strength and stamina to carry out massage treatments on patients.

ORTHOPAEDIC PHYSIOTHERAPIST Assesses and treats patients recovering from surgery on, or accidental damage to, their bones and muscles.

GERIATRIC PHYSIOTHERAPIST Specializes in helping elderly patients improve their mobility, adjust to living at home after surgery, or manage pain from medical conditions such as arthritis.

PAEDIATRIC PHYSIOTHERAPIST Works with children to address birth and developmental problems with muscles and bones and in rehabilitation after surgery or accidents.

PHYSIOTHERAPIST Once working as a qualified physiotherapist, you can take specific courses to expand your skills and knowledge.

SPORTS PHYSIOTHERAPIST Treats a range of sports-related injuries. Also offers guidance on prevention of injury, fitness programmes, and nutrition.

OCCUPATIONAL PHYSIOTHERAPIST Helps people readjust to work following illness or injury, and provides treatment for pain management.

SPEECH AND LANGUAGE THERAPIST

JOB DESCRIPTION

Speech and language therapists assess, diagnose, and support people with speech and communication problems. They also help people who are experiencing difficulties in eating, drinking, and swallowing. They may treat patients recovering from surgery, or those suffering from neurological disorders.

SALARY

Newly qualified therapist ★★★★★
Team leader ★★★★★

INDUSTRY PROFILE

Job opportunities available worldwide • Most speech and language therapists work for public sector health organizations • Increasing number of freelance therapists

CAREER PATHS

A newly qualified speech and language therapist usually joins an expert care team, which includes teachers, nurses, doctors, and psychologists. Once registered, you would have to gain clinical experience on a broad level before specializing in one area of therapy or progressing into a managerial role.

CHILD SPEECH AND LANGUAGE THERAPIST Works alongside hearing specialists (audiologists), and Ear, Nose, and Throat (ENT) doctors, to assess and treat children whose speech and language have not fully developed for physical or psychological reasons.

ASSISTANT After leaving school or college, you can gain invaluable experience assisting a qualified speech and language therapist, while you study part-time for a degree.

GRADUATE You need a degree in speech and language therapy to enter the profession. If you hold a different degree, but have relevant work experience, you may be able to take a shorter postgraduate course to qualify.

SPEECH AND LANGUAGE THERAPIST In this job you assess a client's needs to deliver a course of treatment in consultation with other health professionals and the client's family or teachers. With experience, you can specialize in a number of different fields.

SKILLS GUIDE

 The ability to listen carefully and communicate clearly with both children and adults.

 Good team-working skills to cooperate with teachers, social workers, and health professionals.

 The ability to be sensitive and compassionate towards vulnerable and anxious patients.

 Attention to detail for interpreting measurements to make a correct diagnosis.

 Persistence, a good sense of humour, and the ability to motivate patients.

ADULT SPEECH AND LANGUAGE THERAPIST
Works with adults suffering from speech and communication problems that may have resulted from surgery, stroke, cancer, or from age-related disorders.

TEAM LEADER Takes charge of the work and staffing of a unit, or joins a hospital's management team. This job requires experience as it is a leadership role.

CLINICAL RESEARCHER
Conducts clinical trials on patients with the aim of improving medical procedures and clinical practices.

▼ RELATED CAREERS

▶ **PSYCHOLOGIST** *see p. 254–255*

▶ **PHYSIOTHERAPIST** *see pp. 288–289*

▶ **OCCUPATIONAL THERAPIST** *see pp. 292–293*

▶ **ELOCUTION TUTOR** Provides lessons to help students improve aspects of their speech, such as pronunciation, diction, and voice projection.

▶ **HEARING THERAPIST** Works with adults and children who experience disruptions to their hearing or loss of hearing, and balance problems.

▶ **NUTRITIONIST** Offers advice and information about healthy diets and lifestyles. Nutritionists can also conduct research and make recommendations to food companies and health care authorities.

AT A GLANCE

 YOUR INTERESTS Medicine • Biology • Psychology • Science • Health and social care • Social sciences • English • Languages

 ENTRY QUALIFICATIONS A degree or postgraduate qualification – and professional accreditation – are essential to be able to practise.

 LIFESTYLE Working hours are usually regular. Part-time work and freelance positions are also available, offering more flexibility.

 LOCATION Therapists work in hospitals, community health centres, or assessment units. They often travel to work at different locations.

 THE REALITIES Although patient expectations can be high and the work itself can be relentless and tiring, it is also extremely rewarding.

OCCUPATIONAL THERAPIST

JOB DESCRIPTION

Occupational therapists use individual treatment programmes, exercise, and psychological therapies to help people overcome problems caused by disability, illness, injury, or ageing. The therapist trains patients to carry out their daily tasks, so that they can lead full, independent lives.

SALARY

Occupational therapy assistant ★★★★★
Occupational therapy manager ★★★★★

INDUSTRY PROFILE

Rising demand for occupational therapists • Majority of work in government-sector areas, such as health and social service • Job opportunities worldwide

AT A GLANCE

YOUR INTERESTS Biology • Health and social care • Psychology • Social sciences • Supporting people with mobility problems

ENTRY QUALIFICATIONS An under-graduate or postgraduate degree in occupational therapy is necessary. There may be opportunities to qualify in service.

LIFESTYLE Most therapists work regular hours, but some work shift patterns. Part-time and flexible work options are also available.

LOCATION Occupational therapists work in hospitals, care homes, prisons, and at social services offices. They may need to travel to visit their patients.

THE REALITIES Some patients can be challenging. Occupational therapists need physical strength and agility, as well as patience and a sense of humour.

▼ RELATED CAREERS

▶ **PSYCHOLOGIST** *see pp. 254–255*

▶ **SOCIAL WORKER** *see pp. 258–259*

▶ **SPEECH AND LANGUAGE THERAPIST** *see pp. 290–291*

▶ **HEARING THERAPIST** Works with adults and children who are experiencing hearing loss, hearing disturbances, and balance problems. Hearing therapists mainly work in hospitals and health centres where they assess patients and develop treatment plans.

▶ **MASSAGE THERAPIST** Provides massages to patients and clients relieve any physical discomforts, enhance general wellbeing, and treat specific muscular problems, such as spasms and sprains. Massage therapists also use their skills to provide relief to people with long-term illnesses or sports injuries.

▶ **OCCUPATIONAL HEALTH NURSE** Promotes better health and wellbeing in the workplace, usually as part of a health and safety team.

CAREER PATHS

A degree and professional registration is necessary to practise as an occupational therapist. The work is highly varied with opportunities to specialize in different areas or to progress into management, research, or teaching. Some experienced therapists choose to take up roles in industry or to establish themselves in private practice.

SKILLS GUIDE

 Excellent communication skills in order to interact with patients and other people in medical care.

 The willingness to work in a team with other medical and social care staff.

 The ability to be sensitive and empathize with people who have physical and emotional problems.

 Good decision-making and organizational skills to prioritize and manage caseloads.

 Patience and perseverance in assisting patients unwilling to accept help and suggestions.

Physical strength and stamina to lift heavy equipment and help manoeuvre patients.

SUPPORT WORKER
After leaving school, you can support a qualified therapist while studying part-time for a degree.

GRADUATE You can study occupational therapy as a first degree, or take a shorter conversion course if you have graduated in another subject.

OCCUPATIONAL THERAPIST You assess your clients, draw up suitable treatment plans, then work with them to achieve their targets. With experience, you can specialize in a number of areas.

ORTHOPAEDIC OCCUPATIONAL THERAPIST Works as part of a health care team, helping patients to recover after surgery on, or injury to, bones and muscles.

PAEDIATRIC OCCUPATIONAL THERAPIST Works with children with developmental problems. Also travels to schools to assess children's issues and consult with teachers on appropriate activities.

MENTAL HEALTH OCCUPATIONAL THERAPIST Helps people adjust to living with mental health issues and learning disabilities.

GERIATRIC OCCUPATIONAL THERAPIST Assists elderly clients with age-related problems and medical conditions, such as dementia, impaired vision or hearing, and poor mobility.

OPTOMETRIST

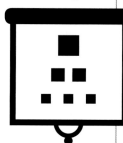

JOB DESCRIPTION

Optometrists examine a patient's eyes to test their sight and check for injury, disease, or other conditions, such as diabetes and high blood pressure. They might use specialist eye-testing equipment to diagnose eyesight problems, prescribe glasses or contact lenses to correct defects in vision, and refer patients to other health care professionals for further treatment where required.

SALARY

Newly qualified optometrist ★★★★★
Consultant optometrist ★★★★★

INDUSTRY PROFILE

Strong competition for jobs • Growing sector with good career prospects • Job opportunities in optician practices, retail stores, hospitals, and doctor's clinics

AT A GLANCE

YOUR INTERESTS Eye care • Health care • Biology • Physics • Chemistry • Mathematics • Science • English • Information Technology (IT)

ENTRY QUALIFICATIONS A degree in optometry and registration with a professional body are required before practising as an optometrist.

LIFESTYLE Optometrists work regular office hours, but evening and weekend work may be required. Part-time consultancy work is also available.

LOCATION Optometrists spend most of their time working in a private consulting or treatment room in an optician's practice, a clinic, or a hospital.

THE REALITIES Most of the work is spent conducting eye examinations inside a small room with no natural light, in close proximity to patients.

CAREER PATHS

After qualifying, most optometrists find work in independent practices or with larger companies that provide eye care to the public. Some work in hospitals, supporting doctors and surgeons to deal with more complex eye problems; others work for manufacturers of spectacles and contact lenses, developing new products.

DISPENSING OPTICIAN If you have qualified as a dispensing optician (*see* Related Careers box), your experience will help when applying for a degree course in optometry.

GRADUATE You need a degree in optometry to begin pre-registration training, which lasts for one year and includes coursework and work placements.

▼ RELATED CAREERS

▶ **DENTIST** *see pp. 282–283*

▶ **DISPENSING OPTICIAN** Fits and supplies glasses and contact lenses according to prescriptions written by optometrists. Dispensing opticians also order and manage a range of optical products, and help customers to choose frames for glasses and contact lenses.

▶ **OPHTHALMOLOGIST** Diagnoses, treats, and prevents eye diseases. Ophthalmologists are doctors who carry out eye surgery in hospital eye departments, as well as in outpatient units and private laser-eye-surgery clinics.

▶ **ORTHOPTIST** Investigates, diagnoses, and treats sight defects, such as glaucoma and cataracts, and any abnormalities in eye movement.

SKILLS GUIDE

 Excellent communication skills for explaining treatments to patients and answering their queries.

 Flexibility to adapt to advances in optometric practice, such as improved scientific techniques.

 Strong interpersonal skills to liaise with and put patients at ease, and interact with colleagues.

 The ability to analyse scientific and mathematical data, and to diagnose patients accurately.

 Good manual dexterity for using sophisticated optometric equipment correctly.

 Concentration, precision, and attention to detail for examining patients' eyesight accurately.

PRACTICE MANAGER
Oversees the running of an optometry practice, managing the business, recruiting staff, ordering stock, and ensuring that sales targets are met.

 CONSULTANT (HOSPITAL) OPTOMETRIST Assesses, treats, and monitors patients suffering from sight loss or complex or serious eye conditions. The role also involves helping patients in their rehabilitation following surgery or disease.

OPTOMETRIST You will need to undertake continued training in order to have your professional registration renewed each year. You can specialize in a particular area (such as children or partially sighted patients), move into management, or open your own clinic.

 OPTICAL DESIGN CONSULTANT Works with technologists in the optical manufacturing industry, helping to shape the design of glasses, contact lenses, and optical products for other purposes, such as telescopes or scanning systems.

SPORTS, LEISURE, AND TOURISM

As the world economy expands, the global demand for recreational pursuits increases every year. Enthusiasm, excellent communication skills, and the ability to help people enjoy their leisure time are prerequisites for working in this growing sector.

SPORTS PROFESSIONAL
Page 298

With exceptional sporting ability, sports professionals are the lucky few who are paid to compete with the best as they try to reach the top of their chosen game.

PERSONAL TRAINER
Page 300

Health and wellbeing is a booming sector, with massive demand for personal trainers who can develop training plans and coach their clients to reach peak fitness.

BEAUTY THERAPIST
Page 302

From massages and nail art to facials and spray tanning, beauty therapists use the latest techniques and products to make their customers look and feel good.

HOTEL MANAGER
Page 304

In this competitive sector where hotels vie with one another for custom, hotel managers strive to make their guests' stays as relaxing and enjoyable as possible.

TRAVEL AGENT
Page 306

Liaising with holiday companies, airlines, and resorts on behalf of customers, travel agents aim to turn their clients' holiday dreams into reality within a specified budget.

AIRLINE CABIN CREW
Page 308

Working on board aircraft, cabin crew attend to the needs of passengers to ensure they have a safe, comfortable, and enjoyable flight.

CHEF
Page 310

Taking a creative approach to ingredients and cooking techniques, chefs combine artistry with a taste for flavours and textures to bring each plate of food to life.

MUSEUM CURATOR
Page 312

Using their knowledge of history, archaeology, or the arts, museum curators display the exhibits and artefacts in their collection to engage and inspire visitors.

SPORTS PROFESSIONAL

JOB DESCRIPTION

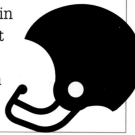

With the talent to be paid to practise their sport, sports professionals compete to achieve individual and team success and to entertain fans. They work hard at training to stay in peak physical condition and perfect their skills. As well as sporting duties, many professionals perform educational or charity work.

SALARY

Low-earning professional ★☆☆☆☆
Top-earning professional ★★★★★

INDUSTRY PROFILE

Extremely competitive, varied industry • Limited opportunities to reach highest level • Work may be part-time • Lucrative profession with international fame and wealth for successful sportspersons

AT A GLANCE

YOUR INTERESTS Competitive sport • Physical Education (PE) • Fitness • Health and nutrition • Business and marketing • Anatomy • Biology

ENTRY QUALIFICATIONS There are no minimum entry requirements to be a sportsperson, other than talent and dedication to a sport.

LIFESTYLE Hours of work may be long and irregular, with some form of training taking place most days. Competitions may occur on weekends and evenings.

LOCATION Sports professionals train and compete indoors and outdoors. Competitive events sometimes require national and international travel.

THE REALITIES Success can make this a highly rewarding and satisfactory career, but many sports professionals have to supplement their income with other jobs.

▼ RELATED CAREERS

▶ **PERSONAL TRAINER** *see pp. 300–301*

▶ **COMMUNITY SPORTS DEVELOPMENT OFFICER** Encourages public participation and access to sports and physical activity. Community sports development officers may work with specific groups, such as young or disabled people.

▶ **PHYSICAL EDUCATION TEACHER** Teaches a range of sports to young people at a school or college, promoting the benefits of physical activity, and encouraging and developing sporting potential.

▶ **SPORTS PHYSIOTHERAPIST** Works with people with sports- or exercise-related injuries, improving their physical capabilities, providing advice on how to avoid further injury, and administering treatment to aid recovery. Sports physiotherapists also diagnose injuries and recommend treatment programmes using non-traditional methods of treatment, such as massage, heat treatment, or hydrotherapy.

CAREER PATHS

There is no defined career path for sports professionals, but most naturally talented individuals achieve some success as children, before working with coaches at amateur level. Early retirement is common due to the physical demands of professional sport, and many ex-professionals move into media or management jobs once their playing careers end.

AMATEUR You can hone your sporting talent by competing at amateur level. Participating in national and international events will develop your skills and increase your chances of being spotted by a talent scout.

SPORTS PROFESSIONAL As a sports professional, your competitive career is likely to be short in duration. Many professionals diversify into areas such as business ownership or commentary in the later years of their careers, or study for qualifications in coaching.

SKILLS GUIDE

 Absolute dedication to improve and maintain individual sporting skill and physical fitness.

 The ability to employ competitive tactics and strategies for gaining an advantage over competitors.

 Strong team-working skills to be part of a competitive or coaching set-up, especially in team sports.

 Physical strength, endurance, and fitness to maintain performance throughout a sports event.

 Good hand-eye coordination and rapid reflexes to excel in competitive sports.

SPORTS JOURNALIST Specializes in a particular sport, using their insight and industry contacts to conduct interviews, attend sporting events, and compile reports for television, radio, the Internet, or print media.

COACH Trains promising competitors or sports teams. This specialist area requires additional qualifications, which sportspeople can study for during their playing careers.

MANAGER Works with professional, school, or college sportspeople to manage teams, resources, and training. Managers may also direct an organization's athletics programme or manage sports facilities.

SPORTS AGENT Represents a professional sportsperson in the negotiation of contracts and sponsorships, and often handles their public relations and finances.

SPORTS PRESENTER Provides live commentary and analysis for sports events that are broadcast on television, radio, or the Internet. This job is open to sports personalities with media presentation skills.

PERSONAL TRAINER

JOB DESCRIPTION

Personal trainers coach people to achieve their health and fitness goals, and help to create fitness programmes to suit the individual. They may also provide guidance on health, diet, and lifestyle changes. An excellent knowledge of the human body enables trainers to set realistic targets for their clients, while motivating them to stay on track so they can reach their goals.

SALARY

Fitness instructor ★★★★★
Personal trainer ★★★★★

INDUSTRY PROFILE

Many freelance personal trainer roles available in gymnasiums • Increasing opportunities due to rise in health awareness

AT A GLANCE

YOUR INTERESTS Sports • Human biology and physiology • Food and nutrition • Sports psychology • Teaching • First aid • Business and management

ENTRY QUALIFICATIONS A diploma in fitness and personal training or a degree in sports science or a health-related discipline is necessary.

LIFESTYLE Personal trainers may stick to regular working hours or adjust according to their client's availability. Self-employed trainers usually travel on demand.

LOCATION Trainers work in a fully equipped gymnasium or a similar facility; those self-employed may also work in resorts, country clubs, and other client sites.

THE REALITIES The competition is fierce. Self-employed trainers often have to work anti-social hours and stay focused and enthusiastic, which can be tiring.

CAREER PATHS

A qualification in sport and fitness is necessary to enter this career. Work may be available at health studios, recreational centres, or hospitals, or for sports clubs or other professionals, and with experience, you can choose to provide customized training to individual clients. With business acumen, you can enter the management side of the fitness industry.

TRAINEE You can usually join a gym or fitness centre as a trainee, studying on the job for a diploma or certificate in fitness.

GRADUATE A degree in sports science is not essential but will give you detailed knowledge of physiology, anatomy, and nutrition that will help your chances of success in this career.

▼ RELATED CAREERS

▶ **OCCUPATIONAL THERAPIST** *see pp. 292–293*

▶ **COMMUNITY HEALTH WORKER** Teaches techniques and behaviours that promote good health to groups and individuals.

▶ **HIGHER-LEVEL TEACHING ASSISTANT** Provides assistance in a classroom or any other learning environment to students who require extra help.

▶ **NUTRITIONIST** Advises clients on eating habits for healthy living and prepares diet plans for them to achieve health-related goals. Nutritionists use scientific knowledge and research to help people on matters of nutrition to improve their health and assist with any related medical conditions.

SKILLS GUIDE

 The knowledge to devise unique health programmes based on a client's physical ability and needs.

 Good leadership skills to motivate and encourage clients to make positive lifestyle changes.

 Sensitivity towards clients who may suffer from a range of health difficulties.

 Good business sense and an ability to market services effectively to make a profit.

A high level of personal fitness in order to demonstrate, guide, and supervise physical activities.

 **FITNESS INSTRUCTOR** Leads classes in activities such as spinning or Pilates, or provides advice and guidance on individual activities and use of weights and equipment at a gym or fitness centre.

 SPORTS COACH Teaches skills in sports such as football and golf to individuals and teams of all abilities, from beginners to professionals. Coaches require a qualification recognized by the sport's governing body to practise.

 LEISURE SERVICE MANAGER Works to ensure that members of a leisure centre receive the best experience there. People in this role manage facilities and staff, with the aim of boosting customer satisfaction levels.

PERSONAL TRAINER As you build your experience and reputation, you may choose to work with clients on the basis of a private arrangement or move into another area of the industry.

 OUTDOOR ACTIVITIES INSTRUCTOR Teaches and leads groups in outdoor activities such as water sports, skiing, hill-walking, and rock climbing.

BEAUTY THERAPIST

JOB DESCRIPTION

Beauty therapists specialize in making people look and feel good. They provide a range of facial and body treatments – such as manicures, pedicures, hair removal, eyebrow shaping, and specialist therapies – to improve the appearance and wellbeing of clients. A beauty therapist may also offer advice on recommended treatments, the use of cosmetics and skin products, and make-up application techniques.

SALARY

Newly qualified therapist ★★★★★
Salon manager ★★★★★

INDUSTRY PROFILE

Growing demand for specialist beauty treatments • Opportunities in a wide range of specialisms and settings, from health salons to home visits • Self-employment common

CAREER PATHS

Beauty therapists start their careers by mastering the basics of a range of treatments, such as waxing, massage, facials, and skincare. Adding to your skills by completing courses in specialist techniques – such as piercings or advanced massage – will increase your career prospects and appeal to employers.

COMPLEMENTARY THERAPIST
Performs a range of specialist health therapies – such as body massage, aromatherapy, reflexology, or hydrotherapy – that complement traditional forms of medical care.

TRAINEE You can combine work experience in a salon or spa with on-the-job beauty therapy training by taking a paid trainee position.

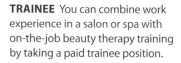

COLLEGE GRADUATE You can become a beauty therapist by completing a vocational college training course, which combines lectures and classes with practical experience. Full-time or part-time courses are available.

BEAUTY THERAPIST As a beauty therapist, you will continue to learn new techniques and utilize new products throughout your career. You may specialize in a type of treatment, or move into salon management or cosmetics sales.

SKILLS GUIDE

 Good communication skills to listen to customer needs and explain treatments clearly.

 Creativity and artistic ability to keep up to date with new techniques and styles.

 Strong customer service skills for interacting with people and making them feel comfortable.

 Excellent manual dexterity to apply beauty treatments such as skincare products and make-up.

 Physical stamina for standing for long periods of time while giving customers their treatments.

Precision and attention to detail for applying make-up and other treatments neatly and accurately.

NAIL TECHNICIAN Carries out manicures and pedicures, and applies lotions, varnishes, and artificial nails. Nail technicians may also offer other treatments, such as foot massage.

HAIR REMOVAL SPECIALIST Uses a variety of techniques, such as electrolysis, waxing, threading, or laser treatment, to remove unwanted hair from clients.

COSMETICS CONSULTANT Visits salons, beauticians, and stores to demonstrate and sell new beauty products and treatments.

▼ RELATED CAREERS

▶ **MAKE-UP ARTIST** *see pp. 32–33*

▶ **HAIRDRESSER** Cuts, colours, shapes, and styles hair, and gives advice on suitable and attractive styles for individual clients. Hairdressers need good people skills in order to build long-term relationships with clients, as well as an awareness of style trends and a willingness to learn new methods of hairstyling.

▶ **IMAGE CONSULTANT** Offers advice to individual clients on their public image, including make-up styles, clothing and dress, and personal presentation. Image consultants also advise companies and corporations on a vast range of topics – such as branding, business etiquette, and understanding corporate culture.

AT A GLANCE

 YOUR INTERESTS Beauty treatments and techniques • Health and fitness • Customer service • Art • Design • English • Fashion

 ENTRY QUALIFICATIONS Beauty therapists can train on the job, but a vocational qualification in beauty therapy is required by most employers.

 LIFESTYLE Most beauty therapists work regular hours, but working during weekends or evenings may occasionally be required.

 LOCATION This job can be done in a beauty salon, hotel, health spa, or on a cruise ship. Some beauty therapists visit clients in their own homes.

 THE REALITIES The work involves close physical contact with clients, which may be uncomfortable. Strong competition means that salaries are low.

HOTEL MANAGER

JOB DESCRIPTION

Hotel managers are ultimately responsible for the safe, comfortable, and profitable operation of a hotel. Their duties might include recruiting and managing staff, ensuring that guests receive a high level of service and enjoy their stay, and overseeing the menu, wine list, and entertainment in the hotel's restaurant or bar. Developing the business and tracking budgets are also key tasks for the manager.

SALARY

Hotel manager ★★☆☆☆
Hotel regional manager ★★★★☆

INDUSTRY PROFILE

Career prospects good due to high staff turnover • Growing industry • Wide range of vacancies globally, with opportunities to work internationally for large hotel chains

▼ RELATED CAREERS

▶ **EVENTS MANAGER** *see pp. 88–89*

▶ **TRAVEL AGENT** *see pp. 306–307*

▶ **RESTAURANT MANAGER** Ensures that a restaurant operates efficiently and profitably, while maintaining the business's reputation and public profile. Restaurant managers coordinate a variety of activities – from maintenance to promotional events – and are responsible for maintaining high standards of food, service, and health and safety.

With a predicted 1.6 billion tourists worldwide by 2020, hotel management is a growing profession.

AT A GLANCE

 YOUR INTERESTS Hotel management • Travel and tourism • Business studies • Economics • Mathematics • Information Technology (IT) • Food and nutrition

 ENTRY QUALIFICATIONS A relevant degree is helpful. Hotel managers usually have at least four years' experience in the hospitality industry.

 LIFESTYLE Working hours are very long, and include evenings, weekends, and holidays. Some managers live in the hotel and work shifts.

 LOCATION Work is mostly based at the hotel, although visiting suppliers is also involved. Managers may have an office for performing administrative work.

 THE REALITIES Dealing with hotel guests can be stressful and tiring, and living in the place of work carries its own pressures. Staff turnover is high.

CAREER PATHS

A degree in hospitality management or a related subject is usually required to work for a larger hotel. The hotel industry also offers good prospects for non-graduates with a positive attitude, sociable nature, and an aptitude for hard work.

TRAINEE As a school- or college-leaver, you can be a hotel manager by taking an entry-level job and working your way up via roles such as accommodation supervisor.

GRADUATE If you have a degree in travel and tourism, business management, or hospitality, you can apply for graduate training schemes run by large hotel groups.

HOTEL MANAGER As a hotel manager, you must balance strategic planning of business affairs with an eye for detail to maintain strong customer service. Working for a larger hotel or chain is a common form of progression.

SKILLS GUIDE

Good interpersonal skills and a friendly approach that makes guests feel comfortable.

The ability to work with staff from a variety of countries and cultures, and adapt to unfamiliar locations.

Excellent communication skills for interacting effectively with senior managers and staff.

Leadership skills to motivate hotel staff and ensure they maintain high standards of customer care.

The ability to come up with effective solutions to everyday problems quickly and efficiently.

Strong commercial awareness to ensure that the hotel is run as a profitable enterprise.

REGIONAL MANAGER Develops and oversees the operations, marketing strategy, and finances of a hotel group in a region or country, taking responsibility for its overall profitability.

HOLIDAY RESORT MANAGER Manages the daily operations of a resort complex, including overseeing the work of event organizers, hotel or restaurant managers, and grounds staff.

CONFERENCE CENTRE MANAGER Provides a venue for business conferences, taking responsibility for staff, finances, marketing, and advertising.

ACCOMMODATION MANAGER Works for a large institution, such as a school, university, or hospital, ensuring that sufficient rooms of appropriate standard are available to meet customer demand.

TRAVEL AGENT

JOB DESCRIPTION

Travel agents organize business or leisure travel for their customers. They may offer advice on national and international destinations, plan the trip itineraries, and take care of any ticket or passport issues that might arise. They may also make additional travel arrangements, including accommodation bookings, and offer guidance on insurance, travel safety, vaccinations, and tours.

SALARY

Junior travel agent ★★★★★
Experienced travel agent ★★★★★

INDUSTRY PROFILE

High-street travel agencies facing growing competition from online travel sites • Specialized providers servicing a particular market, such as business travellers, remain in demand

AT A GLANCE

YOUR INTERESTS Travel and tourism • Geography • History • Business studies • Languages • Economics • Information Technology (IT)

ENTRY QUALIFICATIONS A good basic education is enough for entry-level jobs, but a degree in travel and tourism is advantageous.

LIFESTYLE Travel agents work normal retail hours, including weekends. They may be expected to work overtime during high season.

LOCATION Travel agents usually work in an office or retail outlet. They sometimes get to travel to different destinations as part of their job.

THE REALITIES Agents may have to deal with unhappy customers, which can be challenging, especially when they have to explain situations beyond their control.

▼ RELATED CAREERS

▶ **HOTEL MANAGER** *see pp. 304–305*

▶ **AIRLINE CABIN CREW** *see pp. 308–309*

▶ **CUSTOMER SERVICE AGENT** Answers customer queries and deals with complaints. Customer service agents also take orders and payments, arrange refunds, and maintain computer records of transactions.

▶ **LEISURE CENTRE MANAGER** Runs sports and recreation centres. The job involves arranging timetables for activities, supervising a range of staff, controlling budgets, and promoting and marketing the facilities on offer.

▶ **TOURIST INFORMATION ASSISTANT** Provides information about locations, facilities, and places open to visitors. Often based in airports and major rail stations, tourist information assistants use their knowledge of the transport schedules to advise visitors.

CAREER PATHS

There is no set career path for a travel agent, and a network of contacts in the industry will be the most useful asset in seeking higher positions. You will stand out if you specialize in a few particular destinations or sell to specific kinds of traveller, such as those with special interests.

TRAINEE You will usually start your career as a trainee with a travel agency. This role typically combines on-the-job training with work experience.

TRAVEL AGENT Once you have become a travel agent, industry-run courses in sales or customer care will help you develop your career. With experience, you can seek professional accreditation to move to more senior positions.

SKILLS GUIDE

Good communication skills, telephone etiquette, and sensitivity to cultural differences.

 The ability to complete all necessary arrangements for customers in a careful, well-organized manner.

 The strength to stay calm and polite with clients who are difficult to please.

 Excellent attention to detail to check, order, and relay travel information accurately.

 Knowledge of other languages to be able to talk to people of different nationalities.

TOUR OPERATOR Plans and organizes group travel. The work includes organizing cruises, rail and coach travel, or chartered flights to a selection of destinations.

BUSINESS TRAVEL AGENT Arranges travel and accommodation for corporate clients, negotiating special rates on their behalf.

CALL CENTRE AGENT Sells travel products to customers on the telephone or the Internet, and handles product queries and complaints. May work shifts to deal with customer calls at evenings and weekends.

RESORT REPRESENTATIVE Represents a travel company at a holiday resort or destination, looking after the needs of holidaymakers and liaising with travel and accommodation suppliers.

AIRLINE CABIN CREW

JOB DESCRIPTION

Airline cabin-crew members ensure that passengers experience a safe, comfortable, and enjoyable flight. Duties include checking the aircraft's cabin, greeting and seating passengers, giving safety demonstrations, and selling and serving refreshments. Cabin crew are trained to respond to emergency and security situations, and to administer first aid. They must deal with a wide range of clients and situations.

SALARY

Newly qualified cabin crew ★★★★★
Senior cabin crew ★★★★★

INDUSTRY PROFILE

Strong competition for jobs • Most employees work on a temporary basis – permanent contracts are more rare • Overtime and flight allowances can increase earnings

▼ RELATED CAREERS

▶ **HOTEL MANAGER** *see pp. 304–305*

▶ **AIRLINE CUSTOMER SERVICE AGENT** Checks passengers onto their flight, weighs luggage, and issues boarding passes.

▶ **CUSTOMER SERVICE AGENT** Answers customer queries, handles complaints, and provides information about an organization's services. A customer service agent is often a member of the public's first point of contact with a company.

▶ **RESORT REPRESENTATIVE** Ensures that tourists have a comfortable and pleasant holiday, meeting holidaymakers as their flights arrive, arranging onward transport, and remaining on hand to offer advice once at the resort.

Aviation is expected to expand in the next decade, with more opportunities for cabin crew, especially in Asia and South America.

AT A GLANCE

YOUR INTERESTS Aviation • Travel and tourism • Hospitality • Working with people • English • Mathematics • Languages • Geography

ENTRY QUALIFICATIONS Cabin crew must have a good basic education, be at least 18, and pass fitness tests. Prior customer service experience is helpful.

LIFESTYLE Due to the 24-hour nature of air travel, cabin crew work irregular hours in shifts that include nights, weekends, and holidays.

LOCATION Time is mostly spent working in the cabin of an in-flight passenger aircraft. Significant time away from home is normal in this career.

THE REALITIES Jet lag and standing for long periods make this job physically taxing. Tired or anxious passengers can be difficult to deal with.

CAREER PATHS

Experience in customer service roles and fluency in one or more foreign languages will help gain entry to this profession. It takes between two and five years in the job before achieving promotion to more senior roles, such as dealing with VIP passengers or managing the cabin.

SKILLS GUIDE

Good communication skills for understanding and attending to passengers' needs.

The ability to work efficiently and supportively with colleagues in usually cramped cabin conditions.

Excellent customer service to deal with passengers in a polite, professional, and sensitive manner.

Good numeracy for handling and exchanging foreign currency during in-flight shopping.

Being able to think quickly to keep passengers calm during difficulties, such as emergency landings.

Physical stamina and resilience to deal with jet lag and remain on duty for long hours in the cabin.

SCHOOL- OR COLLEGE-LEAVER If you have a good school education, you can apply for cabin-crew training programmes run by major airlines.

GRADUATE You do not need a degree to work as a cabin-crew member, but undergraduate study in travel, leisure, and tourism, hospitality management, languages, social science, or business, is helpful.

AIRLINE CABIN CREW
You take up your first job after completing training in areas including passenger care, customer relations, and security, customs, and immigration regulations. With experience, you can be promoted to a senior cabin-crew or ground-support job.

LANGUAGES SPECIALIST Works as part of the cabin crew on long-haul flights in which a good knowledge of specific languages is required.

PURSER/SENIOR CABIN-CREW MEMBER Manages part of the cabin on an aircraft – such as the first-class lounge – and oversees other staff. Chief pursers are responsible for managing the whole aircraft.

VIP CABIN-CREW STAFF Looks after very important and prestigious passengers onboard either commercial aircraft or private jets.

CABIN-CREW SUPPORT Supports the work of cabin crew through roles including training, recruitment, and human resources. This role is generally only available to highly experienced cabin crew.

CHEF

SALARY

Commis chef ★★★★★
Head chef ★★★★★

INDUSTRY PROFILE

Most restaurants run independently to tight budgets • Worldwide job opportunities • Industry constantly adapting to changing culinary tastes

JOB DESCRIPTION

A love of food and cooking is vital to succeed as a chef. The role involves planning and coordinating food production at a restaurant or other eatery, managing a kitchen, and directing waiting staff. Chefs may cook food themselves or oversee its preparation by their staff. Many chefs are known to create unique menus and signature dishes. They also handle buying and budgeting for catering operations.

CAREER PATHS

Most chefs train on the job, joining a kitchen as a trainee, or *commis* chef, and studying for vocational qualifications. Ability and commitment are your key to promotion. Working under a rated chef can give your career an extra boost.

HEAD CHEF Devises a restaurant's menu and runs its kitchen. The role also involves making key business decisions with the aim of making the establishment a success.

TRAINEE Following school, you can learn your craft as a trainee in the role of a section chef (or *chef de partie*), rotating through sections such as vegetables, fish, and butchery to become familiar with them all. The type and length of apprenticeship depends on the employer.

GRADUATE As an aspiring chef, you can train in a private academy. Some academies are run by notable cooks. However, fees can be high and there is no guarantee of employment later.

CHEF With experience and sufficient talent, you will climb the ladder of responsibility in the kitchen, through *chef de partie* (responsible for a section of the kitchen) and *sous chef* (the second-in-command, who may schedule staff and buy ingredients), to the position of head chef, or *chef de cuisine*.

SKILLS GUIDE

 Excellent team-working skills to manage staff in a high-pressure kitchen environment.

 Creativity and imagination to devise unique and delicious dishes, and keep the menu fresh.

 Strong interpersonal skills to maintain good relationships with staff at all levels, as well as diners.

 The ability to calculate quantities, price differences, and catering costs to run a profitable kitchen.

 Well-honed practical skills and the ability to use kitchen equipment with ease and speed.

CONTRACT CATERING MANAGER Provides catering services to clients, for business functions, and special celebratory events.

INSTITUTIONAL COOK Cooks in the kitchen of a large organization. Employers include the armed forces, health providers, factories, and other workplaces.

 In the USA, more than 13 million people are employed in the restaurant industry.

▼ RELATED CAREERS

▶ **BAKER** Produces bread and confectionery products within a manufacturing operation, retail outlet, or delicatessen.

▶ **FOOD-PROCESSING OPERATIVE** Works on factory production lines, overseeing the mixing, cooking, and packing of food products.

▶ **KITCHEN ASSISTANT** Performs basic tasks from food preparation and checking deliveries to cleaning the kitchen and all the equipment.

▶ **PUBLICAN OR LICENSEE MANAGER** Runs premises, such as a pub or bar, that serve a variety of beverages. May also branch out into catering or food operations.

AT A GLANCE

 YOUR INTERESTS Food • Cooking • Business administration • Catering, hospitality, and tourism • Food production and farming

 ENTRY QUALIFICATIONS A degree is not essential to become a chef, but food and food production qualifications are an advantage in this industry.

 LIFESTYLE Work often starts very early and finishes very late. Split shifts, evenings, and weekends are a normal part of the working cycle.

 LOCATION Chefs work mostly in restaurant or hotel kitchens. Catering jobs may involve travelling to locations with cooking equipment.

 THE REALITIES Kitchens can be busy high-pressure environments, while equipment, such as knives and hot pans, is potentially dangerous.

MUSEUM CURATOR

JOB DESCRIPTION

A museum or gallery curator manages a collection of historical artefacts or works of art, overseeing exhibitions and new initiatives to attract and educate visitors. This role can involve acquiring, caring for, displaying, and interpreting exhibits, as well as marketing and fundraising activities. Curators also manage budgets and staff, and build relationships with donors and partner institutions.

SALARY

Curatorial assistant ★★★★★
Head curator ★★★★★

INDUSTRY PROFILE

Funding falls during economic downturns • Employers include museums, galleries, and heritage sites • Growth in contract work, but fewer permanent positions available

AT A GLANCE

YOUR INTERESTS Art • History • Languages • Archaeology • Science • Design • Education • Architecture • Information Technology (IT)

ENTRY QUALIFICATIONS A degree is required and postgraduate study is desirable. Larger museums recruit graduates as trainee curators.

LIFESTYLE Full-time curators usually have regular hours, but working on evenings and weekends is common when preparing for an exhibition.

LOCATION Most work is based at a museum, gallery, or heritage site. Travel may be necessary to attend conferences or deliver artefacts.

THE REALITIES Competition for jobs is strong, so working in a lower-paid assistant-level position is necessary to gain sufficient experience to progress.

CAREER PATHS

Museum curators usually hold a degree or postgraduate qualification, and often contribute to research or teaching in their specialist area of interest. Reputation and expertise can lead to a role in a larger, more prestigious collection of exhibits, or a senior position in museum management.

MUSEUM ASSISTANT You can apply for a job as a clerical or visitor-services assistant at a museum or gallery straight from school. You will need good grades in history, English, or a related subject. Previous work experience in a museum is beneficial.

GRADUATE You can take a degree in museum- or heritage-studies, but an undergraduate or postgraduate qualification in a subject relevant to a particular collection may qualify you to apply for junior or assistant curating posts.

▼ RELATED CAREERS

▶ **ANTIQUE DEALER** Uses historical expertise and commercial acumen to buy and sell antique items. Antique dealers may be employed by an auction house or work on a self-employed basis.

▶ **ARCHAEOLOGIST** Investigates past human activities by excavating and analysing material remains, from fragments of bone or pottery to ancient ruins or buried structures. The role also involves recording, preserving, and interpreting remains, as well as publishing findings to improve our knowledge and understanding of the past.

▶ **ARCHIVIST** Stores, catalogues, and maintains documents and other materials of historical significance. Employers can range from national institutions with extensive archives to wealthy individuals with private collections.

SKILLS GUIDE

 Excellent verbal and written communication skills to give talks and write articles and reports.

 Strong IT skills for creating a variety of web-based and printed materials.

 A creative flair for presenting exhibits and displays in engaging and informative ways.

 Good organizational abilities to secure a variety of new exhibits through loans and acquisitions.

 The ability to manage staff and links with stakeholders, such as governors and funding groups.

HEAD CURATOR
Manages the activities of a team of curators and oversees the functions of their individual departments, usually in a larger museum or gallery.

MUSEUM DIRECTOR
Oversees the collection held by a museum, manages personnel and operations, and ensures that the objectives set by the museum's board of governors are fulfilled.

HEAD OF EXHIBITIONS
Specializes in planning, organizing, and marketing permanent or temporary exhibitions at a museum.

MUSEUM CURATOR Most curators spend at least two years as an assistant before becoming a curator. You can choose to specialize in an area of academic research, or move into senior and management roles.

CONSERVATOR Preserves artefacts or works of art by controlling the environment in which objects are stored. A conservator may also restore damaged items using specialist conservation methods.

GLOSSARY

Accreditation
A formal, third party recognition of competence to perform specific tasks. Usually the reason for getting something independently evaluated is to confirm it meets specific requirements in order to reduce risks.

Algorithm
A procedure or formula for solving a problem.

Amateur
A person who engages in a study, sport, or other pursuit for pleasure rather than for financial benefit or professional reasons.

Apprentice
A person who works for another in order to learn a trade.

Arbitrator
Someone chosen to judge and decide a disputed issue.

Assessor
A person who evaluates the merits, importance, or value of something.

Biodiversity
The number and variety of organisms found within a specified geographic region.

Biomedical
The branch of medical science that deals with a human's ability to tolerate environmental stresses and variations, such as in space.

Blueprint
A print of a drawing or other image rendered as white lines on a blue background, especially of an architectural plan or technical drawing.

Business acumen
A keen insight into the workings of the business world.

Commercial
Something that is connected or related to business.

Commission
A duty or task that has been handed to a person or group to perform.

Computer hardware
The collection of physical elements, such as the monitor, mouse, keyboard, and hard drive disk, that make up a computer system.

Computer software
The programs that are used to make a computer perform different tasks.

Consensus
General or widespread agreement, i.e. consensus of opinion.

Conservation
The act of preserving or renovating something from loss, damage, or neglect.

Consultant
A person who gives professional or expert advice.

Conversion Course
A course for graduates who have a degree in one particular subject but who want to learn new skills to forge a career in a different sector.

Conveyancer
A lawyer who specializes in the business of transferring the legal ownership of a property from one person to another.

Curriculum Vitae
A document used by people to present their background, qualifications, and skills to potential employers.

Cyber attack
An illegal attempt to harm someone's computer system or the information stored on it, using the Internet.

Cyber crime
Crimes committed against groups or individuals using modern telecommunications networks, such as the Internet or mobile phones.

Derivative
A special type of contract in the financial world that derives its value from the performance from an asset such as stocks or interest rates.

E-commerce
A type of industry where the buying and selling of products is conducted over electronic systems such as the Internet or other computer systems.

Eco-friendly
A term used to describe a product that has been designed to do the least possible damage to the environment.

Ecosystem
A community of plants, animals, and smaller organisms that live, feed, reproduce, and interact in the same area or environment.

Ethnographic
Relates to ethnography – the systematic study of people and cultures.

Executive
A senior manager in an organization, company, or corporation.

Fellow
The title of a senior teaching position at a university or similar institution. Someone who is a fellow has been awarded a "fellowship".

Freelance
A person who is self-employed and who is not committed to a particular employer on a long-term basis.

Hacker
Someone who breaks into other people's computer systems, for the most part illegally.

Haute couture
A type of clothing, usually made from expensive, high-quality fabric, that is made to order for a specific customer.

Hedge fund
An investment fund, typically formed by a number of different investors, that uses a wide range of techniques to try and generate the highest possible financial return.

Information technology
The study or use of systems (especially computers and telecommunications) for storing, retrieving, and sending information.

Infrastructure
The basic physical or organizational structure needed to operate a business, society, or enterprise.

Interpersonal skills
A term often used in business to describe a person's ability to relate to and communicate with another person.

Legislation
The act or process of making laws.

Module
A standardized part or independent unit that can be used in conjunction with other units to form a more complex structure, such as in a computer programme or in a building.

Networking skills
The ability to build and maintain contacts and relationships with people in the business world. Possibly one of the most important skills for aspiring entrepreneurs.

Overtime
The amount of time someone works beyond normal working hours.

Patent
The official legal right to make or sell a unique invention for a particular number of years.

Periodicals
A publication, such as a magazine or scholarly journal, that is produced on a regular basis: it might appear every week, every fortnight, once a month, once a quarter, or once a year.

Personnel
The people who work for a particular company or organization.

Portfolio
A collection of work intended to demonstrate a person's ability to a potential employer.

Postgraduate
A student who already has one degree who is studying at a university or college for a more advanced qualification.

Private sector
Businesses or industries that are not owned by individuals or groups, usually for profit.

Procedure
A set of established methods for conducting the affairs of an organized body, such as a government, club, or business.

Protocol
A code of correct conduct, often referring to affairs of state or diplomatic conduct.

Prototype
The first example of something, such as a machine or other industrial product, from which all later forms are developed.

Public sector
The portion of the economy consisting of the government and enterprises which are owned by the government.

Revenue
The income a government or business receives from a particular source, such as taxes or the profit made on a property or investment.

Sabbatical
A period of leave from one's customary work. Usually applies to university staff or teachers, who are often granted a period of leave (usually paid) every seven years.

Self-employed
An individual who earns his or her livelihood directly from their own trade or business rather than as an employee of another.

Simulator
A machine, used for training purposes, designed to provide a realistic imitation of the controls and operation of a vehicle, aircraft, or other complex system.

Stakeholder
A person or a group of people who own a share in a business.

Third sector
The part of an economy or society comprising non-governmental and non-profit-making organizations or associations, including charities, voluntary and community groups, and cooperatives.

Trainee
A person undergoing training for a particular job or profession.

User Interface
The visual part of a computer application or operating system through which the user interacts with a computer, often by choosing a command from a list displayed on the screen.

Vocation
A regular occupation, especially one for which a person is particularly suited or qualified.

Welfare
Financial or other aid provided to people in need, especially by the government.

INDEX

ABOUT THE AUTHORS

Consultant and Principal Author: Sarah Pawlewski
Sarah is a careers adviser with more than 20 years' experience. She runs her own consultancy – career-directions.co.uk – and works with clients of all ages across schools, colleges, universities, and industry. She holds degrees in Psychology and Careers Guidance, and is a member of the Career Development Institute.

Contributors: Christine Rowley, Imogen Gray, Heather Towers

ACKNOWLEDGMENTS

The author would like to thank:
The staff and students at Holbrook Academy (holbrookacademy.org) for their insight and progressive views about careers.
Ann Starkie, AS Careers, for her help with the introduction.
Marek Pawlewski, my husband, for his expert advice about technical careers.
Robert Woodcock, for contributing to the journalist and editor profiles.
Marek Walisiewicz, Cobalt ID, for his help, support, guidance, amazing editorial work, and for understanding the complexities of careers guidance.
Paul Reid, Cobalt ID, for bringing the words to life through the graphic design.
Ashwin Khurana, and the editorial team at DK for synchronising all of the material.
And finally, Christine Rowley, Imogen Gray, and Heather Towers for their professional input to the career information.

The publisher would like to thank the following people for their assistance with this book:
Bharti Bedi for proofreading; Margaret McCormack for indexing; Priyaneet Singh and Hina Jain for editorial assistance; Ankita Mukherjee, Heena Sharma, Priyanka Singh, Vidit Vashisht, and Vikas Chauhan for design assistance; and Vishal Bhatia and Pawan Kumar for DTP assistance.